The Neglected Majority:
Essays in Canadian
Women's History
Volume 2

edited by

Alison Prentice and
Susan Mann Trofimenkoff

M&S

Canadian Cataloguing in Publication Data
Main entry under title:
The neglected majority: essays in Canadian women's history vol. 2

(The Canadian social history series)
Bibliography: p.
ISBN 0-7710-8583-4 (v.2)

1. Women — Canada — History — Addresses, essays,
lectures. **2.** Women — Canada — Social conditions
— Addresses, essays, lectures. I. Trofimenkoff,
Susan Mann, 1941 –   . II. Prentice, Alison, 1934 –   .
III. Series.

HQ1453.N44 1977   305.4'0971   C77-116-5

Printed and bound in Canada

McClelland & Stewart Inc.
The Canadian Publishers
481 University Avenue
Toronto, Ontario   M5G 2E9

Contents

Acknowledgements / 4

Contributors / 5

Introduction / 7

1 New France: Les femmes favorisées / 18
Jan Noel

2 Recording Angels: The Private Chronicles of Women
from the Maritime Provinces of Canada,
1750-1950 / 41
Margaret Conrad

3 The Decline of Women in Canadian Dairying / 61
Marjorie Griffin Cohen

4 Birth Control and Abortion in Canada, 1870-1920 / 84
Angus McLaren

5 The Women Ontario Welcomed: Immigrant Domestics
for Ontario Homes, 1870-1930 / 102
Marilyn Barber

6 Changing Relationships: Nuns and Feminists in
Montreal, 1890-1925 / 122
Marta Danylewycz

7 The Peacock and the Guinea Hen: Political Profiles of
Dorothy Gretchen Steeves and Grace MacInnis / 144
Susan Walsh

8 "Weaving It Together": Life Cycle and the Industrial
Experience of Female Cotton Workers in Quebec,
1910-1950 / 160
Gail Cuthbert Brandt

Selected Bibliography: 1980- / 174

Notes / 188

Acknowledgements

We wish to thank the individuals, organizations, and periodicals listed below for permission to reprint the articles in this second collection of essays in Canadian woman's history.

Jan Noel, "New France: Les femmes favorisées." Revised and reprinted from *Atlantis: A Women's Studies Journal*, 6, 2 (Spring, 1981), 80-98.

Margaret Conrad, "Recording Angels: The Private Chronicles of Women from the Maritime Provinces of Canada, 1750-1950." The original version of this paper was published by the Canadian Research Institute for the Advancement of Women/Institut canadien de recherches sur les femmes as #4 in the series The CRIAW Papers/Les documents de l'ICRAF.

Marjorie Griffin Cohen, "The Decline of Women in Canadian Dairying." Reproduced by permission of the author and the review: *Histoire sociale/Social History*, 18, 34 (November, 1984), 307-34.

Angus McLaren, "Birth Control and Abortion in Canada, 1870-1920." Reprinted by permission of the author and University of Toronto Press from *Canadian Historical Review*, 59, 3 (September, 1978), 319-40.

Marilyn Barber, "The Women Ontario Welcomed: Immigrant Domestics for Ontario Homes, 1870-1930." Revised and reprinted with the permission of the author and the Ontario Historical Society. The original article appeared in *Ontario History*, 72, 3 (September, 1980), 148-72.

Marta Danylewycz, "Changing Relationships: Nuns and Feminists in Montreal, 1890-1925." Reproduced by permission of the author and the review: *Histoire sociale/Social History*, 14, 28 (November, 1981), 413-34.

Susan Walsh, "The Peacock and the Guinea Hen: Political Profiles of Dorothy Gretchen Steeves and Grace MacInnis." Reprinted from Barbara J. Latham and Roberta J. Pazdro, eds., *Not Just Pin Money: Selected Essays on the History of Women's Work in British Columbia* (Victoria, B.C.: Camosun College, 1984), 365-79.

Gail Cuthbert Brandt, "'Weaving It Together': Life Cycle and the Industrial Experience of Female Cotton Workers in Quebec, 1910-1950." Reprinted from *Labour/Le Travailleur*, 8 (Spring, 1981), 113-26, by permission of the author and the editor. © Committee on Canadian Labour History.

We also wish to thank Beth Light for her bibliographic assistance.

Contributors

Marilyn Barber is a professor of history at Carleton University.

Gail Cuthbert Brandt is a professor of history at Glendon College, York University.

Marjorie Cohen is a lecturer in social science at York University.

Margaret Conrad is a professor of history at Acadia University.

Marta Danylewycz was a professor of history at Atkinson College, York University, until her tragic death in March, 1985.

Angus McLaren is a professor of history at the University of Victoria.

Jan Noel is a doctoral student in history at the University of Toronto.

Susan Walsh is with Canada World Youth after completing graduate studies at Simon Fraser University.

Alison Prentice is a professor of history and Head of the Centre for Women's Studies in Education at the Ontario Institute for Studies in Education.

Susan Mann Trofimenkoff is a professor of history and Vice-Rector, Academic, at the University of Ottawa.

*This volume is dedicated
to the memory of
Marta Danylewycz (1947-1985),
whom we loved.*

Introduction

In the eight years since the publication of *The Neglected Majority* women's history in Canada has developed tremendously.[1] There are courses at the upper levels of the educational system; in colleges and universities women's history is frequently the backbone of the growing number of women's studies programs. Books of documents and bibliographies are appearing, historiographical essays chart the development of women's history,[2] and increasing numbers of graduate students are unearthing a different past as they comb the archives and libraries of the land. Journal editors and book publishers seek out manuscripts and the Canadian Committee on Women's History, an affiliate of the Canadian Historical Association, has instituted the annual Hilda Neatby Prize for the best article in the subject published in a Canadian journal. There are even jobs in the field as male faculty members agree to hire historians of women. Some of these same men are tentatively restructuring their own courses and carefully watching their tongues as women's history begins to query traditional approaches to the past.

In short, women's history is meeting the scholarly and the political challenge that so excited its early practitioners in the 1970s. The simple and yet startling question – "What about the women?" – posed in the late 1960s because of the development of social history and of the women's movement, has not only produced a new specialization but has also prodded the entire discipline. Indeed, what kind of history could pretend to comprehensiveness when it systematically excluded 50 per cent – or more – of the population? Even the famous French *Annales* school, one of the few historical approaches to gain worldwide notice for its claim to "total history," pays scant attention to women.[3] The disregard is of course understandable when one recalls that historians are very much part of their own society: the questions they ask of the past and the approaches they bring to it are coloured by their own perception of the present. That present remains dominated by men. One need only look at the political, judicial, economic, religious, educational, military, and professional institutions of contemporary society to realize that a disregard for women is a distinguishing trait. In general, women are either non-existent or decidedly subordinate. The exception – or perhaps the confirmation – may lie in the family. How does one reconcile the tremendous regard for women and the terrible violence against them in the same setting? Does the ideological status of wife and mother exact a very high price? For the feminist historian, the answers lie in the past. Committed to changing the present, she is first obliged to change the past.

Changing the past in Canada has, broadly speaking, taken two routes. One of them, more popular with the media and the school system, has sought out those individual women who have made some impact on the largely male world of politics, education, or religion. Such an approach, at least until recently, has tended to take male activity as the norm and to celebrate those few women who have either "made it" themselves within a male world or who have struggled to enlarge that world to make room for women. In general, these individual women are exceptional, gifted by character or fortune. They are the "heroines" of New France, the founders of schools, hospitals, and religious orders, the advisers to bishops and governors; they are the firsts in higher education, professional training, or politics; they are the battlers for women's rights. Once historians have unearthed them, they show up fairly quickly in portrait galleries, popular magazines, and even on postage stamps. Perhaps they serve as role models; perhaps they are just the token women of the past. Frequently they and their causes are mistaken for the sole substance of the history of women.

Uneasy about such limitations, historians have increasingly been exploring a second route toward changing the past. More appropriately (if somewhat protectively) entitled women's history, this route examines groups of women in their own setting and defines importance in their terms. Drawing on the life cycle or life course pattern familiar to demographers and anthropologists, women's historians wonder about growing up as a girl in the past: how was she educated, what did she do, what expectations did she have and how did these contrast with those of other people in her familial, social, or educational milieu? Did the fact that she was a girl make a difference to her upbringing? The middle years of a woman's life then come under scrutiny: occupation, courtship, marriage, sexuality, motherhood, child-rearing, household management, community involvement. How was all this done and did it differ by region, by ethnicity, by religion, or by social class, to say nothing of time? And what if the woman were single, or widowed? How did she approach or experience old age and dying?

As the questions emerge so do the ways of answering them. If the first route to the history of (certain) women summoned the familiar sources of newspapers, private and public correspondence, speeches or writings of the individual concerned, and the records of educational, legal, religious, and political institutions, the second route to women's history conjures up more unusual sources. Census records (particularly the pre-1891 manuscript versions) divulge all manner of information about women who left no other trace: the size of families, the spacing of children, age differences between wives and husbands, the presence of boarders or relatives in households, as well as the usual census categories of religion, origin, and occupation. Medical, parish, and church records can be mined as can recipe books, pattern books, and architectural records, along with more standard popular magazines, diaries, photographs, and novels. The more unusual the source the more the women's historian has to befriend kindred spirits in other disciplines. To make these sources tell us things about the vast majority of women who left no records of their own, the historian has to acquire the skills of demography, psychology, anthropology, medicine, and even nutrition, to name just a few of the relevant areas.

This interdisciplinary approach is another of the characteristics of women's history, and it, too, has become increasingly evident over the past few years. There is, for example, no women's history journal in Canada. One might attribute this to the still small number of practitioners in this country, but even in the United States (where the periodic Berkshire Conference on the History of Women attracts some 2,000 enthusiasts) there is no such journal.[4] In both countries women's history is part of multidisciplinary approaches to the study of women, the two major journals being *Atlantis: A Women's Studies Journal* in Canada and *Signs: A Journal of Women and Culture* in the United States. This reaching beyond disciplinary boundaries, for insight, for support, for understanding, is another of the innovative features of the field; it is helped out tremendously in Canada by the information journal *Resources for Feminist Research/Documentation sur le recherche féministe.* Since 1976 such activity has been promoted by the Canadian Research Institute for the Advancement of Women/Institut canadien de recherches sur les femmes, whose annual meetings bring together feminist scholars from a variety of backgrounds. Historians of women are thus finding that they can actually talk to sociologists, linguists, philosophers, and even the occasional scientist.

While doing so they are constantly refining their own methods and approaches. Like other historians brushing up against the social sciences they are acquiring quantitative skills and theoretical perspectives. In English Canada, particularly, historians have traditionally shied away from methodological or theoretical discussions. Not that such concerns were absent from their work; they were merely subsumed in the very process of documentation and explanation that is the historian's domain. But the political commitment of women's history (both within the profession and the larger society), its interdisciplinary interests, and its self-consciousness have persuaded its practitioners to try to be more explicit. In particular they have had to confront a growing body of feminist theory developed by scholars throughout the Western world. Whether the theory needs grounding in historical experience or whether the theory provides questions for further historical inquiry, the challenge is there. And frequently the interplay reveals the shakiness of earlier, unstated premises. Were the women reformers of the late nineteenth century, for example, merely displaying a female version of their husbands' class interests in regulating the behaviour of the lower orders? Or were they also confined by notions about their own proper behaviour? Were they in fact subject to others' dictates or did they have some measure of control, some exercise of autonomy? Was the separation of the male and female spheres an accompaniment, a result, or a necessary pre-condition of industrialization? There's a theory behind every question and a book before every answer.

From such questions historians are tentatively mapping out a third route toward changing the past. After the history of women and women's history (neither of which is anywhere near completion), feminist history is now boldly proclaiming itself. Whether the label is merely a reflection of the self-confidence and exhilaration historians feel after scaling the heights for a decade or whether it does in fact delineate a new approach is open to debate. Certainly there has always been a feminist purpose to the whole women's history endeavour: to make of women cultural rather than natural beings; to find our bearings in the past in order to chart a course for the future. But the feminist tag also declares a commitment to equality and choice. Much of the little that history does tell us about women's experience, however, is that both equality and choice are very scarce commodities in human, let alone female, experience. Might the name "feminist," then, just refer to an interest in theory, from whatever its geographic or disciplinary source, and its application to a specific historical setting? Or is it a declaration of intent about the nature of history itself? In this latter case, do feminist historians seek to construct a history from women's point of view (in turn raising the question of the specificity of such a point of view and hence of the notion of women's culture)? Or do they seek an integrated history, balanced, whole, and human? Might feminist history be the ultimate in "global history"?

Fortunately, few of the answers are clear, or this book would serve no purpose. Indeed, as the articles indicate, historians tend to work the other way round, deciphering a piece at a time of the overall puzzle in the hope that one day an entirely new edifice will take shape. Some of the authors represented in the first edition of this book have since put their hand to the edifice. Sylvia Van Kirk's *"Many Tender Ties": Women in Fur Trade Society* alters dramatically our notions of the fur trade. Susan Mann Trofimenkoff's *Dream of Nation: A Social and Intellectual History of Quebec* has shocked many a male reader for its calm assumption of the equal significance of women. Veronica Strong-Boag is about to produce not just a book about Canadian women in the inter-war period but the only general account that we have at all of that time. Ruth Roach Pierson is anthologizing her many articles on women during the Second World War; the collective blow to established military history should be devastating. May the authors in this collection have an equally powerful impact.

Now that women are no longer so neglected in Canada's past, and because of the amount of new material since 1977, the choice of articles for this volume was more difficult than the earlier exercise. Some of the traits of the previous volume have been maintained. We have attempted a temporal and regional coverage so that the general reader can glimpse some of the contours of what one day will be a comprehensive history of women in Canada. (The *Collectif Clio* has already produced such a history for Quebec, *L'Histoire des femmes au Québec depuis quatre siècles*, and a group in English Canada is following suit.) We have selected articles to represent the various issues that historians of women have been tackling over the past few years. Where choices had to be made within those areas, we took the texts we particularly liked for their verve of presentation or their daring of question, method, or conclusion.

Most of the articles in this collection thus sit within five broad areas of concern to women's history as it has emerged in Canada over the past fifteen years or so. As will become evident, each area reflects a contemporary concern as well. The women's movement (in both its political and organizational aspects), the work of women (both within and outside the home), ideology, culture, and education, women and the family, and women's health and sexuality are as much on the agenda of contemporary feminists as they are on that of historians of women. Indeed, it was the importance of making sense of these issues today that set historians puzzling over their roots in Canada's past. The results are by no means complete; the picture is by no means comprehensive. But in these five areas, as the essays and the bibliography in this volume indicate, we are beginning to know something.

To understand the women's movement of the late nineteenth and early twentieth centuries, historians have concentrated on the aims, the actors, and the means. There they have documented complexity, subtlety, diplomacy, and frustration, but in this documentation they have found no sure model for contemporary success. Votes for women, for example, did not turn out to be a path to power for women or a recipe for restructuring the world. Rather, women's suffrage represented the culmination of a series of intertwined reform movements where women of a great variety of temperaments and backgrounds exercised considerable political finesse and negotiating skill to bring together labour, farm, women's, and Christian reform groups in support of their cause.[5] Suffrage was of course only the most publicly prominent of the causes advocated by the early women's movement. One of the more sobering revelations of historical investigation is that many of the other causes remain the same: at one hundred years' distance one can hear the same pleas for equal access to education, to training and the professions, for day care, for shared family and household responsibilities.[6] If there is any pattern to the acquisition of women's rights, it is decidedly not one of continual progress. And even if it were, a new problem seems to emerge just as an old one is on its way to solution. No sooner has the evil of unequal pay been recognized, if not yet eradicated, than the horror of pornography becomes evident. Each turn of the Sisyphean rock of women's rights seems to reveal another vile creature.

Somewhat more encouraging messages from the past come from the vast array of women's organizations in turn-of-the-century Canada. They not only kept the women's movement alive but also fostered much of the reform ethos characteristic of the period. From campaigns against alcohol to campaigns for pure milk, women organized vast networks of social reform. They did it in part because of a sexual division of labour that made it fitting for women to undertake familial duties in public. Taking advantage of the contemporary notion of separate spheres, they argued that it was their responsibility to clean up the civic and social disorder created by the male world of industrialization and urbanization. Not that these women were by any means united in their interests or activities. Some were in fact, as early historians have shown, bourgeois, conservative, and quite accepting of class, race, and sex divisions; they neither saw nor challenged the power relations between women and men in the family or the economy. But others are appearing as more recognizable feminists, even socialists, within various reform organizations. Early feminism, historians are now implying, had as many forms then as it does now. One might even suggest that the myriad reforms advocated and undertaken on a volunteer basis by these varied groups of women were at the origin of the welfare state in Canada. If the notion seems far-fetched, one need only consider the present-day dismantling of many aspects of the welfare state by male politicians calmly announcing that the family and community groups (still largely women's sphere) will take up the social burden.[7]

As any investigation of women and work shows, however, women frequently shoulder a familial and an economic burden as well as a social one. Indeed, it was doubtless a recognition in the 1960s – as increasing numbers of married women entered the public labour force – of the double, if not triple, ghetto of isolated household work and subordinate and segregated work in paid employment that led to a search of the past for an explanation of present binds.[8] Initially historians concentrated on paid work. There they discovered the original ghetto: massive numbers of women earning their living as domestic servants in an occupation where the numbers and proportions of men were in decline. This limiting of opportunities was even fostered by women of another social class. Certain women's organizations and reform groups encouraged both domestic science training in the schools and specific immigration policies for the country in order to ensure a steady supply of servants.[9] Of course, they could not put a halt to industrialization, and with that development many young women flocked to the factories. The fact that they preferred such work even though the conditions were demonstrably appalling hints at just how much worse life as a domestic servant must generally have been. But it also suggests the eagerness with which women embraced new economic opportunities: they actively sought industrial work, office work, teaching, nursing, social work, and the professions. And yet in each of those areas, some of which were especially designed for and restricted to women, they were invariably paid less than men and offered fewer chances for training and advancement. Moreover, their vulnerability to the economic order is also evident. During wartime in particular, they could be called into the service of the state only to be summarily dismissed (with palliatives such as family allowances) once the national crisis was over. And yet, all is not subordination and vulnerability in the study of women and work. A much more complex framework is taking shape as historians investigate such topics as the changing age structure of the female labour force, the regional variations in that labour force, as well as women's movement in and out of it according to the needs of parents, husbands, and children.[10]

Less clear, so far, is the history and character of women's unpaid household work. In part this is a reflection of historians' own ambivalence about housework. Being either disinterested in it or burdened by it, few Canadian historians have displayed much interest in its previous manifestations. They have tended therefore to rely on other disciplines and other media to reveal the nature of historical housework. Material culture experts in museums therefore display the vast field of domestic production that was women's work from New France until the 1920s. Feminist theorists influenced by Marxism argue that industrialization and urbanization undermined this work of women, dividing and scattering it to factories that were far from home. Still other theoreticians will say the same about women's reproductive labour: the school, the factory, the hospital, and perhaps even the tavern absorbed the woman's task of tending and shaping present and future generations. Sociologists have documented the process for single towns in the mid-twentieth century;[11] whether it can accurately be read into a common experience for all women remains to be seen. The temptation is to conclude from the theory that women, with less to do, turned their energies to reform or to consumerism, femininity, and even motherhood. But historians of technology from outside Canada advise caution: technological innovations facilitating and even removing some aspects of housework appear not to have reduced the time or energy required of women in households. Quite the contrary.[12]

While investigating such topics, historians keep bumping up against ideas about women. There appears to have been an unavoidable link between the kind of work women actually did, as paid workers, as volunteer social reformers, or as housewives, and ideological notions about what women ought to be doing. Most of those notions have been elaborated by men. Preachers, journalists, doctors, and politicians with their easy access to the media of the day were particularly vocal and historians have had a field day with their utterings. But how disconcerting it is to recognize so many of these Victorian ideas about woman's supposedly innate capacities – generally for tasks that make men comfortable. Even more so is the obvious acceptance of such ideas by women of the time and since. Just how and why this is so has yet to be satisfactorily explained. One of the avenues that historians have been exploring for some time leads to educational systems.[13] Whether segregated and organized by hierarchical religious orders or mixed and carefully scrutinized by elected commissioners or trustees, the message appears to have been the same: women were to be wives and mothers and the intellectual wings of young girls were to be clipped accordingly. Even the feminization of teaching seems not to have altered the message since women teachers were clustered in the lower grades, tending and nurturing. The "real" instruction took place at higher levels and there the teachers were men.[14]

Eventually historians began knocking at the door of the family. Might there be a link here between the domestication of women in the private sphere and the economic and political subordination of women in the public sphere? Were the two spheres in fact as separate as Victorian ideologies liked to pretend? And what happened when different kinds of families interacted, as they did in the Canadian West in the early nineteenth century? "Progress" on the Canadian frontier appears to have meant the introduction – by women – of racism as a means of undermining the essential economic and political roles of Indian and Métis wives of European and eastern Canadian fur traders.[15] The so-called nuclear family in nineteenth- and even early twentieth-century Canada appears to have had an inordinate number of boarders and relatives floating in and out. Even the children were constantly on the move: they either went elsewhere as servants or apprentices or joined the labour force at a very young age. In times of family difficulty they fre-

quented religious or charitable institutions. Their comings and goings were part of entire family strategies for survival in urban
centres where "the working poor" entailed all family members. Just
what the emotional configurations were in such families remains to
be deciphered.

Tackling that area of emotional configurations has been perhaps
the most tantalizing and difficult of historians' endeavours. Snoop-
ing into the hearts and bedrooms of the past seems at first an
exaggerated form of contemporary prurience. And yet so much of
women's identity has traditionally been associated with sexual activity (as mother or prostitute, to cite only the most common of the
dichotomies that accompany the genital demarcation at birth) that
historians would be remiss in ignoring it. Indeed, one could easily
argue that changing contraceptive practices comprise the most significant pattern in the history of wo/mankind. Certainly the topic
reveals power relations between the sexes as doctors, press, and
politicians attempted to keep women ignorant (and pregnant) while
the women themselves fought back with their woman-knowledge,
their access to mail-order potions, and their apparent willingness to
contemplate (and risk) both abortion and infanticide.[16] It may well
be that only an understanding of this private world of femaleness,
coupled with the ideologies that swirl around it, can illuminate the
puzzling patterns of female behaviour in the work world, in the
family, or in the women's movement.

Nor are individual studies easily categorized as belonging to one
area of investigation rather than another. Indeed, nearly all of the
essays in this volume address the *connections* that are so important
to women's lives: between women's work and politics, for example
(Danylewycz's "Nuns and Feminists in Montreal"), or between work
and family life (Brandt's "Weaving It Together").

In all five areas, much more remains to be done. Women's history
has made an impact on the history of Canada, but if these five
areas exemplify the work of Canadian historians of women over
the past decade or so, they by no means exhaust the field. And if
women's history has already made an impact on the nature of
history in Canada, it has by no means been totally integrated into a
new and more complex understanding of our past. We need biographies from a feminist perspective; we need to know about
women's political behaviour, in particular the link between their
personal lives and their political views.[17] What of their interaction
with the law, their participation in the professions, their resistance
to or compliance with social norms, their experience of primary

resource frontiers, of higher education? We need to know how they brought up their children and how they organized their households. We need to explore the idea of women's culture in an immigrant/ colonial society. And we need to know all these things across time and space and social class. May the readers of this book be inspired to continue asking impertinent and important questions of the past – and the present.

1

New France: Les femmes favorisées

Jan Noel

You constantly behold, with renewed astonishment, women in the very depths of indigence and want, perfectly instructed in their religion, ignorant of nothing that they should know to employ themselves usefully in their families and who, by their manners, their manner of expressing themselves and their politeness, are not inferior to the most carefully educated among us.[1]

Les femmes l'emportent sur les hommes par la beauté, la vivacité, la gaité [sic] et l'enjouement; elles sont coquettes et galantes, préfèrent les Européens aux gens du pays. Les manières douces et polies sont communes, même dans les campagnes.[2]

... les femmes y sont fort aimables, mais extrêmement fières.[3]

... elles sont spirituelles, ce qui leur donne de la supériorité sur les hommes dans presque tous les états.[4]

Many a man, observing the women of New France, was struck by the advantages they possessed in education, cultivation, and that quality called *esprit* or wit. Even an unsympathetic observer of colonial society, such as the French military officer Franquet, who visited New France in 1752-53, admitted that its women "l'emportent sur les hommes pour l'esprit, généralement elles en ont toutes beaucoup, parlant un français épuré, n'ont pas le moindre accent, aiment aussi la parure, sont jolies, généreuses et même maniérées."[5] He notes, albeit with disapproval, that women very commonly aspired to stations above those to which they were born.[6] The Swedish naturalist Peter Kalm, who deplored the inadequate housekeeping of Canadian women, nevertheless admired their refinement.[7]

Those for whom history is an exercise in statistics have taught us caution in accepting the accounts of travellers, which are often highly subjective. However, the consensus (particularly that of seasoned observers such as Charlevoix and Kalm) on the superior education and wit of women in New France suggests that their views are founded on something more than natural male proclivity toward *la différence*. Moreover, historians' accounts of society in New France offer considerable evidence that women did indeed enjoy an unusually privileged position in that colony. It is difficult to think of another colony or country in which women founders showed such important leadership – not just in the usual tending of families and farms but in arranging financing, immigration, and defences that played a major role in the colony's survival. It is unusual for girls to receive a primary education better than that of the boys – as many evidently did in New France. One is also struck by the initiative of *canadiennes* in business and commerce. In sum, with respect to their education, their range and freedom of action, women in New France seem in many ways to compare favourably with their contemporaries in France and New England, and certainly with the Victorians who came after them.

Two cautions are in order. First, to arrive at a full appreciation of the position of women in New France would require detailed comparisons with their contemporaries in other Western countries and colonies. The study of *ancien régime* businesswomen, in particular, is a nascent enterprise. In this paper some twenty outstanding figures in business and politics will be examined and hypotheses put forward about what facilitated their rise to positions of influence. To what degree these women were outstanding in the context of their times one cannot yet say with precision. Second, it is not intended to portray New France as some sort of utopia for women. Women, like men, suffered from disease, privation, class inequalities, and the perennial scourge of war. There were also women's particular hardships, such as the dangers of childbirth and the difficulties of assuming double duty when the men were away. A definitive study of women in New France, which will plumb the primary sources and range the continents for useful comparisons, remains to be made. The purpose of this paper is to marshal the fairly extensive evidence that can be found in published works on New France in support of the thesis that women there enjoyed a relatively privileged position, and to discuss why they might have done so.

Why did the women of New France assume leadership positions? How did they acquire a superior education? How did they come to be involved in commerce? There is no single answer. Three separate elements help account for the situation. First, as studies of Western Europe under the *ancien régime* have indicated, ideas about women's roles were surprisingly flexible and varied at the time New France was founded. Second, the particular demographic configuration of the colony gave female immigrants a number of advantages not available to their counterparts in Europe. Third, the colonial economy, with its heavy emphasis on war and the fur trade, seems to have presented women with a special set of opportunities. Thus, as we shall see, the French cultural heritage and demographic and economic conditions in the colony combined to create the situation that so impressed contemporary observers.

Women and the Family under the *Ancien Régime*

The notion of "woman's place" or "women's role," popular with nineteenth-century commentators, suggests a degree of homogeneity inappropriate to the seventeenth century. It is true that on a formal ideological level men enjoyed the dominant position. This can be seen in the marriage laws, which everywhere made it a wife's duty to follow her husband to whatever dwelling place he chose.[8] In 1650, the men of Montreal were advised by Governor Maisonneuve that they were in fact responsible for the misdemeanours of their wives since "la loi les établit seigneurs de leurs femmes."[9] Under ordinary circumstances the father was captain of the family hierarchy.[10] Yet, it is clear that this formal male authority in both economic and domestic life was not always exercised. Of early seventeenth-century France we are told that

> si la prééminence masculine n'a rien perdu de son prestige, si elle n'a eu à se défendre contre aucune revendication théorique ... elle a dû ... souvent se contenter des apparences et abandonner devant les convenances et les exigences du public l'intérêt positif qu'elle défendait.[11]

The idea of separate male and female spheres lacked the clear definition it later acquired. This is in part related to the lack of communication and standardization characteristic of the *ancien régime* – along sexual lines or any other. Generalizations about women are riddled with exceptions. Contradicting the idea of female inferiority, for example, were the semi-matriarchal system in the Basque country and the linen workers' guild, in which a 1645 statute prevented a worker's husband from engaging in occupations unrelated to his wife's business, for which he often served as salesman or partner. More important, because it affected a larger group, was the fact that noblewomen were frequently exempt from legal handicaps affecting other women.[12]

One generalization, however, applies to all women of the *ancien régime*. They were not relegated to the private, domestic sphere of human activity because that sphere did not exist. Western Europeans had not yet learned to separate public and private life. As Philippe Ariès points out in his study of childhood, the private home, in which parents and children constitute a distinct unit, is a relatively recent development. In early modern Europe most of domestic life was lived in the company of all sorts of outsiders. Manor houses, where all the rooms interconnect with one another, show the lack of emphasis placed on privacy. Here, as in peasant dwellings, there were often no specialized rooms for sleeping, eating, working, or receiving visitors; all were more or less public activities performed with a throng of servants, children, relatives, clerics, apprentices, and clients in attendance. Molière's comedies illustrate the familiarity of servants with their masters. Masters, maids, and valets slept in the same room and servants discussed their masters' lives quite openly.[13]

Though familiar with their servants, people were less so with their children. They did not dote on infants to the extent that parents do today. It may have been, as some writers have suggested, that there was little point in growing attached to a fragile being so very apt, in those centuries, to be borne away by accident or disease. These unsentimental families of all ranks sent their children out to apprentice or serve in other people's homes. This was considered important as a basic education.[14] It has been estimated that the majority of Western European children passed part of their childhood living in some household other than their natal one.[15] Mothers of these children – reaching down, in the town, as far as the artisan class – might send their infants out to nursemaids and have very little to do with their physical maintenance.[16]

This lack of a clearly defined "private" realm relates vitally to the history of women, since this was precisely the sphere they later were to inhabit.[17] Therefore it is important to focus on their place in the pre-private world. To understand women in New France one first must pass through that antechamber which Peter Laslett appropriately calls "the world we have lost." Its notions of sexuality and of the family apply to France and New France alike.

In this public world people had not yet learned to be private about their bodily functions, especially about their sexuality. For aid with their toilette, noblewomen did not blush to employ *hommes de chambre* rather than maids. The door of the bed-chamber stood ajar, if not absolutely open. Its inhabitants, proud of their fecundity, grinned out from under the bedclothes at their visitors. Newlyweds customarily received bedside guests.[18] The mother of Louis XIV held court and chatted with visitors while labouring to bring *le Roi Soleil* into light of day. Humbler village women kept lesser court among the little crowd of neighbours who attended the midwife's efforts.[19] On the other side of the ocean, Franquet, arriving at Trois-Rivières in 1753, enjoyed the hospitality of Madame Rigaud de Vaudreuil who, feeling poorly, apparently received her visitors at bedside; farther west, he shared a bedroom with a married couple at Fort St. Jean.[20] From the seventeenth century to the colony's last days, clerics thundered more or less futilely against the *décolletage* of the *élite*.[21] Lesser folk leaned toward short skirts[22] and boisterous public discussion of impotent husbands.[23] Rape cases also reveal a rather matter-of-fact attitude. Courts stressed monetary compensation for the victim (as if for trespass on private property) rather than wreaking vengeance on the lustful villain.[24] There was not the same uneasiness in relations between the sexes which later, more puritanical, centuries saw, and which, judging by the withdrawal of women from public life in many of these societies, probably worked to their detriment.

Part of the reason these unsqueamish, rather public people were not possessive about their bodies was that they did not see them-selves so much as individuals but as part of a larger, more important unit – the family. In this world the family was the basic organization for most social and economic purposes.[25] As such it claimed the individual's first loyalty.[26] A much higher proportion of the popula-tion married than does today.[27] Studies of peasant societies suggest that, for most, marriage was an economic necessity:

> Le travail, particulièrement en milieu rural, était alors fondé sur une répartition des tâches entre les sexes: les marins et colporteurs sont absents plusieurs mois, leurs femmes font valoir les terres; les pêcheurs des marais vont au marché, les femmes à la pêche; le laboureur travaille aux champs, sa femme à la maison, c'est elle qui va au marché; dans le pays d'Auge, "les hommes s'occupent des bestiaux et les femmes aux fromages". Pour vivre il fallait donc être deux, un homme et une femme.[28]

The family was able to serve as the basic economic unit in pre-industrial societies because the business of earning a living generally occurred at home. Just as public and private life were undifferentiated, so too were home and workplace. Agricultural and commercial pursuits were all generally "domestic" industries. We see this both in France and in New France. Removal of the man from home for most of the working day, an event that Laslett describes as the single most important event in the history of the modern European family,[29] was only beginning. The idea of man as breadwinner and woman as homemaker was not clearly developed. Women's range of economic activity was still nearly as wide as that of their husbands. Seventeenth-century France saw women working as bonesetters, goldbeaters, bookbinders, doubletmakers, burnishers, laundresses, woolfullers, and wigmakers. Aside from their familiar role in the textile and clothing industries, women also entered heavy trades such as stoneworking and bricklaying. A master plumber, Barbe Legueux, maintained the drainage system for the fountains of Paris. In the commercial world, women worked as fishmongers, pedlars, greengrocers, publicans, money-lenders, and auctioneers.[30] In New France, wives of artisans took advantage of their urban situation to attract customers into the taverns they set up alongside the workshop.[31] It was in farm work, which occupied most of the population, that male and female tasks differed the least of all. *Habitantes* in New France toiled in the fields alongside the men, and they almost certainly – being better educated than their French sisters – took up the farm wife's customary role of keeping accounts and managing purchases and sales.[32] Studies of Bordeaux commercial families have revealed that women also took a large role in business operations.[33] Marie de l'Incarnation's background as manager of one of France's largest transport companies[34] shows that the phenomenon existed in other parts of France as well.

Given the economic importance of both spouses, it is not surprising to see marriage taking on some aspects of a business deal, with numerous relatives affixing their signatures to the contract. We see this in the provisions of the law that protected the property rights of both parties contracting a match. The fact that wives often brought considerable family property to the marriage, and retained rights to it, placed them in a better position than their nineteenth-century descendants were to enjoy.[35]

In New France the family's importance was intensified even beyond its usual economic importance in *ancien régime* societies. In the colony's early days, "all roads led to matrimony. The scarcity of women, the economic difficulties of existence, the danger, all tended to produce the same result: all girls became wives, all widows remarried."[36] Throughout the colony's history there was an exceptionally high annual marriage rate of eighteen to twenty-four per thousand.[37] The buildup of the family as a social institution perhaps came about because other social institutions, such as guilds and villages, were underdeveloped.[38] This heightened importance of the family probably enhanced women's position. In the family women tended to serve as equal partners with their husbands, whereas women were gradually losing their position in European guilds and professions.[39] We see this importance of the family in the government's great concern to regulate it. At that time, the state *did* have a place in Canadian bedrooms (whose inhabitants we have already seen to be rather unconcerned about their privacy). Public intervention in domestic life took two major forms: the operation of the legal system and governmental attempts at family planning.

The outstanding characteristic of the legal system in New France – the *Coutume de Paris* – is its concern to protect the rights of all members of the family. The *Coutume de Paris* is considered to have been a particularly benevolent regional variation of French law.[40] It was more egalitarian and less patriarchal than the laws of southern France, which were based on Roman tradition. The *Coutume* reinforced the family, for example, by the penalties it levied on those transferring family property to non-kin.[41] It took care to protect the property of children of a first marriage when a widow or widower remarried.[42] It protected a woman's rights by assuring that the husband did not have power to alienate the family property (in contrast to eighteenth-century British law).[43] The Canadians not only adopted the Parisian *coutume* in preference to the Norman *coutume*, which was harsher;[44] they also implemented the law in a way that maximized protection of all family members. Louise Dechêne, after examining the operation of the marriage and inheritance system, concludes that the Canadian application of the law was generous and egalitarian:

> Ces conventions matrimoniales ne nous apparaissent pas comme un marché, un affrontement entre deux lignées, mais comme un accord désintéressé entre les familles, visant à créer une nouvelle communauté, à l'assister si possible, à dresser quelques barrières à l'entour pour la protéger. . . .[45]

The criminal law, too, served to buttress family life with its harsh punishments for mistreatment of children.[46]

The royal administration, as well as the law, treated the family as a matter of vital public concern. The state often intervened in matters that later generations left to the individual or to the operations of private charity. Most famous, of course, is the policy of encouraging a high birth rate with financial incentives. There were also attempts to withdraw trading privileges from voyageurs who showed reluctance to take immigrant women to wife.[47] Particularly in the seventeenth century, we see the state regulating what modern societies would consider intimate matters. However, in a colony starved for manpower, reproduction was considered a matter of particularly vital public concern – a concern well demonstrated in the extremely harsh punishments meted out to women who concealed pregnancy.[48] We see a more positive side of this intervention in the care the Crown took of foundlings, employing nurses at a handsome salary to care for them and making attempts to prevent children from bearing any stigma because of questionable origins.[49]

State regulation of the family was balanced by family regulation of the state. Families had an input into the political system, playing an important role in the running of the state. Indeed, it might be argued that the family was the basic political unit in New France. In an age when some members of the *noblesse* prided themselves on their illiteracy, attending the right college was hardly the key to political success. Marrying into the right family was much more important. Nepotism, or rewarding one's kin with emoluments, seemed a most acceptable and natural form of patronage for those in power.[50] In this sense, a good marriage was considered a step upward for the whole family, which helps to explain why choice of spouse was so often a family decision.[51] These family lines were particularly tightly drawn among the military élite in New France. Franquet remarked that *"tous les gens d'un certain ordre sont liés de parenté et d'amitié dans ce pays."*[52] In fact, with top military positions passing down from generation to generation, by the eighteenth century this élite became a caste.[53]

In this situation, where the *nom de famille* was vastly more important than that of the individual, it was apparently almost as good for political (though not military) purposes to be an Agathe de Repentigny as a LeGardeur de Repentigny. Moreover, women's political participation was favoured by the large role of entertaining in political life. For the courtier's role, women were as well trained as men, and there seems to have been no stigma attached to the woman who participated independently of her husband. Six women, Mesdames Daine, Pean, Lotbinière, de Repentigny, Marin, and St. Simon, along with six male officers, were chosen by the

Intendant to accompany him to Montreal in 1753.[54] Of the twelve
only the de Repentignys were a couple. It is surprising to see
women from the colony's first families also getting down to what
we would today consider the "business" end of politics. Madame de
la Forest, a member of the Juchereau family, took an active role in
the political cliques that Guy Frégault describes.[55] Mme. de la
Forest's trip to France to plead the cause of Governor de Ramezay
was inconsequential, though, in comparison with that of Mme. de
Vaudreuil to further Governor Vaudreuil's cause in 1709. "*Douée
d'un sens politique très fin*,"[56] she soon gained the ear of the Minister of Marine. Not only did she secure the Governor's victory in the
long conflict with the Intendants Raudot (father and son) and win
promotion for his patrons; she appears to have gone on to upstage
her husband by becoming the virtual director of colonial policy at
Versailles for a few years. Vaudreuil's biographer discusses the influence Madame de Vaudreuil exerted with the Minister Pontchar-
train who so regularly sought her comments on colonial patronage
that supplicants began to apply directly to her rather than to the
minister.[57] Contemporaries agreed that her influence was vast:

> Pontchartrain, rapporte Ruette d'Auteuil, ne lui refuse rien, "elle
> dispose de tous les emplois du Canada, elle écrit de toutes parts
> dans les ports de mer des lettres magnifiques du bien et du mal
> qu'elle peut faire auprès de lui," et le ministre "fait tout ce qu'il
> faut pour l'autoriser et justifier ses discours." Riverin confirme
> que ... "ce n'est plus qu'une femme qui règne tant présente
> qu'absente."[58]

Governor Frontenac's wife (though not a *Canadienne*) also played
an important role at court, dispelling some of the thunderclouds
that threatened her husband's stormy career.[59]

As for the common folk, we know less about the political activity of women than that of men. That women participated in a
form of popular assembly is hinted at in a report of a meeting held
in 1713 (in present-day Boucherville), in which Catherine Guertin
was sworn in as midwife after having been elected "*dans l'assemblée
des femmes de cette paroisse, à la pluralité des suffrages, pour
exercer l'office de sagefemme*."[60] Were these women's assemblies a
general practice? If so, what other matters did they decide? This
aspect of *habitant* politics remains a mystery. It is clear, though,
that women were part of what historians have called the "pre-industrial crowd."[61] Along with their menfolk, they were full-fledged
members of the old "moral economy" whose members rioted and

took what was traditionally their rightful share (and no more) when prices were too high or when speculators were hoarding grain.[62] The women of Quebec and Montreal, who rioted against the horsemeat rations and the general hunger of 1757-58, illustrate this aspect of the old polity.[63]

In sum, women's position during the *ancien régime* was open-ended. Although conditions varied, a wide range of roles were available to women, to be taken up or not. This was so because the separate spheres of men and women in *ancien régime* societies were not so clearly developed as they later became. There was as yet no sharp distinction between public and private life: families were for most purposes the basic social, economic, and political unit. This situation was intensified in New France due to the underdevelopment of other institutions, such as the guild, the seigneurie, and the village. The activities of breadwinner and homemaker were not yet widely recognized as separate functions belonging to one sex or the other. All members of the family also often shared the same economic functions, or at least roles were interchangeable. Nor had the symbolic honorific aspects of government yet been separated from the business end of politics and administration. These conditions, typical of most of pre-industrial France, were also found in New France, where particular demographic and economic conditions would enable the colony's women to develop the freedoms and opportunities that this fluid situation allowed.

Demographic Advantages

Demography favoured the women of New France in two ways. First, the women who went there were a highly select group of immigrants. Second, women were in short supply in the early years of the colony's development, a situation that worked in their favour.

The bulk of the female immigrants to New France fall into one of two categories. The first was a group of extremely well-born, well-endowed, and highly dedicated religious figures. They began to arrive in 1639, and a trickle of French nuns continued to cross the ocean over the course of the next century. The second distinct group was the *filles du roi*, government-sponsored female migrants who arrived between 1663 and 1673. These immigrants, though not as outstanding as the *dévotes*, were nevertheless privileged compared to the average immigrant to New France, who arrived more or less threadbare.[64] The vast majority of the women (and the men) came from the Île-de-France and the northwestern parts of France.

The women of northern France enjoyed fuller legal rights and were better educated and more involved in commerce than those in southern France.[65] When they set foot on colonial soil with all this auspicious baggage, the immigrants found that they had yet another advantage. Women constituted a small percentage of the population. As a scarce resource they were highly prized and therefore in an excellent position to gain further advantages.

The first *religieuses* to arrive in New France were the Ursulines and Hospitallers who landed at Quebec in 1639. These were soon followed by women who helped establish Montreal in 1642. Their emigration was inspired by a religious revival in France, which is thought to have arisen in response to the widespread pauperism following the French civil wars of the sixteenth century. The seventeenth-century revival distinguished itself by tapping the energies of women in an unprecedented way.[66] Among its leaders were Anne of Austria and a number of the leading ladies at court.[67] In other parts of France, women of the provincial élite implemented the charity work inspired by Saint Vincent de Paul.[68] Occurring between 1600 and 1660, this religious revival coincided almost exactly with the period when the fledgling Canadian colony, besieged by English privateers and by the Iroquois, was most desperately in need of an injection of immigrants, money, and enthusiasm.[69] It was at this moment that the Jesuits in Quebec appealed to the French public for aid. Much to their surprise, they received not a donation but a half-dozen religious zealots, in person. Abandoning the centuries-old cloistered role of female religious figures these nuns undertook missionary work that gave them an active role in the life of the colony.[70] Thus the great religious revival of the seventeenth century endowed New France with several exceptionally capable, well-funded, determined leaders imbued with an activist approach to charity and with that particular mixture of spiritual ardour and worldly *savoir-faire* that typified the mystics of that period.[71] The praises of Marie de l'Incarnation, Jeanne Mance, and Marguerite Bourgeoys have been sung so often as to be tiresome. Perhaps, though, a useful vantage point is gained if one assesses them neither as saints nor heroines, but simply as leaders. In this capacity, the nuns supplied money, publicity, skills, and settlers, all of which were needed in the colony.

Marie de l'Incarnation, a competent businesswoman from Tours, founded the Ursuline Monastery at Quebec in 1639. Turning to the study of Indian languages, she and her colleagues helped implement the policy of assimilating the young Indians. Then, gradually abandoning that futile policy, they turned to the education of the French colonists. Marie de l'Incarnation developed the farm on the Ursuline seigneurie and served as an unofficial adviser to the colonial administrators. She also helped draw attention and money to the colony by writing some 12,000 letters between 1639 and her death in 1672.[72]

An even more prodigious fund-raiser in those straitened times was Jeanne Mance, who had a remarkable knack for making friends in high places.[73] They enabled her to supply money and colonists for the original French settlement on the island of Montreal, and to take a place beside Maisonneuve as co-founder of the town.[74] The hospital she established there had the legendary wealth of the de Bullion family – and the revenues of three Norman domains – behind it. From this endowment she made the crucial grant to Governor Maisonneuve in 1651 that secured vitally needed troops from France, thus saving Montreal.[75] Mance and her Montreal colleague Margeurite Bourgeoys both made several voyages to France to recruit settlers. They were particularly successful in securing the female immigrants necessary to establish a permanent colony, recruiting sizable groups in 1650, 1653, and 1659.[76]

Besides contributing to the colony's sheer physical survival, the nuns raised the living standards of the population materially. They conducted the schools attended by girls of all classes and from both of the colony's races. Bourgeoys provided housing for newly arrived immigrants and served in a capacity perhaps best described as an early social worker.[77] Other nuns established hospitals in each of the three towns. The colonists reaped fringe benefits in the institutions established by this exceptionally dedicated personnel. The hospitals, for example, provided high-quality care to both rich and poor, care that compared favourably with that of similar institutions in France.[78] Thus, the *dévotes* played an important role in supplying leadership, funding, publicity, recruits, and social services. They may even have tipped the balance toward survival in the 1650s, when retention of the colony was still in doubt.

In the longer run, they endowed the colony with an educational heritage, which survived and shaped social life long after the initial heroic piety had grown cold. The schools that the *dévotes* founded created a situation very different from that in France, where education of women in the seventeenth century lagged behind that of men.[79] The opinion-setters in France sought to justify this neglect in the eighteenth century and a controversy began over whether girls should be educated outside the home at all.[80] Girls in Montreal escaped all this. Indeed, in 1663 Montrealers had a school for their girls but none for their boys. The result was that for a time Montreal women surpassed men in literacy, a reversal of the usual *ancien régime* pattern.[81] The superior education of women that Charlevoix extolled in 1744 continued until the fall of New France (and beyond) – a tendency heightened by the large percentage of soldiers, generally illiterate, among the male population.[82] The Ursulines conducted schools for the élite at Quebec and Trois-Rivières. This order was traditionally rather weak in teaching housekeeping (which perhaps accounts for Kalm's famous castigation of Canadian housewifery). Nevertheless they specialized in needlework, an important skill since articles of clothing were a major trade good sought by the Indians. Moreover, the Ursulines taught the daughters of the élite the requisite skills for administering a house and a fortune – skills which, as we shall see later, many were to exercise.[83]

More remarkable than the Ursuline education, however, was that of the *Soeurs de la Congrégation*, which reached the popular classes in the countryside.[84] Franquet was apparently shocked by the effect of this exceptional education on the colonial girls. He recommended that the *Soeurs'* schools be suppressed because they made it difficult to keep girls down on the farm:

> Ces Soeurs sont répandues le long des côtes, dans des seigneuries où elles ont été attirées pour l'éducation des jeunes filles; leur utilité semble être démontrée, mais le mal qu'en résulte est comme un poison lent qui tend à dépeupler les campagnes, d'autant qu'une fille instruite fait la demoiselle, qu'elle est maniérée, qu'elle veut prendre un éstablissement à la ville, qu'il lui faut un négociant et qu'elle regarde au dessous d'elle l'état dans lequel elle est née.[85]

The second distinct group of female immigrants to New France was the famous *filles du roi*, women sent out by the French government as brides in order to boost the colony's permanent settlement. Over 900 arrived between 1663 and 1673.[86] If less impressive than the *dévotes*, they, too, appear to have arrived with more than the average immigrant's store of education and capital. Like the nuns, they were the product of a particular historical moment that thrust them across the sea. The relevant event here is that brief interlude in the 1660s and 1670s when the King, his Minister Colbert, and the Intendant Talon applied an active hand to colonial development.[87]

There has been much historical controversy about whether the *filles du roi* were pure or not.[88] More relevant to our discussion than their morality are their money and their skills. On both these counts, this was a very selective immigration. First of all, the majority of the *filles du roi* (and for that matter, of seventeenth-century female immigrants generally) were urban dwellers, a group that enjoyed better access to education than the peasantry did.[89] Moreover, the *filles du roi* were particularly privileged urbanites. Over one-third, some 340 of them, were educated at the Paris Hôpital Général. Students at this institution learned writing and such a wide variety of skills that in France they were much sought after for service in the homes of the wealthy. Six per cent were of noble or bourgeois origin. Many of the *filles* brought with them a 50-100 *livres* dowry provided by the King;[90] some supplemented this with personal funds in the order of 200-300 *livres*. Sixty-five of the *filles* brought considerably larger holdings, in the range of 400 to 450 *livres*, to their marriages.[91] The Parisian origins of many *filles du roi*, and of the nuns who taught their children, probably account for the pure French accent that a number of travellers attributed to the colony's women.[92]

These two major immigrant groups, then, the nuns and the *filles du roi*, largely account for the superior education and "cultivation" attributed to the colony's women. Another demographic consideration also favoured the women of New France. As a result of light female emigration, men heavily outnumbered women in the colony's early days.[93] It might be expected that, as a scarce commodity, women would receive favoured treatment. The facility of marriage and remarriage, as well as the leniency of the courts and the administrators toward women, suggests that this hypothesis is correct.

Women had a wider choice in marriage than did men in the colony's early days. There were, for example, eight marriageable men for every marriageable woman in Montreal in 1663. Widows grieved, briefly, then remarried within an average of 8.8 months after their bereavement. In those early days the laws of supply and demand operated to women's economic advantage, as well. Rarely did these first Montreal women bother to match their husband's wedding present by offering a dowry.[94] The colony distinguished itself as "the country of the *douaire* not of the *dot*."[95]

In the social and legal realm we also find privileges that may have been attributable to the shortage of women. Perhaps it is due to the difficulties of replacing battered wives that jealous husbands in New France were willing to forgo the luxury of uncontrolled rage. Some of the intendants even charged that there were libertine wives in the colony who got away with taking a second husband while the first was away trading furs.[96] Recent indications that New France conformed rather closely to French traditions make it unlikely that this was common.[97] But the judgements of the Sovereign Council do offer evidence of peaceful reconciliations such as that of Marguerite Leboeuf, charged with adultery in 1667. The charge was dismissed when her husband pleaded before the Sovereign Council on her behalf. Also leaving vengeance largely to the Lord was Antoine Antorche, who withdrew his accusation against his wife even after the Council found her doubly guilty.[98] In this regard the men of New France differed from their Portuguese brothers in Brazil, who perpetrated a number of amorous murders each year; also from their English brethren in Massachusetts, who branded or otherwise mutilated their errant wives and daughters.[99] When such cases reached the courts in New France the judges, too, appear to have been lenient. Their punishments for adulterous women were considerably lighter than those imposed in New England. A further peculiarity of the legal system in New France, which suggests that women were closer to being on an equal footing with men than in other times and places, was the unusual attempt to arrest not only prostitutes but their clients as well.[100]

Another indication of the lenient treatment Canadian women enjoyed is the level of insubordination the authorities were willing to accept from them. There was a distinct absence of timidity vis-à-vis the political authorities. In 1714, for example, the inhabitants of Côte St. Leonard violently objected to the Bishop's decision to cancel their membership in the familiar church and enrol them in the newly erected parish of Rivière-des-Prairies. A fracas ensued in which the consecrated altar breads were captured by the rebellious parishioners. An officer sent to restore order was assailed by angry women:

> L'huissier chargé d'aller assigner les séditieux, raconte que toutes les femmes l'attendaient "avec des roches et des perches dans leurs mains pour m'assassiner," qu'elles le poursuivirent en jurant: "arrête voleur, nous te voulons tuer et jeter dans le marais."[101]

Other women hurled insults at the Governor himself in the 1670s.[102] An even more outrageous case of insubordination was that of the two Desaulniers sisters, who by dint of various appeals, deceits, and stalling tactics continued to run an illegal trading post at Caughnawaga for some twenty-five years despite repeated orders from governors, intendants, and the ministry itself to close it down.[103]

A further indication of women's privileged position is the absence of witchcraft persecution in New France. The colony was founded in the seventeenth century when this persecution was at its peak in Western Europe. The New Englanders, too, were burning witches at Salem. Not a single *Canadienne* died for this offence.[104] It is not – as Marie de l'Incarnation's account of the 1663 earthquake makes clear[105] – that the Canadians were not a superstitious people. A scholar of crime in New France suggests that this surprising absence of witchcraft hysteria relates to the fact that "depuis le début de la colonie une femme était une rareté très estimée et de ce fait, protégée de la persécution en masse."[106]

Thus, on the marriage market, and in their protection from physical violence, women seem to have achieved a favourable position because of their small numbers. Their relatively high wages and lighter court sentences may also have related to the demographic imbalance. Moreover, the original female immigrants arrived in the colony with better than average education and capital, attributes that undoubtedly helped them to establish their privileged status.

Economic Opportunities

Even more than demographic forces, the colonial economy served to enhance the position of women. In relation to the varied activities found in many regions of France, New France possessed a primitive economy. Other than subsistence farming, the habitants engaged in two major pursuits. The first was military activity, which included not only actual fighting but building and maintaining the imperial forts and provisioning the troops. The second activity was the fur trade. Fighting and fur trading channelled men's ambitions and at times removed them physically from the colony. This helped open up the full range of opportunities to women, whom we have already seen had the possibility of assuming a wide variety of economic roles in *ancien régime* society. Many adapted themselves to life in a military society. A few actually fought. Others made a good living by providing goods and services to the ever-present armies. Still others left military activity aside and concentrated on civilian economic pursuits – pursuits that were often neglected by men. For many this simply meant managing the family farm as best as one could during the trading season, when husbands were away. Other women assumed direction of commercial enterprises, a neglected area in this society that preferred military honours to commercial prizes. Others acted as sort of home-office partners for fur-trading husbands working far afield. Still others, having lost husbands to raids, rapids, or other hazards of forest life, assumed a widow's position at the helm of the family business.

New France has been convincingly presented as a military society. The argument is based on the fact that a very large proportion of its population was under arms, its government had a semi-military character, its economy relied heavily on military expenditure and manpower, and a military ethos prevailed among the élite.[107] In some cases, women joined their menfolk in these martial pursuits. The seventeenth century sometimes saw them in direct combat. A number of Montrealers perished during an Iroquois raid in 1661 in which, Charlevoix tells us, "even the women fought to the death, and not one of them surrendered."[108] In Acadia, Madame de la Tour took command of the fort's forty-five soldiers and warded off her husband's arch-enemy, Menou D'Aulnay, for three days before finally capitulating.[109]

The most famous of these seventeenth-century *guerrières* was, of course, Madeleine de Verchères. At the age of fourteen she escaped from a band of Iroquois attackers, rushed back to the fort on her parents' seigneurie, and fired a cannon shot in time to warn all the surrounding settlers of the danger.[110] Legend and history have portrayed Madeleine as a lamb who was able, under siege, to summon up a lion's heart. Powdered and demure in a pink dress, she smiles very sweetly out at the world in a charming vignette in Arthur Doughty's *A Daughter of New France, being a story of the life and times of Magdelaine de Verchères*, published in 1916. Perhaps the late twentieth century is ready for her as she was: a swashbuckling, musket-toting braggart who extended the magnitude of her deeds with each successive telling, who boasted that she never in her life shed a tear, a contentious thorn in the side of the local curé (whom she slandered) and of her *censitaires* (whom she constantly battled in the courts).[111] She strutted through life for all the world like the boorish male officers of the *campagnard* nobility to which her family belonged.[112] One wonders how many more there were like her. Perhaps all trace of them has vanished into the wastebaskets of subsequent generations of historians who, with immovable ideas of female propriety, did not know what on earth to do with them – particularly after what must have been the exhausting effort of pinching Verchères' muscled frame into a corset and getting her to wear the pink dress.

By the eighteenth century, women had withdrawn from hand-to-hand combat, but many remained an integral part of the military élite as it closed in to become a caste. In this system, both sexes shared the responsibility of marrying properly and of maintaining those cohesive family ties which, Corvisier tells us, lay at the heart of military society. Both also appealed to the ministry for their sons' promotions.[113]

What is more surprising is that a number of women accompanied their husbands to military posts in the wilderness. Wives of officers, particularly of corporals, traditionally helped manage the canteens in the French armies.[114] Almost all Canadian officers were involved in some sort of trading activity, and a wife at the post could mind the store when the husband had to mind the war. Some were overzealous. When Franquet rode into Fort Saint Frédéric in 1752 he discovered a terrific row among its inhabitants. The post was in a virtual state of mutiny because a Madame Lusignan was monopolizing all the trade, both wholesale and retail, at the fort; and her husband, the Commandant, was enforcing the monopoly.[115] In fact, Franquet's inspection tour of the Canadian posts is remarkable for the number of women who greeted him at the military posts, which one might have expected to be a male preserve. Arriving at Fort Sault Saint Louis he was received very politely by M. de Merceau and his two daughters. He noted that Fort Saint Frédéric housed not only the redoubtable Madame Lusignan but also another officer's widow. At Fort Chambly he "spent the whole day with the ladies, and visited Madame de Beaulac, an officer's widow who has been given lodging in this fort."[116]

The nuns, too, marched in step with this military society. They were, quite literally, one of its lifelines, since they cared for its wounded. A majority of the invalids at the Montreal Hôtel-Dieu were soldiers, and the Ursuline institution at Trois-Rivières was referred to simply as a *hôpital militaire*.[117] Hospital service was so vital to the army that Frontenac personally intervened to speed construction of the Montreal Hôtel-Dieu in 1695, when he was planning a campaign against the Iroquois.[118] In the colony's first days, the Ursulines also made great efforts to help the Governor seal Indian alliances by attempting to secure Iroquois students who would serve as hostages, and by giving receptions for Iroquois chiefs.[119]

Humbler folk also played a part in military society. In the towns female publicans conducted a booming business with the thirsty troops. Other women served as laundresses, adjuncts so vital that they accompanied armies even on the campaigns where wives and other camp followers were ordered to stay home.[120] Seemingly indispensable, too, wherever armies march, are prostitutes. At Quebec City they plied their trade as early as 1667. Indian women at the missions also served in this capacity.[121] All told, women had more connections with the military economy than is generally noted.

While warfare provided a number of women with a living, it was in commerce that the *Canadiennes* really flourished. Here a number of women moved beyond supporting roles to occupy centre stage. This happened for several reasons. The first was that the military ethos diverted men from commercial activity. Second, many men who entered the woods to fight or trade were gone for years. Others, drowned or killed in battle, never returned.[122] This left many widows who had to earn a livelihood. This happened so often, in fact, that when women, around the turn of the eighteenth century, overcame their early numerical disadvantage, the tables turned quickly. They soon outnumbered the men and remained a majority through to the Conquest.[123] Generally speaking, life was more hazardous for men than for women[124] – so much so that the next revolution of the historiographic wheel may turn up the men of New France (at least in relation to its women) as an oppressed group.

At any rate, women often stepped in to take the place of their absent husbands or brothers. A surprising number of women traders emerge in the secondary literature on New France. In the colony's earliest days, the mere handful of women included two merchants at Trois-Rivières: Jeanne Enard (mother-in-law of Pierre Boucher), who "by her husband's own admission" was the head of the family as far as fur-trading was concerned; and Mathurine Poisson, who sold imported goods to the colonists.[125] At Montreal there was the wife of Artus de Sully, whose unspecified (but presumably commercial) activities won her the distinction of being Montreal's biggest debtor.[126] In Quebec City, Eleonore de Grand-maison was a member of a company formed to trade in the Ottawa country. She added to her wealth by renting her lands on the Île d'Orleans to Huron refugees after Huronia had been destroyed. Farther east, Madame de la Tour involved herself in shipping pelts to France. Another Acadian, Madame Joybert, traded furs on the Saint John River.[127]

With the onset of the less pious eighteenth century, we find several women at the centre of the illegal fur trade. Indian women, including "a cross-eyed squaw named Marie-Magdelaine," regularly carried contraband goods from the Caughnawaga reserve to Albany.[128] A Madame Couagne received Albany contraband at the other end, in Montreal.[129] But at the heart of this illegal trade were the Desaulniers sisters, who used their trading post on the Caughnawaga reserve as an *entrepôt* for the forbidden English strouds, fine textiles, pipes, boots, lace, gloves, silver tableware, chocolate, sugar, and oysters that the Indians brought regularly from Albany.[130] Franquet remarked on the power of these *marchandes*, who were able to persuade the Indians to refuse the government's request to build fortifications around their village.[131] The Desaulniers did not want the comings and goings of their employees too closely scrutinized.

These *commerçants*, honest and otherwise, continued to play their part until the Conquest. Marie-Anne Barbel (*Veuve* Fornel) farmed the Tadoussac fur trade and was involved in diverse enterprises including retail sales, brickmaking, and real estate.[132] On Franquet's tour in the 1750s he encountered other *marchandes* besides the controversial "Madame la Commandante" who had usurped the Fort Saint Frédéric trade. He enjoyed a restful night at the home of Madame de Lemothe, a *marchande* who had prospered so well that she was able to put up her guests in splendid beds that Franquet proclaimed "fit for a duchess."[133]

A number of writers have remarked on the shortage of entrepreneurial talent in New France.[134] This perhaps helps to account for the activities of Agathe de St. Père, who established the textile industry in Canada. She did so after the colonial administrators had repeatedly called for development of spinning and weaving, with no result.[135] Coming from the illustrious Le Moyne family, Agathe St. Père married the ensign Pierre Legardeur de Repentigny, a man who, we are told, had "an easy-going nature." St. Père, of another temperament, pursued the family business interests, investing in fur trade partnerships, real estate, and lending operations. Then in 1705, when the vessel bringing the yearly supply of French cloth to the colony was shipwrecked, she saw an opportunity to develop the textile industry in Montreal. She ransomed nine English weavers who had been captured by the Indians and arranged for apprentices to study the trade. Subsequently these apprentices taught the trade to other Montrealers on home looms that Madame de Repentigny built and distributed. Besides developing the manufacture of linen, drugget, and serge, she discovered new chemicals that made use of the native plants to dye and process them.[136]

Upon this foundation Madame Benoist built. Around the time of the Conquest, she was directing an operation in Montreal in which women turned out, among other things, shirts and petticoats for the fur trade.[137] This is a case of woman doing business while man did battle, for Madame Benoist's husband was commanding officer at Lac des Deux Montagnes.

The absence of male entrepreneurs may also explain the operation of a large Richelieu lumbering operation by Louise de Ramezay, the daughter of the Governor of Montreal. Louise, who remained single, lost her father in 1724. Her mother continued to operate the sawmill on the family's Chambly seigneury but suffered a disastrous reverse due to a combination of flooding, theft, and shipwreck in 1725. The daughter, however, went into partnership with the Seigneuress de Rouville in 1745 and successfully developed the sawmill. She then opened a flour mill, a Montreal tannery, and another sawmill. By the 1750s the trade was flourishing: Louise de Ramezay was shipping 20,000-*livre* loads, and one merchant alone owed her 60,000 *livres*. In 1753 she began to expand her leather business, associating with a group of Montreal tanners to open new workshops.[138]

Louise de Ramezay's case is very clearly related to the fact that she lived in a military society. As Louise was growing up, one by one her brothers perished. Claude, an ensign in the French navy, died during an attack on Rio de Janeiro in 1711. Louis died during the 1715 campaign against the Fox Indians. La Gesse died ten years later in a shipwreck off Île Royale. That left only one son, Jean-Baptiste-Roch; and, almost inevitably, he chose a military career over management of the family business affairs.[139] It may be that similar situations accounted for the female entrepreneurs in ironforging, tilemaking, sturgeon-fishing, sealing, and contract building, all of whom operated in New France.[140]

The society's military preoccupations presented business opportunities to some women; for others, the stress on family ties was probably more important. Madame Benoist belonged to the Baby family, whose male members were out cultivating the western fur trade. Her production of shirts made to the Indians' specifications was the perfect complement. The secret of the Desaulniers' successful trade network may well be that they were related to so many of Montreal's leading merchants.[141] The fur trade generally required two or more bases of operation. We saw earlier in our discussion that this society not only placed great value on family connections but also accepted female commercial activity. It was therefore quite natural that female relatives would be recruited into business to cover one of the bases. Men who were heading for the west would delegate their powers of attorney and various business responsibilities to their wives, who were remaining in the colony.[142]

We find these husband-wife fur trade partnerships not only among "*Les Grandes Familles*" but permeating all classes of society. At Trois-Rivières women and girls manufactured the canoes that carried the fur trade provisions westward each summer. This was a large-scale operation that profited from fat government contracts.[143] In Montreal, wives kept the account-books while their husbands traded. Other women spent the winters sewing shirts and petticoats that would be bartered the following summer.[144]

The final reason for women's extensive business activity was the direct result of the hazards men faced in fighting and fur-trading. A high proportion of women were widowed; and as widows, they enjoyed special commercial privileges. In traditional French society, these privileges were so extensive that craftsmen's widows sometimes inherited full guild-master's rights. More generally, widows acquired the right to manage the family assets until the children reached the age of twenty-five (and sometimes beyond that time). In some instances they also received the right to choose which child would receive the succession.[145] In New France these rights frequently came into operation, and they had a major impact on the distribution of wealth and power in the society. In 1663, for example, women held the majority of the colony's seigneurial land. The *Veuve* Le Moyne numbered among the twelve Montreal merchants who, between 1642 and 1725, controlled assets of 50,000 *livres*. The *Veuve* Fornel acquired a similar importance later on in the regime. Some of the leading merchants at Louisbourg were also widows. The humbler commerce of tavernkeeping was also frequently a widow's lot.[146]

Thus, in New France, both military and commercial activities that required a great deal of travelling over vast distances were usually carried out by men. In their absence, their wives played a large role in the day-to-day economic direction of the colony. Even when the men remained in the colony, military ambitions often absorbed their energies, particularly among the upper class. In these situations, it was not uncommon for a wife to assume direction of the family interests.[147] Others waited to do so until their widowhood, which – given the fact that the average wife was considerably younger than her husband and that his activities were often more dangerous – frequently came early.[148]

Conclusion

New France had been founded at a time in Europe's history in which the roles of women were neither clearly nor rigidly defined. In this fluid situation, the colony received an exceptionally well-endowed group of female immigrants during its formative stage. There, where they long remained in short supply, they secured a number of special privileges at home, at school, in the courts, and in social and political life. They consolidated this favourable position by attaining a major role in the colonial economy, at both the popular and the directive levels. These circumstances enabled the women of New France to play many parts. *Dévotes* and traders, warriors and landowners, smugglers and politicians, industrialists and financiers: they thronged the stage in such numbers that they distinguish themselves as *femmes favorisées*.

2

Recording Angels: The Private Chronicles of Women from the Maritime Provinces of Canada, 1750-1950

Margaret Conrad

When, over thirty years ago, Catherine Cleverdon wrote her pioneering study of the Canadian women's suffrage movement, she labelled the Maritime region a "Stronghold of Conservatism" and resorted to stereotypes to compensate for the narrow base of her research. The recent decade of productive scholarship in Canadian women's history has, with a few notable exceptions, yielded little on the history of Maritime women and thus the stereotype goes unchallenged.[1] Part of the difficulty lies in the paucity of public documents relating to the participation of Maritimers in the women's movement as it developed at the end of the nineteenth century. Yet, an abundance of Maritime women's diaries and correspondence has not received serious attention, and these offer valuable insights on women's culture not only for the region but for Canadian women's history generally.[2]

Maritime women in the past said a great deal about their lives in their own private chronicles, documents that reflect their assigned "sphere." From the earliest days of European settlement they exhibited a high level of literacy. According to the felicitously detailed 1891 census, women over sixty years of age had a literacy rate ranging from a low of 48 per cent in Prince Edward Island to 68 per cent in New Brunswick. In the same year young women between ten and nineteen had a literacy rate of 85 per cent in New Brunswick, 90 per cent in Nova Scotia, and 91 per cent in Prince Edward Island.[3] Given the cultural values and material conditions of many women in the region, it was inevitable that women's literacy would be put to practical use, writing letters, preserving genealogies, and recording for posterity the rhythm of their life courses.

These documents are especially revealing of the lives of women in the Maritime Provinces, particularly in the period between 1850 and 1950 when the number of women writing diaries seems to be almost unlimited. This period, of course, marks the high point of the so-called "Victorian diary," a largely middle-class document but one that was widespread in the rapidly changing class structure of the period.[4] Taken as a whole, Maritime women diarists, like women who write their autobiographies, exhibit characteristics of (1) straightforward, objective reporting in their style; (2) understatement in their expression; (3) obliqueness regarding personal feelings; (4) silence on sensitive issues such as hatred and sex.[5] On the other hand, they write diaries as revealing and as varied as those of Maritime men. There are, for example, (1) spiritual diaries typical of Puritan and other dissenting religious sects; (2) travel journals; (3) diaries of personal routine; and (4) diaries of public events. Naturally, the balance for women is different. We find far more of the third category than would be found in a similar collection of men's diaries from the region. And we find no examples of what Fothergill categorizes as the journal of post-Freudian sensibility,[6] which has produced such masterpieces as the diaries of Anais Nin. Most of our diarists, it seems, had few literary pretensions – the scribblers, account-books, and tiny pocket diaries hardly being the vehicles for great aspirations.

The amateur nature of most of these endeavours testifies to the private motive that prompted these women to keep diaries: the pleasure of recording events, the drive to trace spiritual and personal growth, the need for a vehicle of self-expression, the fashion of the day. Few, it would seem, had any expectation that their diaries would be published, although we do have one case in which two sisters kept in touch with each other by exchanging copies of their diaries.[7] At least one kept her diary in secret, revealing it only on her deathbed,[8] an indication that some at least saw diaries as a means of ensuring immortality and perhaps some measure of historical understanding. Several of the women probably felt that the discipline of regular diary entry, like regular Bible reading or account-keeping, was an exercise in self-improvement, and some admonished themselves for having failed to write in their diaries when events disrupted their routine. For many, their diaries became life-long friends, while for others, as far as we can tell, diary writing was a brief episode in their lives, prompted as much by the year-span of their diary books as by any sense of obligation.

There are admittedly major limitations in using diary evidence for exploring the history of Maritime women. The most obvious is the class and ethnic bias of our material. Diaries were written overwhelmingly by Protestant, Anglo-Saxon women from rural and small-town environments. Although we have Carrie Best's valuable autobiographical work, *The Lonesome Road*, and Edith Tufts' biographies of Acadian women, we have no diaries of black and Acadian women.[9] Indian women are entirely absent from our archives and Catholic women diarists are rare. This may be explained in part by the early stage of our endeavour but I suspect it also reflects the bias of public record collections and the largely oral culture of Maritimers of non-British origin. In addition, a disproportionate number of diarists came from western Nova Scotia and the Saint John River Valley. Since these areas were settled early and were populated by diary-writing Yankee Puritans who later evolved into Baptists and Methodists, perhaps this bias is not surprising. The Beaton Institute, College of Cape Breton, is also rich in women's documents, a situation that reflects not only the culture of that unique island but also the good sense of the archivists there. The middle-class bias of these sources is diluted in part by diaries of factory workers, domestics, and seagoing women who add occupational dimensions to our largely rural and domestic materials. Moreover, autobiographical letters make it possible to document the lives of mobile women such as missionaries, nuns, and migrant workers. With so many Maritimers on the move in this period and women often the ones who "kept in touch," it was inevitable that we would find several series of letters that take on a diary-like quality.

Space will not permit a discussion of all the fascinating women who kept diaries or wrote such letters. However, a sampling will indicate the richness of the sources. Few pioneer Maritime women left accounts of their arrival in the region. The Loyalist women, whose diaries and reminiscences offer a valuable commentary on the refugee experience of some 30,000 people who came to the Maritime region between 1776 and 1785, are an exception to this generalization. As well as the accounts of Mary Fisher, Sarah Frost, Hannah Ingraham, and Elizabeth Johnston, we have the letters of several Loyalist women, including those of the remarkable Rebecca Byles (Almon).[10] Referring to her regular correspondence (1777-1829) with Boston relatives as a "journal," Rebecca offers a rare glimpse into the mind of an educated eighteenth-century woman whose reading encompassed books on women's rights and whose letters included discussions of the status of women. Equally revealing are the letters of Vénérande Robichaud, who was born in 1758 in Boston to Acadian parents exiled from their homes by the deportation. Vénérande never lived in the Maritimes and therefore her correspondence falls outside our jurisdiction, but her letters from Quebec to her brother in New Brunswick indicate that the treatment of the Acadians at the hands of the British authorities had an indelible impact on the next generation, many of whom came back to "Acadie" after the hostilities between Britain and France had ceased.[11]

Two early diarists are women who wrote what scholars would call "diaries of conscience" or "spiritual diaries." Indeed, one of the recurring themes in our documents is the religious one and anyone hoping to understand Maritime women must take a careful look at the multiple and changing influences that religion exerted on women's culture. The oldest diary we have found – though in published form, not in the original – is that of Mary Coy Morris Bradley of Gagetown and Saint John, New Brunswick. Born in 1771, Mary Bradley is the only Maritime-born woman to have left an account of her childhood memory of the American Revolution.[12] Her journal, which she kept from 1787 to 1848, was published in 1849, and is part autobiography and part diary. It was apparently offered to a wider audience at the advice of a Methodist minister. Although Mary writes within the formal restraints required for spiritual diaries, including rhetorical flourishes, invocation of the deity, and references to spiritual backsliding, she also reveals an enormous amount about the role of women in New Brunswick at the turn of the nineteenth century. Soon after marrying her first husband in 1793, Mary's domestic economy was severely threatened when her husband's lumbering activities failed and debtors threatened to deprive them of everything they owned.

> . . . Just at this critical time, it occurred to me, I will commence the business of weaving. Accordingly I set up my loom, and notified my neighbors, and I soon had plenty of work. I exerted myself to the utmost of my power. I took my pay in such trade as was suitable for our family's use, which made the payment easy to my customers. I soon got into the way of helping ourselves greatly. My labor was hard; but I was favored with a good constitution, and I felt much encouraged and truly thankful for such a providential opening. . . .

> We had been married nine months, and I had been comfortably provided for, and a good prospect for the ensuing winter. I had the privilege of two cows' milk; one my husband brought home, and the other my father gave me; so that by an interchange of milk with my mother, I made plenty of cheese and butter for our

own use. We raised potatoes sufficient for the family, and for fatting our pork; so that with these necessaries of life, milk and butter, potatoes and pork, with but little bread, we lived; excepting particular occasions, I made little use of tea and sugar. I never ran my husband in debt for anything whatever. I endeavored to supply our little wants by my own exertions. I felt quite encouraged to hope, by the blessing of God, that we should accumulate a comfortable living.

In 1805, my husband purchased a house and four lots of land, in Germain street, S[aint] John; and in the year following, we removed to our new abode. The first few years, we kept a grocery, rented a part of the house, and had little prospect of paying for the property. At length times changed for the better, and my husband was enabled to lift the mortgages, and the property became our own. We then felt ourselves greatly blessed by the kind hand of Providence, which had so prospered our labors and we had accumulated a comfortable home; which we esteemed a great blessing. . . .

Despite improved economic circumstances, all was not domestic bliss for Mary.

When I was married to Mr. M., not having much previous acquaintance with his temper and disposition, I expected to receive the greatest marks of attention, kindness, and indulgence from him. But I soon found that, being his wife, I was bound by law to yield obedience to the requirements of my husband; and when he enforced obedience, and showed marks of resentment if his wishes were not met, I was tempted with anger, and felt a spirit of resentment arise in my heart, and retaliating expressions come into my mind; but I had sufficient self-possession to refrain from speaking in an unbecoming manner.

So after I had pondered over it, and ventured to speak to him upon the subject, thinking if he would make some little apology, it would ease my mind, and I should get over it. But instead of the softening southerly shower, it was like the creaking vessel under the harsher breeze. So when I found I had no one to whom I could make known my complaint, my heart was bound up with a hard spirit; and in that state of mind, I could not enjoy communion with my maker.

I was tempted not only to be angry with my husband, but also to hate him. I was afraid to look him in the face or to speak for fear

I should betray the feeling of my mind, which I endeavored to conceal from him and every one beside. I felt as though Satan knew every thought and feeling of my mind, and as if he whispered to me, "Now you may know your husband has no love to you, although he pretended so much; for if he had he would not so frequently hurt your feelings by such harsh expressions, and never seems to care for it afterwards; and at the same time accusing you of hating him. Nothing unites you together; you had better part at once." Those suggestions roused up my mind. O! thought I, part indeed! What a reproach upon my religion, should this take place. No, not for any thing in this world.

These passages[13] reveal Mary's contribution to the rural and urban economy as well as the difficulty of living in a society where women were legally and morally subordinate to their husbands. Mary's solution, like that of many of her contemporaries, was to find solace in religion, but even that had its drawbacks. "I thought, if it were customary for females to preach the gospel, how gladly would I engage in the employment,"[14] Mary noted after recording her conversion experience. Her anguish was not just rhetorical flourish. Her difficulties were distinctly sexist ones as Baptist and Congregational parsons admonished her not to overstep the restrictions placed on women in colonial society and walked out on her when she attempted to pray and preach in public.

I had always heard that women had nothing to do in public, respecting religious exercises, and that it was absolutely forbidden in the Scriptures for a woman to pray in public or to have anything to say in the church of God. Under the consideration of those things, I felt much shame and confusion and knew not how to endure it. I said nothing to anyone upon the subject; but I pondered it over in my heart.[15]

Finally, Mary found a spiritual home in the Methodist Church, where prayer meetings, love-feasts, and community spirit gave her limited scope for her evangelical yearnings. She eventually led a women's Bible class and also continued to write in her diary, which she confessed "so greatly unburdened and comforted my mind."[16] Her first husband died in 1817 and two years later Mary remarried. Though she scarcely mentions her second husband in her diary he left her comfortably well off when he died in 1851. Since she was childless and had no direct heirs, she was able to leave a considerable portion of her estate to the Methodist Church, which had served her needs so well.[17]

Another diary of spiritual odyssey is that of Eliza Anne Chipman, who died in 1853 at the age of forty-six after having borne twelve children and performed the duties as second wife of a Baptist minister in the Annapolis Valley of Nova Scotia.[18] Eliza's rigorous conformity to the rules of spiritual journal-writing makes her diary less revealing than that of Mary Bradley, who seems to have done many things in an unconventional way. So preoccupied was Eliza with her spiritual shortcomings that she even failed to note the birth of one of her many children. Indeed, the restraint in her diary on personal matters is remarkable.

Oct. 7, 1834 What should I render unto the Lord for all his benefits? He has again made me the mother of a fine son and a continued scene of suffering from a broken breast, I am now enjoying a good degree of health – though not fully recovered from the latter.

Eliza's diary reminds us that illness and death were ever-present factors in the lives of colonial women. Four of Eliza's children pre-deceased her, and the death of an invalid daughter reduced her to such despair that, for once, she was forced to abandon her detached recording of personal tragedy. Generally speaking, cousins, siblings, relatives, and friends seemed to die off with unnerving regularity. Of course, we know this to be a fact of colonial life. Demographers inform us that a girl born today has as good a chance of surviving to the age of sixty-five as one born in the eighteenth century had of reaching her first birthday.[19] This drastic change in life expectancy separates us from the experience of Eliza, as does the birth rate. While Eliza had five or six more children than was statistically average even for her day, she bore ten more than women today might expect to bear and was mother to eighteen, since her husband brought to the marriage eight children by his previous wife. The absence of any systematic understanding and control over disease and childbirth almost certainly was a factor in making religion such a dominant feature of women's lives in the nineteenth century, God being even more capricious than the capitalists and bureaucrats of the twentieth century.

The diaries of Eliza and Mary document the restrictions their religious beliefs placed on them; they also testify to the positive contribution of evangelical churches in expanding the public role of women. Mary would have done more if it had been socially acceptable to do so, but Eliza was virtually forced, because of her role as a minister's wife, to take on Sunday School teaching and women's Bible study groups. In doing this she surely established a new role model for the women in her community. Both Mary and Eliza had learned to read to better pursue their Christian duties and Eliza and her husband saw to it that daughters as well as sons received an education. Eliza's daughter-in-law, Alice Shaw, taught school in the Annapolis Valley and after further education at Mary Lyon's famous Mount Holyoke Seminary in 1854-56 returned to Nova Scotia to found the Grand Pré Seminary for young ladies.[20]

Advances in education in New England seem to have had a significant influence on Maritimers. This is not surprising since many Maritime families had come from the old Thirteen Colonies in the Planter and Loyalist migrations between 1760 and 1785 and close ties continued on a kinship, institutional, and commercial basis throughout the nineteenth century. The Maritime-based newspapers of the Baptist and Methodist churches,[21] for example, regularly carried articles from their American counterparts offering suggestions for educational reform. These were quickly seized upon by Maritime church "fathers" anxious to see their churches in the vanguard of nineteenth-century reform. Although there was some debate over the admission of women to institutions of higher learning, it was not protracted and, more important, the negative opinion did not carry the day. Mount Allison and Acadia universities, sponsored by the Methodists and Baptists respectively, were among the first institutions of higher learning not only in Canada but in the British Empire to open their doors to women; and Nova Scotia Normal College founded in 1855 was one of the first institutions in British North America to provide women with an opportunity to take teacher training.[22]

This generation of Protestant women not only had teaching as an option; they also had access to the mission fields overseas, where Christianity and capitalism found increasing scope for their energies. The missions are a curious phenomenon and are rapidly being reinterpreted in the light of fresh insights developed in women's history.[23] It is clear, for example, that women found in the mission fields the opportunities for professional and administrative careers rapidly closing to them at home. Further, much of the effort of organizing and financing the missions came from the women themselves, who established missionary societies to pursue their goals. The first such societies in Canada were established in the Maritimes under the auspices of the Baptist and Methodist churches.[24] Taking their cue from American women as they had on the question of education, Maritime women devoted a great deal of energy to mission work in the same period when the issue of women's rights and suffrage was beginning to percolate in other regions of Canada. Though today we may see their priorities as wrong-headed, it is possible to understand how it was that they saw mission work as a more valuable outlet for their reform activities than putting their own house in order. Given the strong evangelical background of so many of the Maritime women and the tradition of selflessness that was central to the true Christian's life in the nineteenth century, it is difficult to envision them making any other choice than the one they made.

The letters (1871-1916) of Mathilda Churchill of Truro are a good source of information on the moods and methods of women missionaries.[25] Trained as a teacher, Mathilda desperately wanted to be a missionary. Although single women were increasingly acceptable on the mission field by the 1870s, mission boards preferred married couples to represent the "domestic ideal" to the "heathen" and Mathilda eventually married in order to achieve her goal of becoming a missionary. Her description of taking medical training in Philadelphia prior to her departure to India in 1873 documents the seriousness of her purpose, while her work among the native women testifies to the cross-cultural ties binding women together. The sad accounts of death and disappointment during the forty years she spent in mission work are reminiscent of Eliza Chipman's story, despite its vastly different setting.

Another missionary of sorts – or what Sheila Rothman calls a "Protestant nun"[26] – was Marshall Saunders, the daughter of a patriarch of the Baptist Church in the Maritimes. Her diary of a year in a Scottish boarding school at the age of fifteen reveals a homesick daughter sent there by a not untypical Baptist father who believed that women as well as men needed a sound education.[27] Marshall later attended Dalhousie University, taught school, and in 1894 published *Beautiful Joe*, a novel that was destined through the auspices of the American Baptist Publication Society to sell over a million copies. Her social gospel interests meant that her novels had didactic purpose – the protection of animals and children, moral uplift – as well as a patronizing attitude toward the rapidly growing "lower orders."[28] While her middle-class Protestant preoccupations – including her support of women's suffrage – are typical for the period, her single competence suggests the new possibilities that were opening for women. It was no longer necessary to marry in order to have a workshop. It is, indeed, surprising how many of the first generation of university-trained women did not marry.[29] In Marshall's case there were probably some regrets about this for she had an enormous enthusiasm for mothering that found an outlet in the menagerie of animals with which she surrounded herself. The degree of social mothering in which she engaged through voluntary organizations suggests that it was difficult in her day for women to separate self from motherhood, as it still is today.

The single state, of course, had long been an option for Catholic women. The letters (1875-1906) of Sister Teresa McDonald, daughter of Senator William McDonald of Cape Breton, give us a thirty-year picture of a young girl emerging into a competent teacher and administrator through sisterhood in Halifax, Boston, and Sydney.[30] If she ever had any regrets about her choice of celibacy and social service we never hear of them, and one suspects that because of the centuries-long sanction of the church it was easier to choose such a lifestyle. Teresa's choice of a teaching career was far from unusual for women. Many of our chroniclers, especially in the period from 1835 to 1920, were teachers, a fact that accounts for the readability of, and the excellent spelling in, a large number of our documents.

In the same period that Sister McDonald was teaching in Boston and Margaret Marshall Saunders was selling her books there, other women were being attracted to American cities by the opportunities in domestic, clerical, and professional services and in factories and shops. Not all Maritime women were forced to leave the region to find new job opportunities, but the cities on the American seaboard had a head start in industrial development and urban growth and they therefore represented lucrative alternatives to smaller provincial towns such as Halifax, Fredericton, Charlottetown, and Sydney. By 1880, 4,374 Maritime women were employed in Boston alone. Fully 60 per cent were domestics, accounting for 15 per cent of that occupation. Another 18 per cent (767) were dressmakers and 11 per cent (465) were tailors. Fourteen per cent of the nurses (79) were Maritime women, a figure that would rise rapidly by the turn of the century.[31] Between 1881 and 1921 over 165,000 Maritime-born women left the region. This statistic takes on even greater significance when it is realized that it represents a slightly higher number than for men emigrating in the same period and that in 1921 the three Maritime Provinces together contained only slightly over one million people.[32]

The reality of these numerical calculations is brought home when we read the 1872 diary of Hannah Richardson, who worked in a shoe factory in Lynn, Massachusetts, or the letters (1870s and 1880s) of Margaret Connell, who accompanied her husband to the textile mills of Fall River.[33] Both women document beyond any doubt the survival and value of family, kinship, and community networks among those who "went down the road" to the "Boston States." Relatives and friends from home seem to be everywhere, easing the impact of the migration process by securing jobs, finding lodgings, and offering companionship. Moreover, both women considered themselves fortunate to have made the move. Hannah in 1872 earned as much as $3.40 a day at piece work, more than most men in the same period. From her earnings she contributed to the family economy by sending money home to her father and also assisting her brother, with whom she lived for a part of the time that she worked in Lynn. Hannah's diary tells us little of the oppressive conditions of factory life, but we do share her glee at her many material purchases as well as her well-rounded social life, which included church gatherings, sing-songs, parties, and trips to Boston. Hannah worked for only two years before returning to her beloved Sam, who wrote her regularly from Yarmouth. She was nearly thirty when she married, a fact which suggests that Maritime women, like many women elsewhere, were extending the period between school and marriage to take advantage of job opportunities in the rapidly expanding urban industrial sector of the economy. Since Maritimers lived so close to the cradle of North American industrialization, they were among the first to adjust their life courses to it. While Hannah eventually returned to Nova Scotia, Mary Connell, it seems, did not. Instead, she encouraged her relatives to come to Fall River where, she argued, life was easier than in the semi-subsistence farming and fishing communities of Pictou County, which had yet to experience the full impact of the growing coal and steel industry.

Other documents in our collection chronicle less happy experiences south of the border. One young woman wrote letters to her cousin about life in a house for unwed mothers in Boston where she fled to escape the sneering judgement of family and neighbours.[34] Her conclusion that she had "learned" a hard lesson has an ironic truth in it since women alone shouldered the burden of an unwanted pregnancy. While moralists claimed that as many as one-third of the prostitutes in Boston came from Nova Scotia, only second-hand accounts of individual prostitutes have yet been found.[35] Given the well-documented relationship between domestic labour and prostitution, the figure is not particularly surprising.

Factory life and "white slavery" contrast dramatically with the rhythm of events in rural Nova Scotia. The diary of Mary Smith of

Smithville, Cape Breton, gives us an extraordinarily detailed picture of life on a farm in 1891.[36] Mary describes friends and relatives leaving for Boston and Colorado, indicating that urban industrial society is having its magnetic effects on Smithville; nevertheless, the Smiths operate a semi-subsistent farm, making their own home-spun, having their boots fashioned by the local shoemaker, and pulling their children out of school for planting and harvest. Because of the rich texture and detail of her account we learn immediately that Mary's household is made up of Lewis, Flora, Sarah, herself, and at least four children as well as a host of friends and relatives who, it seems, come and go constantly. Yet it is virtually impossible to discern relationships from the duties performed in the household. Mary we know washed her own clothes, is responsible for the dishes, tends the garden, and knits and sews. It came as a real shock to discover that, when she wrote the diary, Mary was seventy-nine years old and a grandmother in an extended household that included her son Lewis and his wife Flora and Mary's unmarried daughter, Sarah. Mary is marvelously aware of life around her, noting political events, reading newspapers, describing the controversy over the proposed new cheese factory in the village, prescribing herbal remedies for friends and relatives. Mary actually died a year after she penned her diary but she left behind a document as complete as any social historian could wish concerning the duties of men, women, and children in rural society. What is remarkable is the sharing of jobs – men hauling water for the weekly washing, women and children picking rock from the fields, everyone gathering in the harvest. It is unlikely that there were any arguments in Mary's house about gender roles. Women were in the home and men in the fields but everyone pitched in and worked when there was work to be done. The following entry well documents the point:

Monday June 22nd
A verry dry high Easterly wind. The first tub Butter full 22 lbs. The little mare verry sick. The boys hear helping doctor her. Flora washed her weeks washing I washed breakfast dishes then cleared the kitchen cupboard and washed all the things that was in it and after dinner the men moved it out of the clothes room into the kitchen. I washed dinner dishes and then had a rest and Sarah moved every thing out of the dinning room took up the carpet and swept and dusted and I washed the windows. The two girls washed up the floor and Sarah got tea ready and after tea she churned. Flora picked the geese and they put them down

into the calf pasture the children and GP [Grandpa] finished picking stone a little while after dinner and then the men fixed the fence to keep the geese in Sarah cleaned up the milk house all ready to wash the shelves and the floor and Flora and the girls finished it up.

Another good farm diary is that of Rebecca Chase Ells of Port Williams (1901-1905).[37] While her husband disappeared to the Klondike for ten years to seek his fortune, Rebecca and her son Manning actually laid the foundations of the family's agricultural empire by churning butter for local consumption and raising apples for the rapidly expanding British market. Rebecca, like Mary Smith, had close family and community networks, but, unlike Mary, she was more fully integrated into a commercial economy and therefore not so dependent on the products of the farm for subsistence. From Rebecca we see how comfortable farm life can be despite the absence of husbands. Her diary provides a good description of the routine of rural life with births, deaths, and social events punctuated by the daily churning of butter, the weekly trip to town, and the annual spring housecleaning. With both of these farm diaries we get a sense of the central position of women in the rural production unit and the rather unsentimental way these women view their roles as hard-working members of hard-working families. The diaries also suggest the ease with which traditional rural occupations were integrated with the new commercial and industrial forces swirling around them. Clearly, for both women and men, rural and urban societies were a continuum not in conflict with each other.[38]

A diary that fits Fothergill's description of "the written equivalent of a moan" is that of Sophia Mary Carman, known, if at all, as the mother of the poet Bliss Carman.[39] This one in many ways is a classic Victorian diary. In Sophia's diary we read of "dear little Bliss," his illnesses and problems. We watch Sophia hold court for the Anglican Bishop, consult the latest faddish French doctor, take cures of quinine and turpentine, read sentimental novels, play draughts, fuss over servants; in short, play the role of the clichéd Victorian lady. Yet it is possible to see how Sophia turned out the way she did. Of impeccable Loyalist ancestry, married to a judge twenty years older than herself, assisted by servants, and, like other women of her day, caught up in a web of friends and relatives of her own class, she had little else to do but read novels and worry about her son. Not raised to hard work like her contemporary rural counterparts, she bought the nineteenth-century definition of "true womanhood" that emphasized purity, piety, submissiveness, and domesticity.[40] In this instance, the Victorian "lady" had every reason to be concerned about her health, for she, and one suspects other similarly maligned Victorian ladies, was genuinely sick. She died in 1886 at the age of fifty-eight.

A good contrast to Sophia Carman is Victoria Burrill Ross, a twentieth-century woman, an educated "lady" to be sure, but one who played golf, encouraged female ambitions, and applauded visiting lecturer Charlotte Whitton. Victoria used what extra time she had as the unpaid mistress of the Mount Allison Ladies' College (1926-35), where her husband was principal, to pen a most literary and sensitive diary, one equal to any written in Canada in the twentieth century and deserving of a much wider readership.[41]

A whole separate sub-set of diary, which has received little attention elsewhere but which is well represented in the Maritime Provinces, is the seafaring woman's journal.[42] Although women rarely went to sea as common hands on deck – in fact, there were superstitions about the undesirability of having women and pigs on ships – they regularly accompanied their sea-captain husbands and fathers, the élite members of the seaborne empire during the "Golden Age of Sail." We have discovered the delightful diary of adolescent Amelia Holder of Saint John, New Brunswick, whom we first meet in 1867 at the age of eleven, reading Gibbon and other classics as part of her shipboard education.[43] She also got on-the-spot geography lessons as her father sailed to Ireland, Gibraltar, South America, and the West Indies. After the first voyage Amelia's mother died, but Amelia and one or more of her siblings continued to accompany their father. One of our last glimpses of Amelia is at seventeen years of age when she and her younger sister are disembarking on a West Indian island, hoping to "snare" rich Planter husbands. With her education and background, one might have expected Amelia to have some professional ambitions but this seems not to have been the fate of most sea captains' daughters of the nineteenth century.

Another fascinating sea diary is that of Alice Coalfleet.[44] Born in Hantsport, Nova Scotia, and educated in an Antwerp convent, Allie accompanied her husband on two around-the-world voyages between 1886 and 1891. Life on board ship included an organ, a Chinese cook, and Christmas celebration with a turkey and all the trimmings. Even the birth of a child is recounted as an idyllic sharing experience between husband and wife:

Dodd and I sat up in the Pilot House. He was making bullets for his gun and I looked on. I retired at 7:30 trying to read, but other matters require my attention. At 10 o'clock a little stranger makes his appearance. He is very welcome a dear pretty little fellow. His head covered with black hair – Dodd is Doctor, nurse and everything else, washes and dresses the little one, lays him alongside me. Then stands and recites funny poetry to make me forget my pains.

Dodd's experience was not that unusual nor that startling to men who were accustomed to delivering farm animals. Allie even describes herself in barnyard terms when an Australian doctor finally has a chance to inspect the thriving mother and baby seven months after delivery. The doctor accused Allie of drinking ale as a means of keeping healthy. But Allie is adamant. "I told him, I only drank water which surprised him – but cows drink water." Allie's happy world crumbles within a brief eight-month period in 1892. First a sister in England dies in childbirth, then another sister is last seen clinging to her sea-captain husband as their flaming ship sinks into the Atlantic. A few weeks after this tragic event, Allie's husband dies at sea. Then to add to the sorrow, both of her grandparents die in rapid succession. Five months after receiving news of her husband's death Allie notes in her diary: "Dodd left no will – nor was he insured. I mentioned insurance just before he left New York. He laughed and said, 'You don't think a fellow is going to die do you?'" But she is not without resources. Her final tantalizing entry reads: "Father writes me encouraging letters – tells me I should write. He always said I was a clever girl – I suppose I might try and teach French in some school."

Allie's tragic widowhood can be compared to that of Laura June Slauenwhite of Pine Grove, Lunenburg County, whose husband died in 1930 when she was fifty years old.[45] Because she, too, was left without provision other than the family farm and was accustomed to more than subsistence survival, she was forced to rely on her earnings as a domestic in the nearby town and on the contributions of her unmarried son, who had difficulty finding work during the "dirty thirties." Laura longed to be back in her own home but was unable to fulfil that wish until World War II made it possible for her son to find permanent work in Halifax driving the teams for a dairy company, common labour for farm boys. When he married in 1944 and brought his new city bride to the household, Laura's role was diminished and she resented sharing her son's affections first with his wife and then with their young daughter. Laura's diary, which she began after her husband's death, is an instructive document on the changing circumstances of elderly women in the twentieth century. Often "sickly" even before her husband's death, after 1944 she frequently took to her bed as she is relegated to a marginal position in a poor, working-class family where her presence is sometimes resented. Only her granddaughter seems to have benefited from a live-in grandmother, since it was from her grandmother that she learned to read, knit, sew, crochet, and play various games. Laura lived to be ninety-six years old. She died in 1976 of old age in a nursing home where she spent the last fifteen years of her life, paying for the privilege from her monthly old-age pension cheque that began arriving in 1951.

Aging appears to have been a perilous experience for women throughout the period that these diaries cover. Women frequently outlived their husbands and were often forced to rely on their scattered family for support. Even when they were physically and materially able to live independently, the prospect of doing so was not always pleasing. Mary Killian MacQuarrie, mother of twelve, writing in 1929 had these poignant words to say about her life after the death of her husband:

> We were left, the younger girls and I, fairly comfortable. However, when the war was over the three girls were married, thus leaving my old mother and me to face the world. The prospect was not very bright in Glace Bay and I had nobody belonging to me there, I sold all my property and bought a home in Sydney, because I had to make a home for my mother while she lived. When she died four years ago I rented my house, sold all my things and started out to visit my scattered family. I sometimes wish I had kept up my old home, but if I were by myself I wouldn't be able to stand the loneliness after always having a full house, and it would be more than I could bear to have to sit at a lonely table and not have people coming in at night. So here I am, at the age of 74, going about from place to place. At present I'm here with Katie in Halifax. I have been with Ethel in Baltimore, three winters and one summer; and with Flora in Buffalo and Syracuse; and with Alice in Montreal. I hope to be for awhile with Flora in Sydney where she is going to live for the next five years.[46]

Two twentieth-century diaries that document new directions for women are those of a secretary in Sydney and an officer in the Canadian Women's Army Corps (CWAC) in World War II.[47] Ella Liscomb gives us a detailed picture of a girl's experience in high school and then as a secretary in a bank. She claims early that she will never marry and she does not. We suspect that the many movie idols whom she lovingly discusses in her 1919 diary gave her an image that the men in Sydney had difficulty living up to, especially since her 1930s diaries document the subordination of women in the modern office, an experience far removed from the romance of Hollywood and in no way conducive to a positive attitude toward her male employers.[48] Our CWAC, on the other hand, hates the bureaucratic double standard that women experience in the army and says so. After being told that she was "out" of the officers' training course at Ste. Anne de Bellevue, she was summoned before a male superior officer who attributed her difficulties to her small-town origins. She resented this "Upper Canadian" chauvinist and eventually singlehandedly vindicated her small-town origins by exposing the inefficiency of the system under which the women were trained.[49] She also got herself reinstated. This diary is a fitting conclusion to this discussion since it points both to a regional sense of grievance and to a more vocal feminist frustration about women's work that would find a collective voice in the 1960s.

It is clear that diaries give us ample evidence on the role of religion, work, family, friendships, migration, class, and gender expectations for women whom we can no longer interview. In some respects, this research has as yet found little that is really new; for the most part Maritime women share the influences that have been documented for North American women generally in this period – the ethnic and class variations in women's culture; the tenacity of the exclusively family role for women; the importance of the church as a vehicle for women's public role; the magnetic attraction to women of the jobs and products available to them in the new urban industrial society; new strategies for survival in the face of industrial capitalism. There are, however, subtle differences in emphasis in the Maritime context that are worthy of mention.

First, almost all of the diaries we have found are written by Maritime-born women, even those for the early nineteenth century. We know, of course, that the Maritime Provinces were largely settled prior to 1850 and that they were settled by families looking for security, economically and spiritually, which in the pre-industrial world was only possible by land ownership and a considerable degree of family self-sufficiency. After 1850 the Maritimes' migration pattern reversed as other regions of North America attracted Maritimers to urban jobs. There was very little immigration to the region after 1850, which differentiates the Maritime Provinces from most of the rest of Canada, where immigration continued unabated until the depression of the 1930s. It is perhaps because of these demographic trends that the family and religious preoccupations identified in our early diaries are continued and "fleshed out" in later ones. By the end of the nineteenth century the centre of gravity had shifted from the farm to the factory and from the Maritime Provinces to other regions of North America. Evangelical feminism may have flourished in the Maritimes but the battles for secular women's rights were fought in dynamic urban environments elsewhere.

The central position of religion and the church in the lives of nineteenth-century Maritime women is not a distinctive trait but it is highly significant. Religion, as we know, served both as a vehicle for resistance to oppression, encouraging equality, self-respect, and public action, as well as a vehicle for accommodating oppression, counselling submissiveness, deference, and restricted options for women.[50] Maritime women, largely because of their rural setting, lived relatively easily with these contradictions while pushing their opportunities for education and church and mission work to the limit. Religious doctrine, especially that of evangelical sects, also steered women away from the vacuous idle pedestal, the ideal that so vitiated many Victorian ladies.[51] Because of the central place of the church in Maritime communities, Maritime women are found in the very forefront of missionary work, temperance activity, and moral uplift, thus participating in what Olive Banks describes as the "evangelical contribution" to feminism.[52] They are less likely to be found leading the agitation for suffrage or legal reform although, as Margaret Marshall Saunders' diary indicates, interest in these areas of women's rights is not wholly lacking. It is significant, I think, that Maritime women were the first in the British Empire to gain access to institutions of higher learning and the first to establish exclusively female missionary societies; they were among the last – though only by a year or two – in Canada to receive the vote.

The rural roots of our diarists is also significant. The industrial underdevelopment of the Maritimes meant that the area lagged behind the rest of Canada in urbanization. In 1921, 50 per cent of Canadians lived in an urban environment. By contrast, only Nova Scotia aspired to the national average while New Brunswick did not become 50 per cent urban until the late 1950s and Prince Edward Island is still predominantly rural.[53] The tenacity of rural life and the real power of women in rural families – especially in the nineteenth century – gave women a sense of purpose. The "weight of indifference," which Catherine Cleverdon notes in the Maritimes with respect to the suffrage movement, stems from the fact that the rural family was a functional unit for a longer period in the Maritimes than in many other parts of North America. There is some irony in this situation, since it was precisely because of the safety valve of out-migration to the United States that life back home could be as prosperous and as satisfying as it ultimately was. The fact that Acadians and Roman Catholics generally were less likely than their Protestant neighbours to roam far afield also suggests that subtle ideological factors were at work in Maritime reactions to the opportunities and ideas in the air in the late nineteenth century. Given the traditional rural suspicion of state interference and the relative political powerlessness of the Maritime region after Confederation, it is possible to understand why it was not entirely clear to Maritime women that the vote would have added substantially to their power.[54] Unlike in Ontario and the western provinces, rural families in the Maritimes did not get caught up in pre-1918 political protest movements that may have sparked a demand for the female franchise. This does not mean that Maritime women were opposed to having a political voice or that they were ignorant of political issues swirling around them. They may have let their men do the voting for them, but their diaries indicate that they were not only aware of political currents of the day but also that the reforms they demanded, such as education reform, temperance, and improved social services, were often shared by the men in their lives.

Finally, it is important to note how easily the rural family in the nineteenth century lived with the new forces of industrialism. While publicists complained of the depopulation of rural communities because of the vast exodus to urban centres, Maritime women found in the city new markets for their traditional farm products, manufactured goods to lighten their workload, and job opportunities to give them an independent income. It is within this context that our chroniclers document what can only be described as the colossal influence of the United States. It was to that country that Maritime women in this period looked for jobs, further education, new consumer products, publishers for their books, and models for their lives. Moreover, the American influence was a two-way process. Cities such as Boston offered opportunities, while women returning to the Maritimes brought new ideas they applied at home – selectively, of course, as befitted the Maritime environment.

While the migration process was a two-way street, out-migration outweighed the reverse: in the final analysis the women's movement in the Maritimes as it developed at the end of the nineteenth century was detrimentally affected because so many Maritime women fought their battles for equality elsewhere. A good example of this trend is found in the career of Annie Marion MacLean from St. Peter's Bay, Prince Edward Island. Annie in 1900 was among the first women to graduate with a doctoral degree in sociology from the University of Chicago. She pursued an active publishing and teaching career, writing scores of books and articles on working women in the United States. Her feminism was rooted in the same rural environment that produced such women as Mary Bradley and Margaret Marshall Saunders, but her active life was confined to areas outside the Maritime Provinces.[55] Another "lost" woman is Elizabeth Hall from Bridgewater, Nova Scotia. Bessie got her first degree from Dalhousie University in 1916, volunteered for hospital service in Halifax during the final years of World War I, and then taught school briefly in western Canada in 1919-20. After taking a Master's degree at the University of Toronto in 1921, she continued her education at Bryn Mawr, where she wrote her doctoral dissertation on mothers' pensions. Such a topic, Bessie confided to her mother, would enable her to make a contribution to social reform policy when she returned to Canada. Unfortunately, the Maritime Provinces were suffering a severe economic crisis in the 1920s, which led to the politically impotent Maritime Rights Movement but not to a significant expansion of social services such as envisioned by Bessie Hall. After receiving her doctoral degree, Dr. Hall found work in the United States, her education and commitment lost forever to the Maritimes and to Canada.[56]

Whether it was Mary Bradley who wanted to be a minister and settled for being a Methodist, Margaret Marshall Saunders who traded off motherhood for social mothering, Laura Slauenwhite who wanted her own home but found only alienation within it, or our World War II CWAC choosing public service but experiencing sexist discrimination in the workplace, the aspirations of women in the past were sadly elusive and have a hauntingly familiar ring. For this reason, the past 200 years of Maritime women's history has an unsettling sense of continuity rather than sharp divisions. As a result, the study of Maritime women's diaries and autobiographical correspondence, in addition to uncovering valuable documents of women's culture, has been a personally important activity for all of us involved in it. As Ann Douglas has noted in connection with her research, we expected to find our foremothers; we ended up finding our sisters.[57]

3

The Decline of Women in Canadian Dairying

Marjorie Griffin Cohen

One of the most productive and important aspects of women's farm work in Canada has been dairying. This, at least, was the case until the rise of the factory system in the production of dairy products. Before the first cheese factories were established Canadian farm women performed most of the actual dairy work and were primarily responsible for most dairy production in Canada. However, as various aspects of dairying moved from the farm to the factory, women's participation was gradually eliminated, particularly on farms that began to specialize in dairying. A variety of complex factors explains why this activity, which was controlled by women, was taken over by men as it moved from a household craft to factory production. The patriarchal structure of the household and the underlying assumptions about the nature of the division of labour between men and women were the most significant forces leading to male control of dairying as capital accumulation became a more important aspect of production. But these factors were reinforced by the economic and cultural forces peculiar to Canadian development and the tendency of governments to support only male efforts in the industry as it became big business.

The focus here is on the changes that occurred in dairying in the second half of the nineteenth and early part of the twentieth centuries in central Canada. Since Ontario and Quebec were major producers of dairy products in Canada and the first provinces to turn to factory production, most of the information will concentrate on the industry in these provinces. However, the experience of women as dairy producers in other provinces will also be elucidated. The development of factory dairying did not occur evenly throughout the country; rather, areas closest to large markets were affected first. Yet, the factors that brought about male control of the industry were common to all areas where the transformation to factory production occurred.

Dairying as Women's Work

A few historians of Canadian dairying have acknowledged, but merely in passing, the significance of female labour before large-scale dairying developed. For example, J.A. Ruddick, in his history of Canadian dairying, says: "The work involved in making cheese and butter on the farm, which had been performed chiefly by women in the household, was taken over by men in the factories."[1] Robert Jones made a brief reference to the extent of women's involvement in dairying in *History of Agriculture in Ontario*, and Vernon Fowke acknowledged "farmers' wives [as] the craftsmen of farm dairies."[2] But for the most part historians have been absorbed in the market conditions of dairying and have been relatively un-interested in the labour aspects of production on the farm itself.[3] In large part this is a result of a preoccupation with transportation, technology, and tariffs, but it is also due to the general tendency to examine issues of labour only when wages are paid.

Although there is infrequent reference to the sex of dairy workers in pre-nineteenth-century records, such records as exist indicate that women as dairy workers were so common as not to merit specific mention. One example is the reaction of a priest visiting New France in 1734. He had no direct comment about women's dairying work, merely expressing dismay that female habitants who worked tending cows during the week wore lace and hoop skirts like ladies of fashion on Sunday.[4] Dairying as a commercial enterprise was slow to develop in New France and in the Maritimes. Most of what was produced was consumed by the household units themselves, but a limited market in which women were active existed even from the earliest days. An advertisement appearing in Halifax in 1776 indicates that dairying was considered a woman's specialty even for some slaves:

> Wanted to purchase, a Negro woman, about 25 or 30 years of age, that understands country work and the management of a dairy, she must be honest and bear good character. Enquire of printer.[5]

By the nineteenth century evidence of women as dairy producers is more plentiful. The most important sources are the accounts of the producers themselves, but observers and critics also frequently commented on women's work in this area. One of the most notable was "Agricola," a well-known critic of inefficient agricultural practices in the 1820s. In criticizing Nova Scotia women for abandoning the labours of the dairy he accepted the notion that dairying was and ought to continue as women's work.[6] However, this tendency of women to abandon dairying was never noted further west and did not continue in the Nova Scotia communities he wrote about.[7] In 1861 James Croil, describing the farm family as a self-contained labour unit, referred to the dairy as the province of women. The "greater part of the labour of the farm in Canada is performed by the farmer himself, his sons and his daughters; the former managing all the out of doors operations, and the latter the dairy and domestic departments."[8] In his reference to dairying the farmer's wife was notably absent; however, Croil did emphasize that her chief role was that of administrator: "Whatever qualifications the farmer should have, mental or physical, all are agreed upon this point, that *a good wife* is indispensable. What is the aim of the husband to accumulate, it becomes the province of the wife to manage, and wherever we hear of a managing wife, we are sure to find a money-making farmer."[9]

However, most of the information about the type of dairying work performed by women, the amount of time spent on it, and its significance in relation to other farm work is the testimony of farm women and men themselves in their letters and diaries. These sources indicate that while dairying was not the exclusive occupation of farm women (as adults, children, or servants) it consumed a considerable portion of many farm women's days. These personal testimonies are extensive and cover most settled areas of the country over long periods of time. While often the reference in a letter or a diary will refer merely to the milking chores or the amount of butter churned in a week, taken as a whole they point very clearly to subsistence-level dairying as the responsibility of females. Accounts that indicate a surplus in production tend to be even more explicit in indicating the importance of dairying to the whole farm operation and in showing that when dairying generated income, the income was recognized by the farm family as having been provided by female labour.

Significance of Dairying to the Farm Economy

In *Wheat and Woman* Georgina Binnie-Clark, a wheat farmer, explained the importance of dairy production to a farm that spe-

cialized in wheat. Her personal law of survival was that the successful farmer should never buy anything in the way of food either for
livestock or for human needs. Whenever possible food should be
raised on the farm and fresh meat and groceries should be obtained
in exchange for dairy produce. Her two cows made a significant
contribution to the farm economy: "I used all milk, cream and
butter necessary in the house, and took several pounds of butter
weekly to the Hudson Bay in exchange for household necessities."[10]
In a speech to the Royal Colonial Institute in London, England,
Binnie-Clark stressed both the precariousness of relying totally on
wheat production and the essential role of dairying in farm operations. She spoke of the experience of "one of the best commercial
women farmers (and her husband)" whose wheat crop on their farm
near Lethbridge had been destroyed by hail. Disaster was averted
only through their dairying. "They have proved their household
expenditure to be covered by the dairy produce of three milch
cows; and had at once bought six more. They were then making
sixty pounds of butter a week, out of this produce they had bought
sixty hens and were prepared to buy winter feed for their thirteen
pigs."[11]

While Binnie-Clark's advice pertained specifically to western
wheat farming in the early part of this century, the strategy of
combining staple production, which was primarily male-oriented,
with subsistence farming, where women's productive efforts on the
farm were concentrated, was common in Canada. The wild fluctuations in prices received for staples during the early stages of
development[12] as well as the general unavailability of certain types
of goods because of underdeveloped markets forced household
units to maintain a significant level of self-sufficiency, particularly
in foodstuffs. Dairying initially arose from the need of household
units to safeguard against the multitude of uncertainties involved in
production primarily for the export market and from the need to
provide for the household. While providing for the household was
the main requirement of women's farm dairying, that activity was
also able in varying degrees to provide an income whenever a
surplus was generated and a market existed. This income was often
critical to the survival of the farm unit, both as a source for investment in initial staple production and as a means of continuing in
years when the vagaries of the market or the climate made staple
production unprofitable.[13]

While dairying remained women's work it slowly grew from an
industry confined to consumption within the producer's household

to one that generated sufficient surplus to be a significant factor in the country's export market. But the process was a gradual one, and the expansion of dairying before factory production rarely involved the specialization of a specific farm unit.[14] Rather it was the result of increasingly larger numbers of isolated farm women producing surpluses for markets.

Conditions of Female Dairying

Early dairying in Canada was performed under difficult conditions that tended to limit farm dairying to small-scale, part-time work for farm women. One of the major disadvantages dairywomen faced as producers for the market was the poorly developed nature of the market itself. Because of the orientation of the economy toward staple exports, transportation facilities to encourage an integrated market internally were slow to develop.[15] In early settlements dairy products were scarce and since dairying was not the primary interest of the farm unit as a whole, the resources available for its use were poor. But problems with inadequate supply were less serious than those of proper methods of distribution, for such surpluses as were generated were redundant without a market for their distribution. Only with the growth of towns and settlements did the markets for dairy produce increase, but even so the production techniques on farms did not change rapidly.

The development of dairying in Canada may well be typical of countries where land ownership is less concentrated and wage labour scarcer than in older countries. In the United States, evidence also points to dairying as the work of individual women's efforts on farms before the factory system. This is particularly evident in midwestern areas where circumstances more closely resembled those found in Canada. There, too, women's dairying appears to have been restricted by limited markets and the tendency for the major effort on farms to have been directed toward staple production for export.[16] The limited nature of markets meant that dairy production and women's work in dairying in North America were very different from what occurred in Europe.[17] In England, for example, the large integrated markets and comparatively small land area stimulated the growth of large dairy farms well before production of dairy products moved to the factory.[18] Within this large-scale farm production dairying methods required much labour. Women not only tended cows and made cheese and butter, but were also primarily responsible for the entire management of the dairy business.[19]

The occupation of dairymaid in Europe was a distinct, skilled, and frequently full-time job.[20] In Canada the dairymaid was a much less common occupation. Female servants worked at dairying in Canada, but most commonly this work was only part of the labour of a general domestic servant.[21] Occasionally, women were hired specifically for farm labour, but even then it was unlikely that the labour would be confined to dairying; normally the work would include such additional farm tasks as poultry raising and fruit and vegetable growing. So while dairying was a feminized industry in Canada, the dairymaid was virtually unknown.

The typical dairy farmer, at least until the 1870s, was the farm wife. Often she performed the work single-handedly. In the winter the labour involved little more than feeding and caring for the cow, for not until the late 1890s was winter milking an accepted practice.[22] Sometimes even these winter activities would be taken over by the male farmer during the months when outdoor work could not be performed.[23] But for most of the year and certainly during the time when dairy production was possible, the labour of dairying was the responsibility of the farm woman. For many who came to the country as immigrants, in particular the "gentlewoman" from England, dairy work was a new skill that had to be acquired quickly and a variety of strategies were devised to overcome the most monotonous aspects of its labour. Mary O'Brien, for example, had the habit of churning butter with a copy of Milton in hand.[24] Even if only one or two cows were kept, dairying was a heavy workload for farm women, both because of the back-breaking conditions under which the labour was performed and because of the multiplicity of additional tasks that were the total responsibility of farm women.

Because dairying was rarely the primary focus of farm operations, there was a tendency to ignore it when capital improvements were considered. Frequently, cows were stabled in miserable sheds so that milking meant exposure to the discomforts of the extremes of Canadian weather.[25] Also, there was a tendency to use land for pasture that was considered unsuitable for ordinary tillage purposes. Usually such land was not well suited for the best grasses for dairying either.[26] Rarely did the farm have a dairy room, the various stages of straining the milk and separating the cream occurring in places such as cellars, barns, and root houses[27] with neither proper temperature control nor proper ventilation. The lack of proper dairy space meant that butter- and cheese-making had to take place in the farm kitchen or on farmhouse porches, conditions that would seldom make the work easier.[28]

Dairy equipment tended to be primitive and improvements in technology were slow to be used widely on farms. Generally this was not because dairy women were sceptical about their use, but because they had little control over capital expenditures on farms. The first dairy commissioner of Canada, in an address at Berlin, Ontario, in 1889, spoke at length about the problem:

> I know the farmers' wives are able to make the very finest butter when they get a fair chance, but the trouble has been that the men have all the good things. *They* [emphasis in original] had to have the horses, and the reaping, and mowing machines, and the driving sheds, and everything else *they* wanted, while their wives had to get along with one pantry for keeping the milk, the butter, the cold vegetables, the pies and everything else.... [G]o round and see the women struggling with an old fashioned churn, working twice as long in churning the butter as there is any need for.... [G]et rid of these old fashioned churns and milk houses and you will revolutionize the butter trade at once.[29]

In fact, he advocated what must have been extreme measures at the time to awaken farmers to the plight of their wives:

> I am not in favour of strikes; but if I could reach the ears of the good women that are such an ornament and joy to the households of Canada, I would have them strike and say "We won't do anything until you give us new churns and milk house."[30]

Farmers in Quebec were no more inclined to invest in dairy equipment for the "ornaments and joys" of their households than were those in other parts of Canada. Elisa Jones, in her book on farm dairying, deplored in 1894 the reluctance of farmers to invest in cream separators.

> Je ne comprends pas qu'un homme ayant le moindre égard pour ses animaux domestiques puisse se passer d'un écrémeur; cet instrument dispense en effet d'une quantité de travail surprenant, et, pour parler d'une manière familière, "*il est généralement moins coûteux d'avoir soin de sa femme* que de l'enterrer."[31]

The assumption in both of these examples is that the male farmer controlled capital expenditure on the family farm, even though the dairy work was in the female domain.[32] The fact that women's work in dairying was less capital-intensive than other aspects of farm production undoubtedly placed female labour and its productive capabilities at a disadvantage, a factor that in turn perpetuated the tendency to concentrate capital in the areas where men worked. But lack of direct investment in women's dairying was not the only problem affecting women's productivity. All aspects of women's farm labour tended to receive less attention than men's when capital improvements were being made. In a study that examined the reasons for the exodus of women from rural areas in the early part of the twentieth century, the problem of the absence of capital improvements in the home was noted as being particularly significant. For example, practices such as locating wells with pumps close to barns rather than houses had the effect of making male labour more efficient at the expense of women's work.[33] To the extent that time on housework was not reduced, women's efforts in other areas of production were affected.

Although women were able to generate surpluses from dairy production, they were frequently unable to generate sufficient money to improve their technology because they traded in small sums or bartered.[34] Until the transformation to factory production, a substantial amount of market activity in dairying did not enter the money economy at all. The small-scale nature of individual production and the problems of adequate transportation to urban markets often forced women to barter their farm produce for groceries or to trade with neighbours who could provide some essential service.[35] This practice lasted well into the twentieth century. At least one analyst saw the prevalence of barter in dairying as the reason for the underdeveloped nature of the industry.[36] In fact, barter was more likely the result of underdeveloped markets rather than the cause of them. In any case, its practice made reinvestment in dairying difficult. Even when money was received for dairy products, women were unlikely to be able to invest it in improved technology. Income from dairying was considered most often to be directly applicable to household maintenance so that the income from the main business of the farm could be reinvested in the farm itself.[37]

Another factor limiting women's dairying was the diversity of labour that farm women performed. Women's main tasks were having and caring for children and performing the housework essential for the reproduction of farm labour. Usually, these household tasks involved a wide variety of activities to provide food and other items for the family's consumption. The type and extent of the activities varied considerably through time and from one part of the country to another. Some activities, such as cloth- and clothes-making, could be carried out in the months when dairy activities were slight.[38] But many extremely time-consuming farm activities had to take place when women were most busy with dairy work as well. For example, the raising of poultry was another important source of income and was carried out on most farms.[39] Many farm women also raised fruit and vegetables and made honey and maple sugar both for family use and to trade or sell. During planting and harvest time women were also expected to work in the fields. In some locations the seasonal pressures on women were extraordinary. In Newfoundland, in the early twentieth century, for example, all but the poorest fishing families kept at least one cow for the family's needs. This was the total responsibility of women at a time when they spent most of their day in the process of drying fish.[40]

For farm women on wheat farms in the western provinces the usual farm duties were compounded by having to cook and clean for a large labour force at regular intervals. One farm woman described a typical day during a busy season:

> In seeding-time she will be up at 4 a.m. to get the men their breakfast. Then she will have to milk, and separate the cream afterwards, if they have a separator. If there are several cows it is quite a back-aching task. Then there will be the house to clean, the breakfast things to wash up, the beds to make, and she must not waste time over that part of her day for there is dinner to cook for hungry men by 11:30. After washing up again the afternoon will mean breadmaking, or clothes washing and ironing, or jam-making, or butter-churning – one of the endless things like that anyway, and at 7:30 or 6:30 (according to the season of the year) she must have "tea" ready. Tea is nearly as big a meal as dinner and the last meal of the day. After that she must wash up, then milk two cows and separate her cream before she can think of going to bed. Probably there will be some darning or mending to do even then. That is a straightforward day, but it is greatly complicated when the children begin to come.[41]

Paid female farm labour appeared to have an equally strenuous workload. An article in the *Grain Grower's Guide* in 1910 pointed to the differences in the amount of work done by men and women hired on farms. The men invariably had regular hours for work, while women were expected to work all the time: "for no farmer will pay a woman wages unless he has work enough to keep her all the long day, and paying work at that, such as butter-making for her to do."[42] This was verified by the testimony of a woman who was offered a job as a home-help on a farm. She was expected to cook for four men and an invalid woman, milk three cows, make butter, and do all the washing and cleaning for the household.[43]

In spite of the workload for female farm servants the work of the farm wife was rarely diminished. Usually the additional female labour made the expansion of the dairy and other market activities of the farm woman possible. One woman who did not have a servant had to keep the size of her dairy herd down because she simply could not manage more. For her it would certainly have made sense to have a servant, if she had been able to find one, because "she would soon pay for herself out of the extra butter I would be able to make."[44] Another farm woman echoed this frustration over not having the time for lucrative economic activities: "I wish I could hire one [female servant] to help me with dairy and chickens, and the pigs, they are all my 'perquisites' and I could make a lot of money by them if I had more time."[45]

The constraints on women's dairy work were significant. The fragmented nature of farm women's work and the problems they faced in accumulating capital and hiring labour tended to keep the production of women's dairying at a relatively low level and served to restrict the size of the dairy herds that could be conveniently handled by a small labour force using rather primitive technology. As markets grew and farmers recognized the advantages of expanded dairying, the small-scale production that women could manage became less tenable.

Growth in Markets

The market in dairy products increased rapidly and exports grew considerably even before factory production began. In 1861 butter production was almost 26 million pounds in Upper Canada and almost 16 million pounds in Lower Canada (Table 1). Cheese-making was less important than butter-making at this time: in Upper Canada little more than 2½ million pounds of cheese were produced and in Lower Canada less than 700,000 pounds. Butter was considered more necessary than cheese to the diet of farm families and was therefore easier to market,[46] but this factor alone did not account for its wider production. It was also easier to learn how to make butter, and the process of butter-making was not as time-consuming or as difficult as cheese-making.[47] Before the rise

Table 1
Homemade Butter and Cheese Production by Province,
Canada, 1851-1891 (in millions of pounds)

		1851	1861	1871	1881	1891
Ontario	Butter	16.1	25.8	37.6	54.9	55.6
	Cheese	3.4	2.7	3.4	1.7	1.1
Quebec	Butter	9.6	15.9	24.3	30.6	30.1
	Cheese	.8	.7	.5	.6	4.3
Nova Scotia	Butter	3.6	4.5	7.1	7.5	9.0
	Cheese	.6	.9	.9	.5	.6
New Brunswick	Butter	3.1	4.6	5.1	6.5	7.8
	Cheese	—	.2	.2	.2	—
P.E.I.	Butter	—	.7	1.0	1.7	2.0
	Cheese	—	.1	.1	.2	.1
Manitoba	Butter	—	—	—	.9	4.8
	Cheese	—	—	—	—	.2
B.C.	Butter	—	—	—	.3	.4
	Cheese	—	—	—	—	—
Alberta	Butter	—	—	—	.1	.4
	Cheese	—	—	—	—	—
Sask.	Butter	—	—	—	—	1.5
	Cheese	—	—	—	—	—
Total Canada	Butter	32.4	51.5	75.1	102.5	111.6
	Cheese	4.8	4.6	5.1	3.2	6.3

SOURCES: *Census of Canada*, 1871, vol. 4, "Censuses of Canada 1665 to 1871," pp. 197, 219, 227, 237, 275, 325, 337, 355, 365, 397; *ibid.*, vol. 3, p. 220; *ibid.*, 1881, vol. 3, p. 248; *ibid.*, 1891, vol. 4, pp. 117-221.

of cheese factories, butter production was also more profitable, mainly because the by-product of butter-making, buttermilk, was in demand for pig-raising.[48]

From about mid-century the market for dairy products grew

considerably. This was initially a result of the opening of American markets to Canadian producers. Rising American prices made Canadian products more attractive[49] and in the short period between 1849 and 1851 it is estimated that butter production increased by more than 350 per cent.[50] Improved transportation with the development of steamships and railways considerably expanded international dairy markets and the Reciprocity Treaty, which permitted free trade in dairy products,[51] made the American market even more accessible.[52] The Civil War in the United States, which caused considerable disruption in dairy production in that country, further enhanced Canadian exports. The greatest impact of the war, however, was on cheese production, and ultimately this had important ramifications for women's control over dairying. From 1860 to 1862 Canadian exports of butter increased by over 60 per cent. While this was dramatic, the increase in cheese exports was even more startling. From 1860 to 1863 these exports increased by over 700 per cent.[53] The high prices paid in the United States for Canadian cheese lured many Canadian farmers into specializing in dairy farming.[54] The move was particularly sensible in the face of uncertain wheat production and the new technology that permitted cheese to be manufactured in greater quantities and more profitably in cheese factories.[55] Butter production at this time did not develop in the same way. Rather, it remained as a part-time activity for women on farms where most productive resources were concentrated on wheat growing or mixed farming. The amounts of butter produced in home dairies, however, were considerable and continued to rise until the second decade of the twentieth century.

Paradoxically, while the opening of the American market was a great boon to the Canadian dairy industry, the closing of the same market with the end of the Reciprocity Treaty further stimulated cheese and butter production. The return of the tariff gave Canadian producers greater control over the domestic market for dairy produce at a time when farmers were being deprived of good markets for cereals in the United States. Dairy exports to Great Britain were stimulated, too. From 1865 to 1870 exports of butter increased from about 7 million pounds to almost 15½ million pounds and butter was still considerably more important than cheese in the value of exports.[56] But the introduction of cheese factories rapidly changed the nature of the dairy industry. By 1874 the amount and the value of cheese exports were considerably higher than those of butter.[57]

Rise of Cheese Factories

The rapid transition of cheese-making from the farm to the factory almost completely removed women from this form of dairy production in a very short period of time. By contrast, the factory production of butter was much slower to take hold, so women's displacement from this aspect of dairying was much more gradual.

Cheese-making was the first aspect of dairying to move to the factory and for some time remained the only form of dairy production taking place off the farm.[58] The first cheese factory in Canada began operations in Ontario in 1864 with technology imported from the United States. Seven years later there were 353 cheese factories in the country.[59] By 1881 the production of homemade cheese in Ontario, the province with the greatest number of cheese factories, was about half what it had been in 1871 (Table 1). And the *First Annual Report of the Dairy Commissioner of Canada* in 1890 stated that 99 per cent of the country's cheese production occurred in factories.[60] By way of contrast, in the same year less than 3 per cent of the butter of Canada was made in creameries.[61] With the rise of cheese factories, the character of dairying on the farm changed considerably, especially the division of labour in dairy work. The specialization of farms in production of milk to supply cheese factories meant males increasingly became involved in the production process. As large dairy herds developed, dairying ceased to be a part-time occupation for farm women and more and more became the major work of the males on the farm.

Milking was the first type of female dairy labour to be more regularly performed by men. When the family farm had one or two cows, milking was usually women's work. The cow, as part of the wife's dowry,[62] had become part of the family's wealth, and it was her responsibility and its products belonged to her. As farms grew, there was a tendency for milking to be assigned to the hired help. The larger farms and larger farm households greatly added to the household responsibilities of farm women and their dairy work increasingly became confined to indoor activities. As long as any aspect of production involved the farmhouse, it remained within the female domain, but outdoor dairy activity gradually became the preserve of men. Certain activities, such as barn-building, feed-growing, barn-cleaning, and the preparation of silage had been primarily male responsibilities, but increasingly the pasturing, feeding, calving, and milking were also taken over by men.[63] In a textbook from 1911 widely used in dairying colleges, the passing of women as milkers was lamented.

Much might be said in favor of women as milkers. The withdrawal of women from the cow stable has been detrimental to
the dairy industry. A woman has naturally greater patience and
more innate kindness and a higher ideal of cleanliness than a
man. The exercise of these virtues tells on the cows and on the
milk-flow. Milking comes at such inconvenient hours for the
housewife, and her duties are already so manifold, she should
not be asked to go to the stable to milk. Moreover, many stables,
I am sorry to say are not fit for her, with her skirts, to enter. It is
well for the woman on the farm to learn how to milk, so that in
case of sickness or absence of the men, they may attend to the
cows.[64]

The introduction of cheese factories made it possible for greater
amounts of cheese to be made by a small labour force, but for the
farms supplying the raw material the labour involved in dairying
increased. Milking remained a labour-intensive task on most farms
because the use of milking machines was slow to be accepted. Until
well into the twentieth century milking was usually done by hand,
so it became essential, as herds grew, for the farm unit to invest
more in its dairy labour force, a force that was mostly male.[65]
The move to factory cheese production did not immediately
separate women from cheese-making. In the early stages of factory
production women were a considerable portion of the labour force
although, admittedly, the labour force itself was not large. In 1871
37 per cent of the labour in cheese factories was female (Table 2).
Because production methods in early cheese factories were similar
to those used in domestic production and because the factories
themselves were often located on the farm, it was not unnatural for
the makers of farm dairy cheese to participate in factory work. But
even from the beginning it was recognized that factory production
would eventually eliminate women from cheese-making. In the
year in which the first dairy factory in Canada was established, the
Canadian Farmer noted that the innovation in cheese-making
would mean farm women would no longer have to do this heavy
and difficult work: "The old method of cheese-making has done
more to injure the health of women in cheese-dairying districts
than any other cause."[66] As cheese production in factories became
more regular, women's presence was eliminated. By the turn of the
century there were no women working in cheese factories in Canada.

Women continued to make some cheese in farm dairies but the
amount was insignificant compared to factory production.[67] Some

Table 2
Employment in Cheese Factories by Gender,
Ontario, Quebec, and Canada, 1871-1911

Year	Ontario Males	Females	Quebec Males	Females	Canada[a] Males	Females	Females as % of total
1871	577	332	37	40	624	374	37.0%
1881	1,348	287	262	62	1,652	351	18.4%
1891	1,755	175	876	95	2,726	287	9.5%
1901[b]	2,733	—	3,630	—	6,886	—	—
1911[c]	2,446	1	3,255	—	6,143	1	—

[a] Cheese production outside Quebec and Ontario was negligible for these years. Even by 1911 over 97 per cent of factory production of cheese took place in these two provinces.

[b] The figures for 1901 and 1911 represent employment in both cheese and butter factories. There were 126 males and 25 females employed in creameries in Canada in 1881 and 401 males and 24 females in creameries in 1891.

[c] In 1911 there were also three individuals of unspecified sex under sixteen years of age who were working in cheese factories in Ontario.

SOURCES: *Census of Canada*, 1871, vol. 3, p. 372; *ibid.*, 1881, vol. 3, p. 406; *ibid.*, 1891, vol. 3, pp. 93-98; *ibid.*, 1901, vol. 2, pp. 306-19, vol. 3, pp. 18-39; *ibid.*, 1911, vol. 3, pp. 52-83.

small cheeses required too much time and trouble for cheese factories[68] and were still profitable for farm women, but frequently this type of work was considered more trouble than it was worth.[69] On the whole, cheese-making by farm women ceased to be an important source of income for farm families. By 1910 the total value of homemade cheese was placed at $154,000. In the same year the value of homemade butter was over $30 million.[70]

Changes in Butter-making

Creameries for butter-making were much slower than cheese factories to become established, so women continued to be Canada's butter-makers until well into the twentieth century. The first Canadian creamery began in Quebec in 1873,[71] but by the turn of the century the greatest proportion of Canadian butter was still being made by farm women. The 1901 census shows that while 36 million pounds of butter were being made in factories, over 105 million pounds were being produced on farms (Table 3).

Table 3
Butter Production in Creameries and on Farms by Province,
Canada, 1901-1941 (in millions of pounds)

Province		1901	1911	1921	1931	1941
Ontario	Creamery	7.6	13.9	37.2	77.5	86.3
	Farm	55.4	63.2	33.5	24.3	24.5
Quebec	Creamery	24.6	41.8	41.6	69.7	76.5
	Farm	18.3	19.6	15.5	13.7	10.2
Nova Scotia	Creamery	.3	.4	2.5	5.9	6.5
	Farm	9.1	11.0	8.7	6.1	5.9
New Brunswick	Creamery	.3	.8	1.1	2.4	4.5
	Farm	7.8	9.1	8.4	8.1	5.2
P.E.I.	Creamery	.6	.7	1.2	2.0	2.7
	Farm	1.4	2.3	2.1	1.8	1.3
Manitoba	Creamery	1.6	2.1	7.6	21.1	31.1
	Farm	8.7	10.9	8.4	9.1	9.4
B.C.	Creamery	.4	1.2	2.1	5.4	6.1
	Farm	1.1	1.2	1.9	1.6	2.5
Alberta	Creamery	(.7)[a]	2.1	11.8	23.0	35.3
	Farm	1.2	7.7	9.1	11.9	14.0
Sask.	Creamery	(.7)[a]	1.5	6.6	19.0	37.1
	Farm	2.3	12.1	15.9	21.0	21.3
Total	Creamery	36.1	64.5	111.7	226.0	286.1
	Farm	105.3	137.1	103.5	97.6	94.3
Farm butter as % of total production		75%	68%	48%	30%	25%

[a] Alberta and Saskatchewan combined.

SOURCES: *Census of Canada*, 1901, vol. 2, pp. 210-17; *ibid.*, 1911, vol. 4, pp. 348-57; *ibid.*, 1921, vol. 5, p. 56; *ibid.*, 1931, vol. 8, pp. 12, 52, 82, 152, 205, 389, 545, 597, 669, 736; *The Canada Year Book*, 1924, pp. 242-43; *The Canada Year Book*, 1933, p. 252; *The Canada Year Book*, 1942, p. 214.

By 1911 only in Quebec did the factory production of butter exceed home production. For the country as a whole less than a third of butter production took place in factories.[72]

Butter production remained in women's hands for a variety of reasons. First, domestic butter-making was a much simpler operation than domestic cheese-making. Making cheese on the farm required more space and equipment than making butter and required a skill less readily learned.[73] But also significant were the much higher costs involved in butter production in factories. The capital costs for creameries were more than two and a half times greater than for cheese factories, and the costs involved in hauling materials were considerably higher as well.[74] Until separators were widely used on farms, whole milk was hauled to the creamery. Milk was also transported to cheese factories, but these establishments used the entire product, while butter factories used only cream in production. This involved transporting six times the bulk necessary for production to creameries.[75] Also, the methods of separating cream, even at the creamery, were slow and labour-intensive.[76] Production in cheese factories was both less wasteful and provided a more reliable product. The result was that cheese exports soared while those of butter declined. Cheese exports increased from 6 million pounds in 1868 to over 88 million pounds in 1889. During the same period butter exports dropped from 13½ million pounds to fewer than 2 million pounds.[77] This development of the cheese export market also served to retard the growth of creameries.

Even though there were several factors that perpetuated butter-making on the farm, this method of production was frequently criticized. The uneven quality of homemade dairy products was a common complaint. Usually the blame was placed on inadequate production methods and sometimes even outright fraud.[78] In butter-making, careless and unclean production methods, the use of ordinary Canadian salt instead of specially prepared factory salt, and holding cream until sufficient quantities to churn were produced all tended to result in a less than ideal product.[79] So did feeding cows indifferently or with substances that strongly affected the taste of milk. But more deliberate actions also resulted in inferior products. In 1872 a public analyst examined forty-nine samples of butter and found that twenty-three of them had been adulterated.[80]

The problems with the quality of Canadian butter and in particular its lack of uniformity prompted petitions to government "praying that the inspection of butter may be made compulsory."[81] While the domestic methods of production were most often considered the source of the problems the entire blame cannot be laid here. In fact, many women had acquired reputations as especially fine butter-makers.[82] The fact that butter made in the western parts of Ontario was notoriously bad while that in the eastern townships was very good suggests less that women in the western part of the province were more slovenly in their production methods than that marketing problems played a major role in creating the bad reputation for Canadian butter in general. Most women had few outlets for their butter. They could either trade with their neighbours or with local merchants in nearby towns. Often the merchant could not sell the butter immediately and would store it for as much as six months in his cellar, usually without proper packing, ventilation, or ice, until a travelling butter dealer took it off his hands.[83] Individual women who had to sell their produce where and when they could had no control over the quality of the article once it left their hands.

Gradually the handling and transportation facilities for butter improved in some areas of the country. In 1877 a special train with refrigeration and ventilation ran from Stratford, Ontario, to Montreal every Saturday during the dairy season.[84] When it reached Montreal, the dairy products designed for export to England were immediately put on ships fitted with special compartments for butter and cheese, and to minimize the amount of time the produce would spend in unrefrigerated conditions these items were the last freight loaded and the first unloaded. But mechanical refrigeration was not introduced on ships until 1897 so the quality of butter exports to England remained poor.[85] Moreover, the widespread use of refrigeration did not occur until considerably later.

By the end of the last decade of the nineteenth century several important changes occurred that were significant for transferring butter production from the farm to the factory. The change usually considered to be most important was the introduction of the centrifugal cream separator to Canada, the first one having been brought to the country in 1882 from Denmark.[86] This new technology revolutionized the old methods of recovering cream from milk and radically reduced the amount of labour for farm women in the process of butter-making. However, while the separator made butter-making on the farm easier and contributed to a more reliable product, its advent also made the use of factories more practicable. The separator worked as follows: the milk was placed in the separator bowl and was then subjected to a strong centrifugal force. The heavier substance, the skim milk, was thrown from the centre and was drawn off from the inside wall of the bowl. The lighter cream was forced inward and channelled off through an outlet near the centre of the bowl.[87] Separating cream from milk could then be done in a relatively short period of time and thereby very much reduce the common risks of contamination and souring in the earlier methods of separating the cream. The introduction of the separator also meant that whole milk did not need to be transported to creameries, making the cost of creamery-produced butter much lower than it had been. Not only was the cost of haulage considerably reduced, but also the skim milk could be left for use on farms. Altogether the new separator was heralded as an important advance. Not only would yields be higher and costs lower, but there was an added bonus: "The farmer's wife is saved the labor and worry of making butter on the farm."[88]

Government Aid

The introduction of the separator was an important step toward creamery production of butter. However, it was not sufficient inducement to farmers to turn to creameries in large numbers.[89] Only with considerable government encouragement and money were farmers enticed into the industry and was butter-making thus removed from farm women.

Substantial government aid was necessary to promote the rise of factory dairying in Canada.[90] As is not untypical of government subsidies in development projects in general, aid in Canada was biased toward increasing male activity in the dairy industry.[91] This is not to imply that government action, realistically, could have been different. The forces that restricted women's access to capital and tied their labour to work in the farm household were powerful deterrents to women's participation in capitalistic development. Rather, government promotion of dairying as a male activity was a reflection of the economic position of women and the notion that a more capital-intensive industry outside the home was rightly the sphere of males. Nevertheless, although government action cannot be seen to be the cause of women's decreasing participation in dairying, it certainly served to accelerate the trend in this direction.

Government aid to the dairy industry was motivated by a desire to stimulate and improve production as competition from American, Danish, and Australian butter increasingly threatened the Canadian market. These countries were able to produce better products at lower costs because of improved transportation and production methods.[92] If Canada was to continue exporting dairy products the government recognized that production methods would have to change. Governments in Canada had begun to subsidize male dairy enterprises early in the history of cheese factories. Beginning in 1873 with the Ontario government, provincial governments instituted the practice of giving grants to dairymen's associations to encourage factory production. According to one dairy historian, money was given "ever since there has been any organization among dairymen competent to administer such funds."[93] With the money the organizations were expected initially to provide factory inspection and education on new dairy methods. After 1890 these activities were slowly taken over by government itself, but aid to dairymen continued in the form both of new factory equipment and of direct financial assistance to farmers who started dairy factories.

Gradually, government help took on a variety of other forms. In some cases governments became involved in the actual production of cheese and butter, although not with the understanding that this would be a permanent public venture, but to prove that the enterprise could be profitable to dairymen. Often government management was instituted in a factory primarily because male farmers simply did not possess the skills or experience necessary for butter- or cheese-making. In these cases some investment in the factory would be made by the farmers, but government agents would operate and manage the factory until the farmers acquired sufficient knowledge of the manufacturing end of the business themselves.[94] Model creameries and cheese factories were frequently established to teach new dairying techniques. Also, improvements in transportation facilities and refrigerated storage areas were made by the government.

Educational promotion was an important part of government efforts to stimulate factory dairying among male farmers.[95] Dairying schools and travelling dairies were instituted in a number of provinces to teach new dairying techniques. The first travelling dairy was sent by the federal government to Manitoba in 1894 to give demonstrations on the use of the cream separator, the testing of milk samples, and the proper way to churn cream and work butter. Similar travelling dairies were sent to Saskatchewan, Alberta, and B.C. The success of travelling dairies prompted some provincial governments to institute their own. Of particular note is that which was begun in Nova Scotia because it is the only one that appears to have been carried out by a woman. Laura Rose's travelling dairy, which began in 1901, was so popular that it was continued for six successive seasons and a second travelling dairy had to be added.[96] Several dairy schools were open to women. In fact, at the Agricultural College at Guelph, Ontario, the dairy department was the only branch of the college open to women at the turn of the century. Of the eleven students in the Government Dairy School in Winnipeg, four were female. Unfortunately, in most schools, a certificate-granting program was a longer course of study and few women embarked on it. The National Council of Women reported in 1900 that while the Kingston Dairy School provided courses open to women, none had yet entered the longer certificate-granting course. The reason given was that the hours were long, and there was a great deal of lifting and heavy work involved. However, it should be considered that the women simply could not meet the preliminary work requirement for the course: it was necessary to have worked at least three seasons in a cheese factory or creamery.[97] Since the census for 1901 reports that no women were working in cheese and butter factories at that time, they would have had difficulty complying with this regulation.

Government education efforts constantly stressed an important change in the nature of dairying. It had become "scientific" and was therefore more worthy of the serious farmer's attention than it had been before. Women's dairying was viewed as an instinctive type of process, although, as was noted by a well-known dairy expert who specifically discussed the value of women's intuition, this approach could often be effective.

> In the domain of cheese-making these [i.e., those who acquire mastery by intuition] will generally be women, at all events in private dairies; they hit upon one scientific truth after another by a process of reasoning which neither they nor anyone else can explain, but which is often correct nevertheless, and they do the right thing at the right time without caring to inquire into the why and wherefore of it.[98]

Whatever success women achieved was seen as having less to do with learning the trade well or acquiring skill through practice than through some haphazard approach associated with women's nature. The big business of dairying was seen as requiring a different type of approach, one that was more systematic, more intensive, and more masculine:

> To combine the home-grown fodders with the more concentrated

bought feeds so as to obtain the best results; to delve into the mystery of how the cow can take this food and manufacture the same into creamy white life-giving milk; scientifically to separate the cream and make the fat into golden bricks of fragrant butter; to get this butter to the best market and obtain for it the highest price; surely to accomplish all this demands a man of no small calibre.[99]

It was this type of man that governments wanted to encourage to specialize in dairying.

There is no evidence to show that women butter- or cheese-makers received any form of government subsidy. The various government agencies involved in promoting dairying at times expressed sympathy with farm women for the difficult conditions under which they laboured, but the only solution deemed feasible (outside of encouraging male farmers to provide better equipment for their wives) was to remove women from dairying altogether.

In some areas of the country women did move in the direction of trying to establish co-operatives to sell their eggs, cream, and butter.[100] In the West in particular the poorly developed markets and the monopoly power of the merchants clearly placed the isolated woman at a disadvantage when selling her produce. Elizabeth Mitchell described the situation on the prairies just before World War I:

> The farmer's wife might drive in ten miles or more, in time she could ill afford, and go to the first store to offer her goods, butter, eggs, cream, vegetables, all very perishable in hot weather. A low price would be offered, which she would refuse, but by the time the second store was reached the second store-keeper would be warned by the first, by telephone, not to go above his price.[101]

Some sort of co-operative marketing venture certainly could have improved the farm woman's position. But the efforts of women to organize were slow to develop and did not serve as an alternative to the growing tendency for the industry to be controlled by males. Dairymen's associations had already been well established and the various governments had found them useful channels for subsidizing dairying efforts. Homemakers' clubs and Women's Institutes had become interested in providing information to farm women on dairying techniques,[102] but the focus of these organizations regarding dairying was less on organization and distribution than on production techniques on the farms themselves.[103] By this time the future of dairying was clearly in the factory and done by men. To be sure, dairy production in the western provinces was still almost exclusively taking place on the farm and was being done by farm women, but the impetus toward factory dairying for the country as a whole was firmly established.[104]

No evidence so far suggests that women on farms perceived the government aid to males as a threat to their interests. However, one of the difficulties in understanding the relations of production within the family context is in ascertaining the extent to which changes in activities are understood by family members as being significant shifts in areas of control. Because the farm family is an economic unit where men and women share in a standard of living that is a product of their mutual and interdependent labour, the effect of change on individuals within the unit is often obscured by the perception of the benefit to the family as a whole. The close personal relationships within families undoubtedly meant that whatever antagonisms and contradictions arose in the production process were less likely to be recognized as arising from different relations in production than from the ordinary business of getting along in a marriage. Understanding the effect of change on women was undoubtedly complicated by the slow and uneven process of transforming dairy production from farm to factory, a process which meant that women were not abruptly displaced from the control of dairy production. Undoubtedly some women welcomed the reduced workload when dairying was no longer their responsibility, but to others it meant a certain loss of independence. In a recent study of farm women's labour, Linda Graff quotes a woman who felt the loss of income from her own work for the market: "That's one thing about years ago when we had cows and hens, the women got the egg check and you had your own money to handle where you don't have your own money nowadays which is different and I don't like it as well."[105] Of course, even today some farm wives are involved in the work of dairying, but the distinction is that where women had the primary responsibility for dairying in the pre-factory period, their role now is mostly to "help."[106] Ultimately, the inability of women to develop their household craft into capitalist production resulted in male domination of the industry.

4

Birth Control and Abortion in Canada, 1870-1920

Angus McLaren

In the spring of 1908 the congregation of Toronto's St James' Cathedral was informed by the Reverend C. Ensor Sharp that the Almighty interested himself directly in the demographic details of Canada's declining birth rate: "God abhors the spirit so prevalent nowadays which contemns [*sic*] motherhood. How it must grieve Him when He sees what we call race suicide; when He sees the problems of married life approached lightly and wantonly; based on nothing higher and nobler than mere luxury and gratification of passion."[1] This fear of "race suicide" to which Sharp referred had been popularized in North America by President Theodore Roosevelt, whose statement, "The woman who flinches from childbirth stands on a par with the soldier who drops his rifle and runs in battle," was only the most famous remark to be made by a generation of social observers who attributed the shrinking size of the Anglo-Saxon family to the "selfishness" of women. By the turn of the century Canadians were well acquainted with such concerns. In the Canadian edition of Sylvanus Stall's *What a Young Man Ought to Know* (1897), the author expressed his horror that many women married, not to bear children, but "for the purpose of practically leading a life of legalized prostitution."[2] Crown Attorney J.W. Curry, KC, addressing the city pastors of Toronto in 1901, claimed that employment opportunities permitted women to avoid marriage or to fall back on "crime," which led to a "low birth rate."[3] According to Professor H.E. Armstrong, speaking at the 1901 Winnipeg meeting of the British Association, all attempts to bring women into competition with men were dangerous, "for she will inevitably cease to exercise her specific womanly functions with effect, so delicate is the adjustment of her mechanism."[4] A contributor to the *Canadian Churchman* (1900) went so far as to assert that even the pressures of existing society encouraged "to put it bluntly, in nine cases out of ten, women to murder their unborn children."[5]

What exercised the imaginations of these writers was the belief that women were responsible for the fall in marital fertility. In fact this fall was only a symptom of the major social and economic transformations Canada was undergoing at the turn of the century. Later commentators would speak of the confidence and optimism of the age, but when one examines the population discussion one uncovers many expressions of fear and foreboding. What had been a rural, agrarian society was becoming an urbanized, increasingly industrialized community. These shifts, though only partly understood at the time, were seen as posing major dangers. The population increased from 4.3 million in 1881 to 8.5 in 1920 but much of this growth was due to foreign migration. In 1871 60 per cent of the population had been of British stock; in 1921 only 40 per cent could claim this heritage. Could the new arrivals be Canadianized or would they overwhelm the young nation? The population was, moreover, increasingly drawn to the cities. By 1921 the dividing line was reached when over half of all Canadians were urban dwellers. It was a commonplace that city life was inherently anonymous and immoral and the question was posed if it would succeed in undermining the virtues of rural newcomers. And the virtue of young women was felt to be particularly at risk. By 1921 there were 58,000 more women than men in the cities. The largest contingent of these "surplus" women were in the 15-29 age group. This imbalance was due in part to the new employment opportunities offered women in textile mills, tobacco companies, food processing plants, retail stores, and domestic service. In 1896 women made up 20 per cent of the active work force, by 1931 25 per cent.[6] The vast majority of these women would eventually leave their jobs, marry, and raise families, but the anxious expressed their concern that they would have already formed tastes and habits of independence that would render them unfit to raise the traditionally large family. Middle-class women, on the other hand, were accused of restricting family size simply out of a desire for greater luxury and self-indulgence.

The same fears of race suicide were expressed in Britain and the United States, but in Canada the anxieties of the middle-class English were exacerbated at the beginning of our period by both the fertility of the Irish and Quebec's successful "revanche des berceaux," and later by the influx of non-British migration. In an article on "The Canadian Immigration Policy," W.S. Wallace, a future editor of the *Canadian Historical Review*, warned: "The native-born population, in the struggle to keep up appearances in the face of the increasing competition, fails to propagate itself, commits race suicide, in short, whereas the immigrant population, being inferior, and having no appearances to keep up, propagates itself like the fish of the sea."[7] And turning to the threat of eventual Catholic domination, the *Canadian Churchman* bemoaned the fact that, "As France is to Germany, so seemingly is Ontario to Quebec...." Such attempts by the protestant churches in Canada to wake the populace to the perils of the situation won the applause of Lydia Kingsmill Commander in *The American Idea: Does the National Tendency Toward a Small Family Point to Race Suicide or Race Degeneration?* (1907). "The French Canadians alone," she informed her readers, "being devout Roman Catholics, primitive and simple-minded, and given to agricultural pursuits are extremely prolific."[8]

As bizarre as these outbursts might first appear they are nevertheless worthy of note because they point to one of the major social phenomena of Canadian history that has yet to be carefully examined – the late nineteenth-century decline of the birth rate. The most dramatic aspect of the decline took place in Ontario (falling by 44 per cent between 1871 and 1901), so that from 1881 to 1911 it had the lowest fertility of any province. Even Quebec's general fertility rate dropped by 21 per cent between 1851 and 1921 while that of Canada as a whole fell by 41 per cent[9] (see Table 1).

Table 1
General Fertility Rates, Canada and Selected Provinces, 1871–1931
(annual number of births per 1,000 women aged 15–49 years)

Year	Canada	N.S.	Quebec	Ontario	Manitoba	Sask.	B.C.
1871	189	174	180	191			
1881	160	148	173	149	366		202
1891	144	138	163	121	242		204
1901	145	132	160	108	209	550	184
1911	144	128	161	112	167	229	149
1921	120	105	155	98	125	135	84
1931	94	98	116	79	81	100	62

SOURCE: Jacques Henripin, *Trends and Factors of Fertility in Canada* (Ottawa, 1972), p. 21.

Given the fact that despite relatively stable marriage rates and improving fecundity the birth rate of English-speaking families fell, some form of birth control must have been employed. Discovering exactly what form of control is a problem.[10] Traditional histories of birth control assume that the decline of fertility in the late nineteenth century in Europe and North America was due to the diffusion of some new knowledge or technique. It has to be recalled, however, that there were several traditional methods already available. To space births Canadian families had long relied on simple continence and the margin of safety from conception provided when a woman was nursing.[11] In addition, two major methods of family restriction were to be used right into the twentieth century – coitus interruptus and self-induced abortion.

Abortion was to be of special importance. At a time when withdrawal was the most widely used method of contraception – and all studies show that this was the case in Europe and North America until at least the 1930s – numerous couples would discover that a "mistake" had been made.[12] What then? Clearly those who were intent on limiting family size would have to contemplate the option of abortion as a second line of defence against an unwanted pregnancy. An examination of the history of abortion is, moreover, of special interest to the historian in that more references were made to it by medical and legal observers than to employment of contraceptives. By studying this "back-up method" of birth control that was called into play when other means failed, it is possible to cast a fresh light on the general question of family limitation. In what follows I will review the means of contraception available to Canadians at the turn of the century and then proceed with an examination of the abortion issue.

How would young Canadian couples of the 1890s seek to control their family size? The information available to them in published form on means of contraception was limited. Section 179C of the 1892 Criminal Code (substituted with section 207 in 1900) restricted writing on the subject: "Everyone is guilty of an indictable offense and liable to two years' imprisonment who knowingly, without lawful excuse or justification, offers to sell, advertises, publishes an advertisement of or has for sale or disposal any medicine, drug or article intended or represented as a means of preventing conception or causing abortion." The English draft code on which the Canadian law was based had only a general section on "obscene libel"; in making the sale or advertisement of contraceptives and abortifacients a specific indictable offense, the Canadian government was following the more stringent line of the American Comstock laws.[13] Partly as a result of the law there was no organized birth control movement in Canada until the 1930s, by which time the birth rate had already reached a low level and, indeed, was about to turn upwards.

Discussion of family limitation was restricted but it did take place. It is clear from the mass-produced medical and self-help literature, mostly of American origin, which circulated widely in Canada that doctors and popular practitioners recognized the growing desire of the public to avoid overly large families.[14] Although respectable physicians would not countenance the use of "mechanical" contraceptives, they would on occasion advise the use of certain "natural" means of control. The first means were simple continence – Emma F. Angell Drake in *What a Young Wife Ought to Know* (1908) recommended twin beds – and prolonged nursing, which was widely believed to provide protection against a subsequent conception.[15] The second advised natural method was restriction of intercourse to what was thought to be the "safe period" in the woman's ovulation cycle. Unfortunately the cycle was completely misunderstood and the so-called "safe period" was mistakenly calculated to fall at mid-month. The correct cycle was not established until the 1920s, but in the meantime several generations of physicians vaunted the reliability of their schedule. Augustus K. Gardner, for example, in *Conjugal Sins Against the Laws of Life and Health* (1874) advised waiting twelve days after the menses: "This act of continence is healthy, moral and irreproachable. Then there need be no imperfection in the conjugal act, no fears, no shame, no disgust, no drawback to the joys which legitimately belong to a true married life. Thus excess is avoided, diseases diminished, and such a desirable limitation to the number of children, as is consistent with the peculiar nature of the individuals concerned, is effected."[16] Canadian readers received similar advice in John Cowan, *The Science of the New Life* (1869), George H. Napheys, *The Physical Life of Women* (1873?), and Winfield Scott Hall, *Sexual Knowledge* (1916).[17] The information was not always consistent. H.W. Long in *Sane Sex Life and Sane Sex Living* (1919) claimed that ten days after the period a woman entered her "free time"; B.G. Jefferis and J.L. Nichols in *Searchlights on Health: Light on Dark Corners* (1894) asserted that from mid-month to within three days of the menses one enjoyed "almost absolute safety."[18] For women with short, regular cycles the suggested schedules might have offered some protection but for most they would have been disastrous.

A third natural method, but one not as well supported, was the practice of coitus reservatus or intercourse without ejaculation. This method met with some success in John Humphrey Noyes' Oneida Community in upstate New York and its benefits were proclaimed by Alice B. Stockham in *Karezza: Ethics of Marriage* (1896) and in *Tokology: A Book for Every Woman* (1916). The former book was so highly thought of by some Canadian women that it was enthusiastically reviewed by the superintendent of the Department of Purity in Literature, Arts and Fashion of the Women's Christian Temperance Union.[19] The problem with this form of contraception was that although its advocates claimed it raised the sexual relation to a higher spiritual level, it demanded a degree of self-control available to few Canadian males.

But what of the most reliable forms of contraception known of in the nineteenth century – the sheath, douche, and pessary?[20] Doctors would not discuss their use because such appliances were associated in their minds with the libertine, the prostitute, and the midwife, and were thus outside the realm of respectable medicine. The importance of the rhythm method and the reason why it was greeted by physicians with enthusiasm was that it was not tainted with such associations; it had been "scientifically" determined and so offered a means by which the medical profession could claim to extend its expertise into the most intimate area of human life.

When one looks for references to "mechanical" means of contraception one finds, because of both legal restrictions and medical distaste for the subject, little direct information. Women who did know about the prophylactic benefits of douching would, however, have been able to read between the lines in the advertisements for the "Every Woman Marvel Whirling Spray," which offered, according to its producer, the Windsor Supply Company, the advantages of "vaginal hygiene." The company's advertisements appeared in such diverse publications as the T. Eaton Company catalogue, Jefferis and Nichols, *Searchlights on Health*, the Toronto *Daily Mail and Empire*, and even in the staid pages of the *Dominion Medical Monthly*.[21] Of course, to be fully effective a douche would have to be used in conjunction with a pessary. A recipe for a homemade one concocted of cocoa butter, boric acid, and tannic acid found in the papers of the feminist Violet McNaughton suggests that Canadian women were not slow in producing their own protective devices.[22]

For men the most effective contraceptive was the sheath or condom. By the 1890s they were being mass produced in Britain and the United States and distributed by druggists in Canadian urban centres. A sensational report on their easy availability was made in 1898 by the purity campaigner C.S. Clark in *Of Toronto the Good*: "I saw a druggist's advertisement a short time ago in a Toronto paper with this significant line: *Rubber Goods of ALL KINDS For Sale*. There is not a boy in Toronto, I dare say, who does not know what that means .... A young fellow of sixteen once handed me a pasteboard coin, silvered over. When I mentioned to him that I saw nothing in the possession of such a coin, he laughed and told me to tear off the outside layer. I did so, and discovered one of the articles I have endeavoured to describe."[23] What is noteworthy in Clark's report, however, is that such contraceptives were assumed to be employed, not so much to control marital fertility, as to permit extra or premarital liaisons. They were no doubt used by some to control family size but their relatively high price, their association with venereal disease and prostitution, and the claims of doctors that they caused dangerous inflammation all restricted their employment. This left coitus interruptus as the simplest and most widespread form of contraception. Doctors might condemn it as "mutual masturbation," or "conjugal onanism," but until well into the twentieth century it was the main way in which Canadian couples sought to "cheat nature."[24]

Canadian couples had a fairly wide variety of contraceptive measures available to them by 1900 but they were all to a greater or lesser extent lacking in reliability.[25] If they failed, those who were adamant in their desire to limit family size would then have to face the serious decision of whether or not to seek an abortion. The necessary linkage of abortion with contraception was recognized by Gardner, who warned his readers: "You have no right 'to take precaution,' or failing in this, to resort to murder."[26] He recognized that the very fact that a couple used other methods could prepare them psychologically, when necessary, to fall back on abortion. As the use of contraceptive measures in general increased at the turn of the century, so, too, would the recourse to inducement of miscarriage.

Abortion is often left out of the histories of birth control but the issue raises a number of vital questions: women's responses to their physical functions, the medical profession's views of women's health, and male and female attitudes toward sexuality. If women resorted to such dangerous remedies it was because legal and medical authorities were withholding from them information necessary for the safe control of their fertility. The fact that significant numbers of women (including working-class women) sought abortions is, moreover, strong evidence that they were not, as was frequently assumed, passive in relation to their own fertility: they wanted to control it and were willing to go to considerable lengths to do so. And, finally, the issue reveals that the development of new methods of birth control and the controversy over their use at the turn of the century took place in the presence of a reality not yet fully perceived by historians – a widespread tradition of abortion based on folk remedies.[27]

The abortion question was brought forcefully to the Canadian public's attention in 1908 by "Kit," the writer of the "Women's Kingdom" column in the Toronto *Daily Mail and Empire*.[28] In an article of March 21 entitled "Race Suicide," she noted that though one was inclined to say hard things "of married women trying by every desperate means to avoid motherhood," the real scoundrels were the doctors. "Some fashionable physician living in a grand house, driving his motor, commits – every time he gets the price – a sordid murder, and goes scot free."[29] On the previous March 16, Dr. A.G. Ashton Fletcher, graduate of the University of Toronto and surgeon to the Queen's Own Regiment, was charged along with Harry Saunders, electrician, with the death of Jessie Helen Gould. Gould, a waitress at the Cadillac Hotel, had, it was later reported in court, paid twenty dollars to Ashton Fletcher to induce a miscarriage and died shortly afterwards of acute septic peritonitis.[30] The inquest sparked a series of articles and letters to the editor. One writer to the *Daily Mail* quoted the coroner to the effect that, "for every physician arrested for the crime there are 50 going 'scot free,' and for every physician there are 500 women guilty without the physician's aid."[31]

The Jessie Gould case was not an isolated affair. A perusal of the newspaper advertisements of the time reveals the widespread advertisement and sale of abortifacients and abortionists' offers of aid. Amongst the pills and potions of quacks surreptitiously claiming to have abortive powers were Radway's Pills for "female irregularities"; "The New French Remedy: Therapion"; Sir James Clarke's Female Pills; Madame Duvont's French Female Pills; Dr. Cowling's English Periodic Pills; Chichester's English Diamond Brand Pennyroyal Pills; Dr. Davis' Pennyroyal and Steel Pills; Old Dr. Gordon's "Pearls of Health," which, according to its producer, the Queen Medical Company of Montreal, "Never fails in curing all suppressions and irregularities ... used monthly"; the "Ladies Safe Remedy: Apioline" of Lyman and Sons of Montreal, who asserted that it was superior to such traditional remedies as apiol, tansy, or pennyroyal; Cook's Cotton Root Compound: "Is successfully used monthly by over 10,000 ladies," claimed Cooks of Windsor, Ontario;[32] and finally Karn's "Celebrated German Female Treatment." We know quite a bit about F.E. Karn of 132 Victoria Street, Toronto, because in 1901 he was tried under section 179C. His advertisements contained such statements as: "Thousands of married ladies are using these tablets monthly. Ladies who have reason to suspect pregnancy are cautioned against using these tablets .... They will speedily restore the menstrual sections when all other remedies fail .... No name is ever divulged, and your private affairs, your health, are sacred to us." Did such claims, which accompanied in this case what Karn was advertising as "Friar's French Female Regulator," amount to an announcement that the product was an abortifacient? The lower court judge was taken in by the warning against pregnant women using the product; the appeal court justices recognized that this was in fact the best way to vaunt the efficacy of the product.[33]

These advertisements of abortifacients are important for two reasons. First, they reveal that women seeking an abortion could obtain drugs and potions without directly involving themselves with an abortionist. Secondly, these announcements in their assertions that they are superior to traditional methods indicate that quacks were competing with and borrowing from traditional medical lore. In the *Physiology of Marriage* (1856) William Alcott wrote: "True it is that many who find themselves pregnant resort to tradition and household practice for what they call relief. Some field, or swamp, or grove contains the needful poison; and forthwith it is swallowed."[34] A woman would first seek to "put herself right" by drinking an infusion of one of the traditional abortifacients such as tansy, quinine, pennyroyal, rue, black hellebore, ergot of rye, savin, or cotton root. Ergot of rye was long used by midwives to induce labour and today in the form of ergometrine is still employed by obstetricians. Savin was as early as 1879 "well known as a popular abortive" in Toronto.[35] The effectiveness of these drugs is hard to determine but since they were employed generation after generation it must be assumed that they could on occasion induce miscarriage.[36]

If the drugs failed a woman might try bleedings, hot baths, violent exercises, and consumption of large quantities of gin. After this would come the riskier step of attempting a dilation of the cervix with slippery elm, a sponge tent, or catheter. It would only be as a last resort, and if it were still not beyond the sixteenth week when the quickening of the foetus caused an abandonment of all attempts, that the woman would turn to the abortionist. How would one find the help required? It was only necessary to glance at the advertisements in the personal and medical columns of the local paper. In the Toronto *Daily Mail* for March 21, 1908, there were five advertisements for "Ladies Home Before and During Confinement" and one for a Mrs. M. Summers who offered to cure "uterine tumours" and "irregularity" and in addition would send a "Women's Own Medical Adviser."[37] In the *Manitoba Free Press* for 1909 one finds similar announcements: "Ladies Avoid Unnecessary Delay and Disappointment," "Notice to Women – Have You Ever Used our Female Regulator?" with the guarantee that all information provided will remain confidential.[38] And finally the papers carried the advertisements of physicians and surgeons who by referring to their specialization in "sexual disorders" could attract the attention of the desperate.[39]

In 1908 Judge Winchester of Toronto complained that scarcely a week went by without a doctor being named in a criminal abortion and asked that the Medical Association take some action.[40] In the circumstances the timid reply made by the medical profession was revealing. The editor of the *Canadian Practitioner and Review* admitted that in Toronto alone there were probably half a dozen doctors practising abortion but he insisted that they were practically ostracized by their colleagues and at least kept out of the Toronto Academy of Medicine. They should be deprived of their licences, he conceded, but how could that be done?[41] In the following year the *Dominion Medical Monthly* went further in an article entitled, "When a doctor is accused of criminal abortion ...." The author declared, "All doctors in a great city have probably been approached some time or other in this respect."[42] If some gave in to the temptation of a large fee it was because the "open door policy" in medical education had resulted in an oversupply of poor young doctors. The obvious remedy was to improve the lot of practitioners by restricting entry to the profession. What was good for doctors would eventually be good for society at large.

As far as abortion itself was concerned the medical profession took the illegality of the operation as reason enough to continue to support the notion that it was both medically and morally wrong. There were of course individual doctors who in the privacy of their consulting rooms alluded to birth control and even helped induce miscarriages. But in public doctors would condone the termination of pregnancy by a surgeon only if a mother's life was in grave danger and full medical consultation took place. What was ignored was the fact that many women had to rely on self-induced abortions as a form of fertility control because the profession, though it might advise the restriction of family size, failed to provide the information on contraception that would make this safely possible. Earlier in the century doctors might have opposed abortion because of the dangers it posed to the mother's health, but by 1900 hospital abortions could be performed with relative safety. As early as the 1840s Dr. Alfred A. Andrews of Windsor was successfully carrying out therapeutic abortions.[43] By the 1890s the processes of dilation and curettage were well advanced but such operations were refused to all but a few.[44]

What was most striking in the medical discussion of abortion was the fear voiced by numerous doctors that they could be "victimized" by women seeking help. The medical journals carried numerous articles warning physicians to turn a deaf ear to the pleas of patients. Dr. Andrews estimated in the 1870s that in Windsor there were fifty criminal abortions a year. He called on his colleagues to steel themselves against the heart-rending tales of seduced young girls, but assumed that married women could be more easily dealt with: "As for cases of married women, who, in order to shirk the responsibilities of maternity, seek to make you accomplices in a felony, you can have no difficulty. I have hundreds of such applications. The crime of foeticide is fearfully prevalent, and rapidly increasing, and corrupting and debasing the country both morally and physically."[45] The same line was followed by an editorial in the 1889 *Canada Lancet*: "What physician, in practice for any length of time, has not had many applications, often accompanied by a considerable bribe, to relieve the victim of the seducer from the social disgrace attached to her sin, or the selfish and degraded married female from the care and trouble naturally devolving on her?"[46] To spurn such pleas was to put one at the possible mercy of a vengeful woman, the editor warned, to assist her was of course out of the question, but even to see her, if she had already attempted to induce her own miscarriage, could put the physician in a position in which he could be held responsible for the consequences. Under such pressures, claimed the writer, some doctors committed suicide. But who were they? The editor gave no examples and the lack of evidence suggests that such scenes of entrapment were only to occur in the fervid imaginations of medical journalists.

When it came to explaining the apparent rise in abortion, physicians attributed the blame to the greater education of women and their declining interest in maternity, the advertisement of aborti-facients, and the presence of quacks and popular practitioners.[47] The remedies suggested by the medical press included a call for the closer supervision of druggists, a more thorough registration of births and miscarriages, a restriction of medical advertising, and the reportage of all requests for abortion to "some competent exec-utor of the law."[48]

Doctors saw the usefulness of drugstores and newspapers being kept under surveillance but they did not accept the notion that their own profession, though it, too, contributed to the ranks of the abortionists, should be interfered with. Doctors sought to maintain the privilege of the secrecy of the consulting room, which was as sacred as that of the confessional. In fact they saw themselves as rivalling priests in upholding the moral values of society against the onslaught of abortion: "I had for many years noted and wondered at the fact [wrote Dr. Andrews] that of the married women who sought my co-operation, nearly all were Protestants . . . the Roman Catholic priesthood, have in their confessional an opportunity of instructing and warning their flock. Protestant women do not go there, but we, and we only, have the private ear of the whole sex, and it is, I conceive our duty, to lose no opportunity of diffusing the information we possess in this regard."[49] Similarly, a contributor to the *Canadian Practitioner and Review* would assert in 1908: "It is probable that the two classes who are fighting against the evils of race suicide in all civilized countries are practitioners of medicine and priests in the Roman Catholic Church."[50] Doctors thus turned the abortion issue to their own purposes in advancing their claim to be the counsellors and confessors of Protestant Canada.

Who were the women seeking abortion and what was their view of their right to do so? Mrs. Mary Wood-Allen in *What a Young Woman Ought to Know* (1898) cautioned that a woman who mar-ried but sought to limit family size inevitably would have to face the question of abortion. "If she proposes deliberately to avoid motherhood she puts herself in a position of moral peril, for such immunity is not often secured except at the risk of criminality."[51] The approach the woman would make to the doctor was described by Emma F. Angell Drake, herself a physician. To her came many a young wife who asked to be "helped out of her difficulty." "Again they say, 'There is no harm until there is life.' 'Doctor I have missed my monthly period and have come in to have you give me some-thing to set me right.'"[52] McFadden referred to such women as having "many ways of hiding the actual facts from themselves."[53]

Thus women did not say they sought an "abortion," but rather wanted to be "made regular" or to "bring on a period." Doctors accused such patients of using euphemisms and circumlocutions, but what is clear is that many women did not consider what they were doing to be wrong. This was brought out in all the testimony on the subject. They assumed that abortion was permissible before the third month or quickening and when not induced by another person. It was this absence of guilt that most enraged and confused male physicians. Hugh L. Hodge complained: "And when such individuals are informed of the [illegal] nature of the transaction, there is an expression of real or pretended surprise that any one should deem the act improper – much more guilty...."[54] Dr. E.L. Tompkins expressed the same concern in the *American Journal of Obstetrics* (1896): "There seems to be no incompatibility between high moral and religious views on other subjects and utter lack of the same in regard to abortion. I have been asked recently by a lady who is a typical Christian and a woman of the highest honor and integrity in all other matters, to produce an abortion for a young married friend whom she thought too poor to raise children."[55]

Women and doctors took different views of antenatal life. Women remained true to the traditional idea that until the mother felt the foetus "quicken" it was permissible to take what measures were necessary to make herself "regular." Dr. Ballock asserted that "I am not able to recall one who was ever particularly distressed over such an act, especially if it happened in the early months of pregnancy."[56] The thought that women rather than doctors should decide on whether life was present was what raised the ire of men such as Hodge. "What it may be asked, have the sensations of the mother to do with the vitality of the child? Is it not alive because the mother does not feel it?"[57] Many women would have answered it was not. What one finds in examining the nineteenth-century abortion issue is that doctors were seeking to instil in the public a new belief in the vitality of foetal life from the moment of conception. It is important to note how new this concept was. Abortion had not been made a statutory crime in British law until 1803 and even then the concept of quickening was retained, as it was in the revised statute of 1828, and only removed in 1837. In a similar fashion the Offenses Against the Person Act of 1861 made it a crime for the woman to abort herself whereas the acts of 1803, 1828, and 1837 had all been aimed at the abortionist.[58] In short, the notion that a woman less than three months pregnant who sought to "put herself right" was committing a crime was a recent development and had not yet been fully forced on the public conscience. In 1922 O.A. Cannon could still write in the *Canadian Medical Association Journal*: "The moral conscience of the public, including that of some physicians, needs educating, and it should be some one's business to make it known that from conception the unborn child is a human creature whose destruction is equivalent to murder."[59]

Doctors were never to be totally successful in convincing women of the immorality of abortion. For many it was to remain an essential method of fertility control. This group included single women seeking to avoid an illegitimate pregnancy and the hardships that such a birth would entail. We know more about these women than the married because their names appeared frequently in court cases.[60] There were, for example, Jessie Gould, a waitress at the Cadillac Hotel in Toronto who died of acute septic peritonitis in 1908, Mary Ellen Janes of Victoria who died of blood poisoning in 1895, Kate Hutchinson Gardener, a chambermaid of the Tecumseh Hotel in London who died of an overdose of chloroform in 1878.[61] Doctors could sympathize with the plight of the seduced young girl who was a victim of male lust. But by the beginning of the twentieth century there were reports that some women were seeking abortion, not because they could not marry, but because they wanted to retain their independence. "As one of this sort pithily put it," reported Dr. Edward A. Ballock, "she was not going to give up a hundred-dollar place for a fifty-dollar man."[62] For whatever reasons single women sought abortion, the odds are that the relative number of their attempts would be exaggerated simply because they would more likely be found out. Dr. J.F. Scott noted that married women who already had borne children recognized the signs of pregnancy earlier than the single and could thus take more effective action.[63] Moreover, a married woman who miscarried raised few suspicions; with a single woman there was the chance of the doctor, neighbours, or even the police investigating. In a time of trouble a single woman would have fewer resources at her disposal, she would have fewer people to whom she could turn, and the likelihood of dangerous complications was therefore all the greater.

The evidence suggests that most women seeking abortion were married but the numbers involved are difficult to determine. The number of arrests for abortion would be of some interest but such figures would bear no necessary relationship to the actual numbers of women seeking to terminate their own pregnancies. An abortion only came to the authorities' attention if something went seriously

wrong, and the figures of the police indicate, if they indicate anything at all, only the *unsuccessful* attempts. In a popular self-help
medical manual such as J.H. Kellogg's *The Home Hand-Book of
Domestic Hygiene and Rational Medicine* (1906) one was told that
though abortion was fifteen times more dangerous than birth, only
one woman in a thousand was ever punished. Where Kellogg drew
his figures is not known but some credence could be given to a
report in the *Canadian Practitioner and Review* of 1916 entitled
"Race Suicide":

> Mrs. McKerron died in the Toronto General Hospital December
> 19, 1915, after a short illness. An Inquest was held, and the jury
> brought in a verdict that death was due to blood poisoning
> caused by an illegal operation performed by Mrs. Cull. In his
> address to the jury the coroner, Dr. Millen Cotton, said: "The
> question of race suicide is growing to alarming proportions in
> this city." He also said there were between three and four hundred
> cases in the hospitals last year as a direct result of illegal opera-
> tions, and in addition to these there were many cases in private
> houses which were not discovered.[64]

Such claims were further substantiated when the activities of pro-
fessional abortionists were brought to light. The Toronto *Evening
Telegram* reported that the police investigations of the activities of
Dr. Andrews gave some idea of the extent of the practice:

> Inspector Stark took possession of all the correspondence in the
> house, which consisted of between 200 and 350 letters, involving
> beyond doubt a number of criminal operations, performed on
> both married and single females, all over the country. Some of
> these letters are couched in the plainest language by educated as
> well as ignorant women, written confidentially but confessing to
> the greatest acts of shame and seduction, and offering to pay
> large sums of money for advice and successful treatment. Some
> contained grateful acknowledgement of what the doctor had
> done for them, and begging him to keep their secrets from the
> world. Others asked for immediate advice, and suggest secret
> interviews, when the would-be patients would be the least likely
> observed.[65]

The danger of abortion is hard to establish. Doctors frequently
spoke as though it was inevitably followed by death but their own
figures did not bear this out. It is also evident that complications
arising from instrument-induced miscarriage declined as women

turned to their own purposes the antiseptic lessons of Pasteur.[66] Here would be yet another reason why the number of discovered abortions would have less and less relevance to the number of undiscovered. Yet even with these qualifications some idea of the social significance of abortion can be gained if the figures on maternal mortality are viewed as the "tip of the iceberg" of all attempts at induced miscarriage. Though the infant mortality rate declined in the first decades of the twentieth century, maternal mortality remained high.[67] Studies carried out in the 1930s revealed that in the previous twenty-five years the rate remained at 5.1 to 5.5 per 1,000. A contributing cause could have been the fact that as families became smaller a higher percentage of all births became the more dangerous first births. But even with the large percentage of primaparous births, the lower age of mothers and the improvements in medical care should have led to a decline in maternal mortality. Bungled abortions kept the rate high. In a study of 334 maternal deaths in one year in Ontario it was discovered that fifty-nine or 17 per cent were due to abortion, thirteen were deaths of unmarried women, and of the abortions one-third had been self-induced.[68] Again, these figures could only represent a small fraction of the number of successful abortions.

It is of course impossible to determine exactly the rate of abortion in Canada but all reports indicated that here as in the United States it was to play a major role in lowering the birth rate. In 1896 Scott cited a "Report of the Special Committee on Criminal Abortion" of the Michigan State Board of Health, which estimated, on the basis of one hundred doctors' reports, that 17 to 34 per cent of all pregnancies were aborted.[69] In 1922 Dr. O.A. Cannon wrote in the *Canadian Medical Association Journal* that of the 314 women he had attended during pregnancy, fifty-one had aborted. "Of fifty-one women attended by me during abortion, twenty-two admitted criminal interference. This percentage of forty-three would have been materially increased if all the patients had been equally frank."[70] Cannon placed the abortion rate at somewhere between 7 and 14 per cent of living births – a figure remarkably close to that established once the practice was legalized and reliable statistics made available.

Before concluding this brief overview of the early history of birth control and abortion in Canada it is necessary to reiterate that the concern for the "slaughter of the innocents" at the turn of the century was sparked not so much by the fall of English Canadians' birth rate *per se* but by its decline relative to that of the French

Canadians and the immigrant population. It was a cruel irony that many of the eugenically-minded doctors who opposed the family limitation of the "fit" were clamouring in the decade before the First World War for the forced sterilization of the "unfit." In such works as A.B. Atherton's "The Causes of the Degeneracy of the Human Race," R.W. Bruce Smith's "Mental Sanitation, with Suggestions for the Care of the Degenerate, and Means for Preventing the Propagating of the Species," and James B. Watson's *Who Are the Producers of Human Damaged Goods?* (1913), doctors calmly took it upon themselves to decide who should and who should not be allowed to breed.[71] Though they claimed to be protecting "quality" of race, their own criterion of "fitness," namely high socio-economic status, predisposed them to categorize those of a lower class or different culture as genetically inferior.[72] But this eugenic concern for fit stock was, despite the reactionary premises on which it was based, eventually to provide a rationalization for tolerance of family planning. As it was made ever more obvious that women could not be prevented from seeking to control their fertility, the argument began to be voiced that safe contraception might be the lesser of two evils. In the *Canadian Medical Monthly* of 1920 A.T. Bond would argue that more reliable mechanical means of birth control would have to be accepted if only to lower the abortion rate.[73] In the same year the government demonstrated its preoccupation with the unacceptably high levels of infant and maternal mortality by establishing the Council on Child and Family Welfare.[74] Abortion and the deaths it entailed had slowly forced upon the state and the medical profession the acknowledgement that if they were seriously concerned with the bearing of healthy children they would have to take some steps in easing the burden of motherhood.

At this preliminary stage of investigation of the history of abortion in Canada it must be admitted that a large number of questions remain to be answered. We would like to know more about the dangers of self-induced miscarriages, the techniques employed, and changes of practices over time. This paper will have served some purpose if it has shown that these problems deserve further inquiry. The importance of the evidence that we have garnered is that it reveals, despite the assumption of women's passivity in relation to their fertility, the extraordinary risks they would run to control it. That they had to continue to resort to old-fashioned and frequently dangerous remedies was a consequence of the medical profession's refusal to provide them with adequate information on contraception. An examination of what was frequently simply a second line of defence against unwanted pregnancies in addition indicates the strength of the desire of couples to limit family size. Finally, if this review of the recourse to quack potions, home remedies, and back-street abortions teaches us anything, it is that there was at the turn of the century – as there is today – a demand for abortion and if that demand is not met by the medical profession it will be met by others.

5

The Women Ontario Welcomed: Immigrant Domestics for Ontario Homes, 1870-1930

Marilyn Barber

"Female Domestics Wanted for Ontario, Canada: Situations Guaranteed at Good Wages." Such was the message of an Ontario advertising poster used in Britain in the 1920s, but the appeal was an old one, unchanged from the 1870s. Throughout the period from 1870 to 1930, domestic servants were actively recruited for Ontario by both the federal and provincial governments. Domestics were the only unaccompanied female immigrants so solicited and they were treated as preferred immigrants along with farm families and single male farm labourers. The number of women who responded to the appeal and came specifically to the province of Ontario cannot be accurately tabulated. However, between Confederation and the depression of the 1930s, over 250,000 women immigrated to Canada stating their intended occupation as domestic service. For those from the British Isles, Ontario was the favoured destination, although Montreal and the western provinces also attracted many. In addition, in the 1920s, Ontario began to receive an increasing number of women from continental Europe. Domestic service played a vital role in enabling single women to immigrate to Ontario and to begin life in a new country. And, conversely, immigrant domestics formed a significant proportion of the women working in Ontario homes and helped shape the character of domestic service in the province.

The servant girl problem, as it was called in the periodicals and newspapers of the day, was a dominant concern of many Ontario women because the province suffered from a chronic shortage of domestic servants. Servants were employed not simply by the rich, but also by the wives of professionals and small businessmen in towns and villages as well as cities. In addition, there was a strong unsatisfied demand for household help on the farms of the province. The majority of domestics in Ontario, therefore, were not engaged in homes with a large staff but rather worked in one-servant households as generals or cook-generals.

In part, servants were employed as a symbol of status. A "lady" did not do her own work, or at least not all of it. If she could not afford the luxury of complete leisure from household duties, employing a servant to assist her maintained her standing in the community. Attitudes were changing regarding the social accept-ability of doing one's own work, but slowly. In 1878, a columnist in *The Farmer's Advocate*, published in London, Ontario, com-mented:

> Does Her Own Work, Does she? What of it? Is it a disgrace to her? Is she less a true woman, less worthy of respect than she who sits in silk and satin and is vain of fingers who never knew labor? ... In matter of fact, is it more dishonorable for the merchant's wife to do her own work than for the merchant to do his? For her to look after her house than for him to look after his store?[1]

The very protest, however, showed that contrary ideas persisted. Indeed, almost thirty years later, the president of the Ontario Women's Institutes was still emphasizing the recent acceptance of doing one's own work. In her words:

> Of late years, since domestic help has been so hard to procure, and wages have advanced so rapidly, many housewives have been compelled to do all their own work, and, when one would enquire of a friend as to how she was getting along, she would perhaps acknowledge with reluctance that she was doing "all her own work," and in a tone that would indicate that she was owning up to poverty or something of the kind. But now a lady will announce with pride to her friends, without even being asked, "I am doing all my own work," and we never give the condition or circumstance a second thought.[2]

Many women had to give the circumstances a second thought, because they desperately needed help simply to accomplish their work. Without electricity or many labour-saving devices, household work was both strenuous and time-consuming. A servant could greatly ease the burden of laundry day with its tubs of boiling water to be heated early and tended by hand, of ironing day with the heavy flat irons, and of cleaning, baking, and cooking. Especially was a servant a necessity rather than a luxury in homes with a young family where the wife might well be expecting another child, or in farm homes where the wife helped with outside chores – the dairy, the poultry, and the garden – in addition to coping with her inside housework. Improved technology, which came earlier to middle-class city homes than to rural districts, eased some of the physical drudgery of housework but did not reduce the demand for domestic servants. The growth in affluence of the middle class with industrialization meant that more families could afford to hire domestic help. In addition, any decrease in physical labour through technological assistance was offset by higher standards of home and child care and by the increasing activity of women in affairs outside the home, often through the churches or organizations such as the WCTU, the Local Councils of Women, or the farm women's associations. Women were told that it was their responsibility to be concerned with issues such as prohibition, child welfare, or farm co-operation, and that they must organize their work to allow themselves time for these activities. Therefore, the demand for domestic servants, whether as status symbols or as essential assistance, constantly exceeded the supply in Ontario, as in the rest of the country, throughout the period from 1870 to 1930.

The servant girl problem existed because women in Canada entering the labour force shunned domestic service if possible. Thus, while the proportion of women in the paid labour force relative to the female population increased in the twentieth century, the percentage of the female labour force in domestic service decreased. In 1891, approximately 40 per cent of working women in Canada were domestic servants, but the number declined to less than 20 per cent after World War I and had only increased slightly at the time of the 1931 census. In Ontario, the proportion of the female labour force in domestic service was similar to but slightly lower than the national average, probably because of the greater opportunities for women in Ontario in other occupations.[3] Unfortunately, the division between live-in and live-out or daily domestics is not revealed in the census statistics. In the United States, domestic service in the early twentieth century was in the process of changing from predominantly live-in to predominantly live-out work. By the 1920s, live-in service was dying out and the modern system of day work had become entrenched.[4] The same trend was taking place in Canada, but at a slower pace, because Canada did not have the black married domestics who were the first and most substantial basis of live-out domestic service in the United States. In Canada, to the end of the 1920s, live-in domestic service was still very important, but it was definitely not popular with Canadian women seeking work.

Objections to domestic service centred on the lack of freedom, the isolation or loneliness, and the low status of the occupation. Canadian women preferred clerical, shop, or factory work, even at lower net wages than domestic work, because of the greater freedom and independence. They had every evening off instead of one or two a week, and, as their home environment was separate from their work environment, they were not always under the direct supervision and authority of their employers. Young women working outside the home also had more opportunity to make social contact with others of their own age, whereas those in domestic service complained of being ostracized as "only a servant" by other young people on the rare opportunities when they were free for social activities. Employers were aware of the problem and throughout the period discussed means of elevating the status of housework, but with little success. In 1900 *The Farmer's Advocate* accurately described "The Problem of Domestic Service":

> From one side comes the cry of the worried and harassed housekeeper: "Where, and oh! where are our household helpers gone?" And from the other side comes the reply: "To the factories and to the stores, where, if our positions are not always of certain tenure, and our salaries leave something to be desired by way of margin after our board bills are paid, yet, oh! glorious privilege, we are, after business hours, our own mistresses, and we can go to the theatres and band concerts, to big balls and little 'hops', with Jack to-day and Tom to-morrow, and who shall say us 'nay'.[5]

The Advocate believed that the problem soon would be solved because:

> The trend of present-day teaching being to elevate domestic service and to remove from it the old mistaken idea that it is a step lower in the social scale than employment on other lines – a mistake which is at the bottom of nearly all the trouble – we can afford to leave the future to take care of itself.[6]

The introduction of domestic science in Ontario elementary schools at the turn of the century, the development of Macdonald Institute at Guelph for the professional teaching of domestic science, and the recommendations of the Royal Commission on Industrial Training and Technical Education in 1913 that women be trained for housework all were intended to elevate the status of household work in the province. Ontario women remained unconvinced by the argument that household work was the best preparation for their ultimate careers as wives and mothers. The attempted change in terminology in the 1920s from "domestic servants" or "maids" to "houseworkers" or "household workers" also failed to change the common view of the occupation. In 1928, an article in *Chatelaine* titled "What's the Matter with Housework?" continued to point to the lower social status of housework. At the end of the 1920s, as at the turn of the century, the reply to the question of why young people did not respect housework as much as other occupations remained "Simply because of the old feudal conditions generally attached to it – because the worker's life and time is not her own. To them she is not an adult of free will, to live as they do and share their recreations and social life. She is to them a chattel, a shut-in."[7]

Because Canadian women did not enter domestic service in sufficient numbers, employers and governments turned to immigration to find the solution to the servant girl problem. All those influential in the formation of immigration policy agreed that the immigration of domestic servants should be actively encouraged. As one Member of Parliament commented, nothing he could do pleased his constituents as much as obtaining maids for their wives.[8] Cabinet ministers, leading members of the civil service including those in the Immigration Branch, important businessmen, and socially prominent women had a personal as well as a community interest in the importation of domestic servants. From a party of Scottish domestic servants specially selected for western Canada in 1898, one was left in Montreal for Sydney Fisher, Minister of Agriculture, and two were left in Ottawa for Clifford Sifton, Minister of the Interior, and James Smart, Deputy Minister of the Interior. Similarly, the resources of the Immigration Branch were used to secure Scottish servants for Mackenzie King's mother in Toronto, Mr. Harvey, manager of the Bank of British North America in Ottawa, Dr. King, director and chief astronomer of the Dominion Observatory, Mr. White, inspector of U.S. Agencies for the Immigration Branch, and many others.[9] Against this interest in procuring domestic servants, there was no opposition. The demand was so great there was little danger that the market might be flooded. In addition, Canadian domestic servants were unorganized, had no union to represent their interests or to protest that large-scale immigration might lower the wages of native workers. Hence, female domestic servants joined farmers and farm labourers as the only class of immigrant the government openly and actively recruited throughout the period.

Since immigration is a joint responsibility of the Dominion and the provinces under Section 95 of the BNA Act, the Ontario government as well as the federal government worked to promote the immigration of domestic servants. From 1874 to 1899, Ontario maintained a separate Department of Immigration whose work was then taken over in the twentieth century by the Bureau of Colonization and the Department of Agriculture. In its recruitment efforts throughout the period, the Ontario government concentrated on the British Isles, as British domestic servants were preferred. Ontario agents were stationed in Britain to advertise the advantages of the province and at the port of Quebec to oversee the forwarding of immigrants for Ontario and to protect Ontario parties against the raids of Quebec agents.[10] While the Dominion government for much of the nineteenth century offered special low fares to domestic servants to attract them to Canada, Ontario gave its own additional bonus to domestics to entice them to make Ontario their Canadian destination.[11] Immigrant domestics coming to Ontario were placed in employment by government immigration agents at Ottawa, Kingston, Toronto, Hamilton, and London. The supply was never equal to the demand, and, year after year, agents reported that applications could not be filled. In particular, it was difficult to persuade servants to accept situations in rural districts or to travel west of Toronto. For example, the unequal regional distribution is shown by statistics for 1882 when the Ontario agent at Quebec sent 1,087 domestics to Toronto, 404 to places east of Toronto, but only seventy-five to the region west of Toronto, including Hamilton, London, and Stratford.[12]

The competition for immigrant domestics was strong. Most prospective employers visited the district immigration offices – the Toronto agent reported in 1887 that as many as thirty a day called at the office and had to go away disappointed[13] – or wrote letters of varying degrees of literacy to the Toronto headquarters. They specified their requirements or preferences and the inducements they offered. A woman near Chatsworth wrote: "I want a girl Scotch or Irish Protestant if you have one must be able to milk and wash and shall have a good home and as high wages as are going in this part of the country."[14] A farmer near Armow was even more detailed in his instructions: "I am a farmer and want a girl to help do house work and cook. I want a good strong healthy good looking English speaking girl to such a girl I would give good wages steady employment and a good home."[15] However, the Rev. W.J. Smyth at Uxbridge was prepared to be flexible, within certain limits, if necessary: "I would be glad if you could [send] me a servant girl from among the Immigrants. One about 16 or 17 would suit us – but it would not matter about the age if we got a good trusty girl. If such could not be got a trusty and respectable old lady would do us."[16]

Some, however, were not content with the official channels of application. In order to prevent girls being spirited off the immigrant train before they reached their destination, the department arranged with the Grand Trunk Railway in 1884 that the baggage of assisted immigrants was not to be given up except at the station to which it was checked.[17] The Ontario agent at Quebec carried the supervision of assisted domestics even further on at least one occasion. In his words:

> I have some difficulty occasionally keeping girls from sailors and cattle men as an instance by last mail steamer, were three pretty girls with their mother – after giving them passes (3) for Toronto I had occasion to go over to the hotel at noon and to my astonishment, I saw these same girls drinking beer with two sailors. I waited for nearly an hour and counted 8 glasses of beer. Barkeeper stated they had in all 12 glasses each. I lost patience and had the two sailors locked up and took the passes from the three girls who bought their own tickets to Montreal.[18]

Concern for women travelling unaccompanied, together with the problems of women in both Britain and Canada, led women's organizations on both sides of the Atlantic to join the government in promoting female immigration. The most important of these organizations was not Canadian but British: the British Women's Emigration Association, formed in 1884. The founders of the BWEA wished to solve the problems of surplus or unemployed British women in the context of imperial development. The imbalance of the sexes in both Britain and the colonies – too many women in Britain, not enough women in the colonies – might be solved by encouraging more women to emigrate. In addition, the association emphasized careful selection of the women to be sponsored, for "the requirements of the Empire must come before the needs of the individual," and "only the best were good enough to carry on overseas the finest of British traditions."[19] With these principles, Canadian women would heartily agree. British and Canadian interests, however, were not so easily reconciled when it came to deciding more specifically which women should be encouraged to move across the Atlantic. Good experienced domestic servants were scarce in the British Isles, too, as was noted by Ontario immigration agents as early as 1868.[20] The class of female immigrant Canadian women's organizations most wanted to attract, therefore, was the class that British women definitely did not want to see depart. The BWEA was quite willing to encourage British women to take work in Canadian homes, provided the prospective emigrants were not already in domestic service in Britain. Hence, when the BWEA established a loan fund to assist women with passage fares, loans were not granted to British domestic servants but only to factory workers who would agree to enter domestic service in Canada. Similarly, the association made loans available to educated gentle-women who wished to immigrate to Canada as home-helps. In addition, the BWEA advised British women that Canada offered a wide range of employment possibilities for women. The association co-operated with factory owners in Canada who wanted to obtain female workers for their mills and also sponsored educated women seeking opportunities in Canada in teaching, nursing, or secretarial work. However, the majority of women who emigrated with the association's parties were destined to domestic service, and many had already been in service in Britain.[21]

The British Women's Emigration Association insisted on careful protection for the women whom it sponsored, sending them over-seas in escorted parties. The association provided hostels for the initial assembly of its parties at London and Liverpool and em-ployed matrons to supervise the journey. In addition, parties were sent only to Canadian centres where satisfactory reception and placement arrangements had been made by local correspondents. The BWEA first sent the majority of their immigrants to Montreal, where a hostel had been begun in 1881, and later included Win-nipeg, when Octavia Fowler founded the Girls' Home of Welcome there in 1896. Toronto ladies were anxious to receive domestics from the association, and the BWEA equally wished to send women to Toronto. Consequently, Agnes FitzGibbon, a committed im-perialist and president of the Toronto Local Council of Women, became, in her words, the "instrument through the use of which the work has been done."[22] While in England in 1902 for the corona-tion, FitzGibbon became actively interested in women's immigra-tion, writing on the topic. At the request of Lady Aberdeen, she addressed an Edinburgh meeting of the National Union of Women Workers of Great Britain and Ireland, and she was urged to become a correspondent of the BWEA. Upon her return to Toronto, Fitz-Gibbon organized a small committee of the Local Council of Women to meet and place BWEA parties, but, in effect, did nearly all the work herself. Because of the difficulty of procuring suitable temporary quarters for housing the women, FitzGibbon again took the lead in insisting that the work could not continue unless a receiving home be established. Largely as a result of her initiative and pressure, the Women's Welcome Hostel was opened in 1905 at 66 Wellesley Street, where it remained until larger quarters were secured in 1911 at 52 St. Alban's Street.[23] Agnes FitzGibbon's contacts with influential Torontonians assisted her greatly in her work. She was well known in Toronto circles, not only as the president of the Local Council of Women and founder of the Women's Canadian Historical Society of Toronto, but also as a popular writer descended from the Strickland family. She was the granddaughter of Susanna Moodie, an English immigrant of the 1830s, who in her best known book, *Roughing It in the Bush*, made some rather acerbic remarks about the character of domestic servants in Upper Canada. Her grandmother undoubtedly would have been interested in the work Agnes FitzGibbon directed as secretary-manager of the Women's Welcome Hostel until her death in 1915.[24]

Begun with a provincial government grant and private subscription, the Toronto Hostel offered twenty-four hours' free board and lodging to immigrant domestics so that they might have a chance to rest – one day – before being sent to work. Because the hostel was supported by a provincial grant, a deliberate effort was made to distribute the maids around the province. After 1907 the hostel also received a federal grant in recognition of the national importance of its work with immigrant women. The hostel kept complete records of the women it received, collected loans, and corresponded with both prospective immigrants and employers.[25] In the hostel report for 1906, FitzGibbon noted that:

> A book with a full entry of the history of the immigrant is kept, giving name, nationality, age, calling, religion, date of arrival, destination, name and address of employer, wages received, whether the immigrant has received a loan and the amount returned by her from time to time. Many of these girls are only enabled to emigrate because of loans made them by organizations in Great Britain and these loans are repaid by the girls through our agency.[26]

Such records, unfortunately, do not seem to have survived. The largest parties at the hostel came from the British Women's Emigration Association, but women sent by other agencies, including booking agents in the British Isles, were also received. In addition to being a control agency, the hostel was intended as a social centre where domestics could come during their afternoons off or between placements. For many immigrant domestics the hostel thus served as a home away from home and it received high praise from the chairman of the British Emigrants' Information Office when he visited Canada in 1909. In his view: "The hostel is most comfortable and evidently well managed and appears to be conducted on the most highly commendable lines. Miss FitzGibbon herself is a lady of great force of intellect and of high character."[27]

While the British Women's Emigration Association and its Canadian associates, the Local Councils of Women and the YWCA, emphasized care in the selection and placement of domestics, all agencies were not so scrupulous. Because many prospective immigrant domestics could not afford the expense of the journey to Canada, a number of practices developed to overcome the difficulty. Sometimes the Canadian employer advanced the fare to an agent and then deducted a set amount monthly from the servant's wages until the advance had been repaid. More frequently, the fare was advanced by one of the numerous societies or agencies that sprang up to deal with the trade in female domestic servants. The system was unorganized, chaotic, and open to abuse by both the immigrants and the agencies. Servants left their employers before repaying their passage advance, and employers found themselves not only out of pocket but also with no servant. Few employers were able to follow the example of Peter Bryce, chief medical inspector of the Department of the Interior, who tracked down his servant when she left after five days, and, as she seemed "utterly callous as to her responsibility to the extent of £5.7.9," brought her before a police magistrate to ensure that the money would be repaid.[28] On the other hand, some agencies were in the business solely for the object of gain as it was possible in the immediate pre-war period to earn a bonus of $5 from the federal government, a similar bonus from the Ontario government, a $2 commission from the federal government for placing the domestic, a sum from the immigrant herself for the advance of passage money, and a fee from the employer for providing her with a servant. Agencies primarily interested in financial rewards wanted to bring as many domestics as possible and gave little attention to either careful selection overseas or proper placement in Canada.[29] The situation before the First

World War thus often exacerbated the difficulty of reconciling the personality and interests of the newly arrived domestics and the Canadian employers.

The First World War cut off overseas immigration to Canada and gave the government a chance to assess old policies and work out new ones. In 1914 and 1915, as a result of the recession and unemployment, the demand for domestic servants was at a low ebb in Canada. In Ontario, it was reported that while there was still a need for domestics in the rural areas, there were women idle in the cities who were willing to take domestic work.[30] Therefore, for the first time, the immigration of domestic servants was not encouraged. The government withdrew the bonus for domestic servants from Canadian agencies and paid it to British booking agents only on experienced domestics who could show by references that they had been at least one year in service.[31] As the war brought full employment, the demand soon fully revived. Canadian women, like British women, left domestic service to take up war work, and new recruits were not available. However, immigration could not be revived because the British government in 1917 forbade, for the duration of the war, the departure of women capable of war work.[32] The war, accompanied by a reform sentiment that a new and better society must emerge in Canada to justify the war, thus gave both the opportunity and the impetus for change in women's immigration.

At the end of the war, the Canadian government expected and prepared for a sudden mass influx of pent-up British immigrants. The most immediate concern was to protect the country against undesirable immigrants. The Women's Advisory Committee of the Repatriation Committee, formed to look after the interests of returning soldiers and their dependants, feared that women of questionable character would come to Canada following the soldiers.[33] Even leaving aside the question of female army followers, reformers and social workers believed that much more care needed to be taken in the selection of domestic servants in order to safeguard Canadian society from mental and moral misfits, especially of the factory worker class. Helen Reid, a member of the Repatriation Committee and the Dominion Council of Health, wrote:

> stricter measures must be taken to encourage the admission of
> the best class of household worker and to prevent the entry of
> unqualified women from British mill and factory, who, in addition to their lack of training for domestic service, bring with

them only too often, serious mental and moral disabilities. These women either glut the labor market here, reducing the wages of working men, or end up, alas! too frequently, in our jails, hospitals and asylums.[34]

The anticipated influx did not occur in spite of the free ocean passages offered by the British government to ex-service men and women. Attention in Canada soon was forced to focus, not on careful selection from large numbers available, but on the increasingly more difficult task of combining careful selection with the need to attract scarce domestic servants. The shortage of domestic servants in Britain in the 1920s was even more acute than in the pre-war years. As reported to the Canadian government: "400,000 women left domestic service during the war. Girls of 14, who in ordinary times would have started in as scullery maids, started clerical and other work at 30s a week, and having tasted blood, as it were, refused to enter housework."[35] At the same time, Canada had to continue to compete for British domestic servants with other Dominions, especially Australia, which offered free passages.

To promote more effective recruiting, as well as to ensure both careful selection and protection of immigrant domestic servants, a new and much more extensive government organization dealing with women's immigration developed. The Women's Division of the Immigration Department resulted from the belief that the immigration of women was best supervised by women.[36] In the 1920s, it expanded to include not only a permanent supervisor in Ottawa, but also a staff of women officers in both the United Kingdom and Canada. The Women's Branch undertook the control and supervision of British domestics from the point of initial investigation in the British Isles to the provision of follow-up services after placement in Canada. A British woman who wished to come to Canada to engage in domestic service first was interviewed by a Canadian woman officer and, in addition, had to pass a medical examination. The medical examination was a source of controversy because not only was the giving of a medical exam overseas a new procedure but also it was initially required only for unaccompanied women. By the end of the 1920s, the examination overseas was made compulsory for all immigrants, replacing the examination at Canadian ports and eliminating the expense and heartache of rejection after a long ocean journey. In the early 1920s, however, the implementation in Britain of a medical examination only for unaccompanied women seemed to discriminate against those women as much as it favoured them. The implication seemed clear that not only were women with medical problems, or those assisting them, to be spared the expense of the ocean journey, but also that the medical examination could be used to ensure more careful selection of unaccompanied women than of other groups. The latter concern is evident in a memorandum from the Supervisor of the Women's Division in 1920, who wished to have included the question, "Has the applicant ever suffered from a loathsome disease," noting that "undoubtedly this latter question, although the most important to us, will raise considerable question in England."[37] The applicant who successfully passed the medical exam and the interview was issued a sailing permit and came to Canada in a conducted party, supervised on board ship by a woman conductress appointed by the shipping company and on the train journey by a travelling conductress of the Immigration Department. Her destination most often was one of a chain of Canadian women's hostels established across the country to receive immigrant domestics. The Women's Welcome Hostel at Toronto, taken over by the government in the 1920s, provided the Ontario link in the chain, and women taken there were placed in situations by the women's branch of the government employment service, another development of the 1920s. Toronto was fortunate in having a very competent woman, Jessie Duff, at the head of its women's employment service, and thus avoided some of the problems that arose elsewhere in the country.

The establishment of such a government network for the selection and placement of British domestics reflected both the more restrictive immigration practices of the 1920s and the increasing involvement of government in social services in co-operation with voluntary agencies. In part, the protection seems to have been an outgrowth of the social purity movement, of the concern that women as the centre of the family must be kept pure to safeguard the values of the nation, and of the fear that lower-class women were both exposed to danger and prone to stray. However, the authorities also definitely viewed the system as encouraging rather than discouraging unaccompanied female immigrants. A better class might be induced to immigrate if they and their relatives knew that they would be well cared for on the journey and placed in satisfactory situations in Canada. The old adage that a satisfied immigrant made the best immigration agent was always kept firmly in mind.

The emphasis on quality always had to be balanced against the need for domestic servants. A joke from Toronto that circulated in the Immigration Department in the mid-1920s illustrated the problem:

> A Magistrate remarked to a man brought up before him for speeding.
> "The Officer tells me that you were going forty miles an hour."
> "Yes Sir, your honor" the culprit admitted, "I was. I had just received word from the Employment Office that they had found a COOK who would agree to come to our house in the suburbs and stay at least a week."
> Fortunately the magistrate, too, lived in the suburbs.
> "Officer," he ordered, "Get my car for this man at once. It does at least sixty miles an hour easily."[38]

Competition among the Canadian provinces for domestics was almost as great as competition between Canada and other countries. To attract experienced domestics to Ontario, the Ontario government in 1920 renewed its pre-war offer of passage assistance to be repaid out of wages. The most significant measure of assistance to British immigrant domestics in the 1920s was the Empire Settlement Act, a British act passed to promote migration within the Empire. Under the Empire Settlement Act, the Ontario government as well as the federal government entered into agreements with the United Kingdom government to assist on a fifty-fifty basis the immigration of British domestics to Canada first by passage loans and later by drastically reduced ocean fares.[39] By entering into a separate agreement, the Ontario government was able to continue its own work of recruiting domestics specifically for the province, as well as share in the proceeds of the Dominion government's activities. The province, indeed, received more than its fair share of British domestics, with Toronto becoming the favourite destination for British immigrant domestics in the 1920s, much to the distress of non-Torontonians.

The dominance of Toronto became a problem for the Ontario government as well as for other provinces. Many immigrant domestics chose to go to Toronto because relatives or friends had preceded them to the city, because Toronto seemed to offer more opportunities, or simply because the name became known to them through government advertising overseas. The presence in Toronto of the main Ontario distribution centre for domestics, the Women's Welcome Hostel, also served to channel British domestics into that city, and, once there, they refused to leave. Working near the hostel could, in itself, be an attraction. As one Irish immigrant recollected,

"It was home. The Hostel was home and you always met your friends there. It was great."[40] In an attempt to achieve a more equal distribution of immigrant domestics around the province, the Ontario government reduced the prominence of Toronto in Ontario publicity overseas. In addition, instructions were given to the Ontario agent in London, England, to send women directly to Ottawa, London, Hamilton, and Kingston to be accommodated at the YWCA on arrival and placed through the government employment bureaus in those cities.[41] Such efforts did direct some immigrant domestics away from Toronto, but, at a time of scarcity of domestic servants, did not significantly alter Toronto's position as the main receiving centre.

Even the low passage fare and guaranteed employment offered by the Empire Settlement Act did not procure enough British houseworkers to fill the demand, and Ontario was forced to turn to other expedients. In 1928, Ontario, along with Manitoba, Saskatchewan, and Alberta, agreed to co-operate with the Canadian government in providing financial assistance to inexperienced girls who trained for Canadian domestic service in British hostels. Previously only those with satisfactory domestic experience in service or in their own homes had been eligible for assistance under the Empire Settlement Act. The training hostel experiment was designed to extend this assistance to factory and shop women who showed a willingness and ability to enter domestic service by taking an eight-week course of training in Canadian household methods, including cooking, laundry, ironing, and cleaning. British authorities ran the training hostels that were established at Lenzie (near Glasgow), Newcastle, Cardiff, and London, but the Canadian government paid half the cost of the Canadian equipment installed in the hostels and provided a woman officer to screen applicants and give final approval to each trainee before emigration. The Canadian government also paid $20 toward the passage of each trainee and each participating province contributed $5 of the $20 for each trainee it received.[42]

The training experiment was cut off in 1930 because of the depression but it was not considered a success during its short period of operation. The scheme did not greatly increase the number of immigrant domestics coming to Canada. Ontario both requested and received more trainees than the other participating provinces but the total number of trainees who came to Canada was only 507. More importantly, Canadian authorities reported an abnormally high number of problem cases among the trainees.[43]

The high failure rate was attributed to the background of the women and to the inadequacy of the short training course. The British government, which took the initiative in urging the hostel training program, was most concerned to aid those in depressed areas by enabling them to emigrate. Canada chose to co-operate with the local training program of the British Ministry of Labour because the cost to the Canadian government was minimal. Hence, three of the hostels – Lenzie, Newcastle, and Cardiff – were established near districts experiencing a mining slump and preference was given to girls from the depressed areas. Although the Canadian woman officer sought to approve only "girls over seventeen with good tonsils, sound teeth, and of refined appearance," she stressed their ignorance of "decent home life."[44] In her words:

> The girls were recruited from Pit-Head workers, Mill hands, Factory workers, Shop assistants, a very few Out-door workers and still fewer girls from their own homes. With few exceptions these girls came from one and two-roomed homes where there would be a family of possibly 6, 8, or 10 people. They, therefore, had little or no opportunity of learning routine house work and cooking, in fact many of them did not know how to keep themselves clean.[45]

For such inexperienced girls, an eight-week course hardly provided an introduction to even the rudiments of housework in Canadian homes. Yet the first trainees were placed in Ontario as trained domestic servants with resulting frustration for both employer and employee. As a result of complaints, the Ontario employment service later tried to take great care in placing the trainees as inexperienced workers in specially selected homes, mainly in Hamilton, Toronto, and Ottawa. Nevertheless, as the supervisor of the Women's Divison reported, the Canadian centres that took the trainees came to regard them "as about the most troublesome and inexperienced type of women workers that we get from the Mother Country."[46] The training hostel experiment seemed to create more problems than it solved, and Canadian officials were not sorry when changed economic conditions brought it to an end.

Another solution to the inadequate supply of domestic servants in the later 1920s was the recruitment of women from continental Europe. As the Agent General for Ontario in London reported in 1923:

I am still of the opinion that sooner or later should we wish to increase the supply of domestic workers in Canada, especially the Eastern portion, that we will have to go further abroad than English-speaking people. All our large industries have required to bring in certain nationalities to do certain classes of work, and it seems to me that sooner or later our household demands cannot be filled excepting they are willing to take on certain other domestic workers than English-speaking.[47]

In 1925 his advice was followed as continental Europe was opened up to Canadian immigration activity by the Railways Agreement negotiated by the Department of Immigration and the Colonization Branches of the CPR and the CNR. The Railways Agreement authorized the railways to recruit, transport, and place in Canada farmers, farm workers, and domestic servants from what were called the "non-preferred" countries of central and eastern Europe, such as Poland, Russia, Hungary, and Roumania. Domestics could be brought to Ontario only if they were directly nominated by name by someone in the province who guaranteed to ensure employment for them. For the Prairie Provinces the railways could also bring forward what were called "bulk orders" of domestics to be placed in rural homes, and once in Canada a number of these women found their way back to friends or relatives in Ontario.[48] A letter from a woman in Banff to the Calgary placement office of the CPR in 1928 is illustrative:

Here I am in trouble again. This Mary Virgolova whom you sent me July 19 has been quite bright and satisfactory with her work and apparently happy. At first she was specially dumb – but she responded nicely to teaching. She has been corresponding a little and claims to have a brother in Toronto. Yesterday she received a registered letter from him – containing $50 and she says he wants her to go there. . . . Had I ever thought that she would leave so soon, of course we wouldn't have undertaken the nerve-wrecking job of training her. . . . I wish we could take steps to have Toronto taken off the map.[49]

With the Railways Agreement and with restrictive American laws that turned European immigrants to Canada, the proportion of Ontario domestic servants born in continental Europe increased in the 1920s.[50]

From 1870 to 1930, the women Ontario wished to welcome were experienced domestics from the British Isles. However, because of the scarcity of domestic servants in Britain, inexperienced women from Britain or women from continental Europe who agreed to enter domestic service in Canada were also welcomed, although not always by their first employer. Those engaging immigrant women included both employers who believed that experienced domestics from the British Isles were superior to others and employers who believed that immigrant meant cheap labour. In general, though, with the scarcity of domestic servants, those who hired immigrant domestics were those who could obtain them. Immigrant domestics were concentrated in urban areas in Ontario, but that was a result of immigrant preference, not employer choice. The 1911 census, the one published census that tabulates domestic servants by city and birthplace, shows half of the immigrant domestics in Ontario were in cities with a population of 15,000 or more. The distribution is more striking when it is noted that in those Ontario cities, domestic servants were divided evenly between Canadian-born and immigrant, whereas outside the larger cities 70 per cent of domestic servants were Canadian-born and only 30 per cent immigrants. Even the urban concentration of immigrant domestic servants was largely accounted for by the cities of Toronto and Hamilton. In Ottawa, the second largest city in Ontario in 1911, only 30 per cent of domestic servants were classified as immigrant.[51]

The interests and aims of governments, agencies, and employers are much clearer in the literature than are those of the immigrants themselves. Who were these women and why did they choose to come to Canada? What were their hopes and fears, successes and failures? How did they view domestic service in Canada? For both British and continental European women, beyond providing an entry to the country, the main attraction of domestic service was economic. It offered them the certainty of immediate employment and, with board and room provided, the opportunity to save more money than was possible in factory or shop work. Many of the women were acutely aware of the need to earn money beyond their immediate expenses because they usually had to pay back their passage fare, and often were also sending money home or were saving to bring relatives to Canada. Hence, they looked for the position that paid the highest wage, one of the reasons for the reluctance to go to the lower-paying rural areas. Disputes between mistress and maid frequently centred on the question of wages, the employer insisting that the girl should accept a low wage because of her inexperience in Canadian ways or complaining that as soon as she acquired some training the girl left for a better-paying position. Many immigrant women regarded domestic service as a temporary occupation, as the bridge that enabled them to cross to the opportunities of the new world, of America, where freedom, money, marriage, or other careers awaited them. They came with a spirit of adventure, seeking to build new lives for themselves, and in the process contributed to their new country. Nearly all suffered initial problems of adjustment. Most were placed alone as cook-generals in middle-class households where, in urban areas, uniforms, servants' quarters, and a formality of manner distanced servant from employer. For those who had expected greater equality, more free time, or higher wages, the reality was a shock. The loneliness of being in a strange household was accentuated by the strain of learning new ways, and, for European domestics, a new language. Many minor irritants could lead to major dissatisfaction and help to explain the frequent movement of domestics from one position to another. Cooking, in particular, required adjusting to new equipment and new foods, especially for women from poorer homes. Complaints that supposedly experienced domestics from Ireland could not cook resulted in the report in 1924 that their experience had been with cooking over a turf fire made on the floor of the house and that therefore they would be entirely lost if asked to do cooking on a gas range or an electric stove.[52] Health problems could be even more serious than work problems. While some employers were very kind, others refused to allow a domestic to remain in their house if she became ill. There were frequent reports from the Toronto hostel of domestics returning to the hostel because they had bad colds, asthma, eczema, mumps, tonsillitis, ulcers, and even a brain tumour.[53] Such illness not only caused physical problems, but also a heavy drain on the slender finances of a recently arrived domestic. For most immigrant women, pride and determination led to overcoming the obstacles. Others, because of circumstance or character, were not so fortunate, and there are hostel or deportation records of domestics who were considered major problems for reasons of illegitimacy, immorality, bad conduct, or mental deficiency.[54] For the most part, the lives of the immigrant domestics remain obscure, and it is impossible to determine how many married, went into other employment, or returned to their country of origin.

As the decade of the 1920s ended, an era in the immigration of domestic servants for Ontario homes also drew to a close. From 1870 to 1930, Ontario employers relied on governments, women's associations, and private agents to recruit immigrant domestics for their homes. Throughout the period, the British Isles remained the preferred and dominant source of supply. However, by December, 1929, the Toronto bureau of the Ontario employment service was reporting that there were "a great many industrial and clerical workers who are unfortunate in finding employment trying for domestic positions. The local supply of inexperienced help more than equals the demand."[55] With the unemployment crisis of the 1930s, attention shifted from recruiting immigrants to training Canadians for household work. By the time immigration resumed after World War II, immigrant domestic servants from the British Isles no longer figured prominently among the women Ontario welcomed.

6

Changing Relationships: Nuns and Feminists in Montreal, 1890-1925

Marta Danylewycz

Two distinct ways of seeing feminism in late nineteenth-century Quebec have emerged in recent years. The first examines the politics and organizational activities of Montreal's leading feminists and grounds them in the objective historical circumstances that created conditions favourable to their development. Unravelling the contradictions in the feminists' positions and highlighting the extensive opposition in clerical and political circles to the most innocuous of women's demands help to explain the weakness and the relative short life of the first surge of feminist activity in Montreal.[1] A radically different approach begins with religious women, whose presence pervaded nineteenth-century Quebec society, and places them at the centre of the inquiry. According to its proponents, the impulse that in Protestant and secular cultures underlay the organization of women's work took the form of religious vocations in Quebec. There the Catholic Church played a dominant and inspirational role in education and social service. Francophone women who joined active (as opposed to contemplative) religious orders to work for the benefit of society behaved like lay women elsewhere who organized charitable work. The child-centred, family reinforcement objectives of many English-Canadian and American social feminists were items of abiding concern among sisters in Quebec. Nuns taught men and women their familial and social responsibilities. When that failed, they provided victims of poverty, ignorance, disease, and delinquency with shelter and surrogate families. For some, convents offered a socially sanctioned alternative to marriage and motherhood as well as an escape from the loneliness and poverty that often accompanied spinsterhood. For a few women religious life also opened the door to a variety of occupational opportunities that women in other cultures strove to attain through the women's movement.[2]

122

The second interpretation adds religious women to the usual cast of characters in the history of feminism. What were their roles and how did their presence affect the balance between feminist and anti-feminist forces? Part of the answer lies in the long-standing nun-lay woman relationship that feminism modified, first to expand lay women's role as social activists, and later to win for them greater educational opportunity. By re-examining the circumstances that gave rise to the mobilization of women at the end of the nineteenth century, the creation in 1907 of the Fédération Nationale St-Jean-Baptiste, the opening of the École d'enseignement supérieur pour les filles a year later, the mushrooming of women's study circles, and finally in 1923 the founding of the Institut de Notre-Dame-du-Bon-Conseil, this paper traces the unfolding of the nun-lay woman relationship and highlights the ways it served feminism. At the same time, it shows how the relationship and the limits of co-operation between feminists and nuns were defined not only by the two parties involved but also by forces fighting against changes in the occupational and political status of women. Threatened by women's demands for equality and by their actual intellectual achievements, the Church hierarchy and its political allies tried to discourage nuns from sympathizing with feminists by suggesting that the interests of religion were at odds with women's emancipation. But before examining these themes, it is necessary to scan the activities of nuns and lay women on the eve of the feminist movement.

One-sixth of the 6,500 nuns working in the province of Quebec at the turn of the twentieth century ministered to the social needs of Montreal's growing female population.[3] For instance, the Sisters of Miséricorde and the Sisters of the Good Shepherd gave refuge to unwed mothers. The Sisters of Providence and the Grey Nuns ran day-care centres for working mothers, boarding homes for the aged, taught primary schools, and educated the blind and the deaf. As rural migration to Montreal intensified and industrial production and commerce in the city diversified, religious communities took on new responsibilities. In 1895, Sister Pelletier, a Grey Nun, opened Le Patronage d'Youville, where rural emigrants were given shelter as well as some training in domestic science. Responding to social change as well, the Congregation of Notre Dame and the Sisters of the Holy Name of Jesus and Mary in the 1880s added typing and stenography to the curricula in their academies.[4]

Next to the powerful, dynamic, and well-organized religious communities, francophone lay women occupied a marginal place in social service. Theirs was a supportive role. With the exception of the enterprising handful who headed charitable associations and created half-way houses for the destitute and the needy, the majority participated in philanthropic activity as assistants to religious women. The build-up of religious forces in philanthropy was set in motion in the 1840s and 1850s during Mgr. Ignace Bourget's administration. Committed to building a powerful Church, Bourget encouraged French religious communities, then under attack by the French state, to pull up their stakes and migrate to Quebec. Several orders responded. Bourget nurtured religious vocations in Quebec as well and coaxed lay women active in benevolence to place themselves and their work under his rule. After many years of caring for sick and homeless women, widow Émelie Tavernier-Gamelin took Mgr. Bourget's advice and founded the Sisters of Providence. Similarly, Mme. Rosalie Cadron-Jetté, who gave refuge to unwed mothers and shelter to abandoned infants, exchanged her lay apostolate for a religious vocation. She called herself and her newly established community the Sisters of Miséricorde.[5]

At times lay teachers and providers of charity took the initiative in forming religious communities and inadvertently strengthened clerical control in social service and education. Esther Blondin, a teacher and principal of a boarding school and former novice of the Sisters of the Congregation of Notre Dame, used her administrative and pedagogical skills to form the Sisters of St. Anne in 1850 just as a former student of the Congregation, Eulalie Durocher, had done seven years earlier in establishing the Sisters of the Holy Name of Jesus and Mary. Under less favourable circumstances in the remote region of Rimouski, the order of the Sisters of the Holy Rosary was founded in 1880. Louise Turgeon conceived and persistently built, despite Mgr. Langevin's opposition, a community devoted to the education of rural children.[6] At other times, insolvency sounded the knell of lay women's associations and facilitated religious control. Consider the case of the Montreal Orphanage. Founded in 1832 by the Ladies of Charity in the wake of the cholera epidemic that left many children parentless, it remained under their care for fifty years. In the 1880s mounting and seemingly unresolvable financial difficulties led to the resignation of its managers, Elmire and Delphine Morin. With their departure, the orphanage was entrusted to the Grey Nuns.[7]

The domination of social services by the Church was favoured also by the half-hearted involvement of lay women in, or their intermittent absences from, charitable work. Disinterest, apathy, family commitments, and child-rearing, or simply the attitude among some middle-class women that "that hardest and most unpleasant task" of ministering to the poor could be left to the sisters, reinforced religious control.[8]

Just as all these personal and political factors seemed to guarantee religious hegemony in the social and educational sphere, lay women began voicing their discontent with their self- and socially-imposed roles. They looked to the feminist movement, around which women in similar predicaments but under different political and religious systems were rallying. In 1893, *Le Coin du Feu*, a pioneering woman's magazine, took Quebec society by surprise by demanding "un regain du prestige de la femme."[9] In addition to exploring ways in which women could improve their social and political status, Joséphine Dandurand, its editor, gave speeches to audiences of lay and religious women.[10] In them she urged that a new, more equal relationship between the two be developed, denying that her services in benevolence were as an auxiliary and second-class participant. Readers of *Le Coin du Feu* shared and elaborated upon Dandurand's concerns. While nursing her youngest child, Marie Lacoste-Gérin-Lajoie, who became Montreal's leading feminist and a self-educated legal expert, mulled over the idea of transforming every woman's home into "un bureau d'affaires, un atelier, une étude, soit des professions libérales, de la science ou des arts."[11] Absolutely committed to her role as homemaker and mother, she nevertheless refused to be enslaved by it and to become "un être déformé, une créature manquée."[12] Single women also expressed the need for change. Robertine Barry, journalist, editor of *Le Journal de Françoise*, feminist, and later factory inspector, was the antithesis of the "spinster of yesteryear," the recluse who lived in the shadows of her parents or siblings. Donning a professional cloak, Barry championed the cause of women's emancipation and welcomed the political and social changes she believed would improve the condition of single women.[13]

The overcrowding, unsanitary conditions, disease, unemployment, and poverty that accompanied the transformation of Montreal from a commercial centre to a sprawling, industrial metropolis in the last decades of the nineteenth century threatened to tear apart the fragile social fabric. The prospect of urban decay and growing incidents of labour unrest alerted the middle and upper classes to social reform, forcing them to institute more extensive and effective methods of alleviating social distress. As changing material conditions led to new forms of public assistance, they opened avenues of action for women who felt constricted by their assigned sphere. Gérin-Lajoie, Barry, and Dandurand, who were the first to voice publicly their discontent with prescribed roles, seized the opportunity provided by the vacuum of social reform.[14] Their speeches popularized the plight of the working woman, called for protective legislation, demanded an improvement of working conditions, and proposed the creation of working women's associations. At the same time, to make good their commitment to help the poor and the exploited, they demanded greater political and legal rights for themselves. "Secourir les humbles, aller vers ceux qui jusqu'ici sont restés sans défense: se mettre au service des opprimés et donner par là une expression nouvelle à la charité"[15] was possible only if women had the legal and political means at their disposal to implement and enforce social reform.

This process of politicization among the privileged few generated the formation of a feminist ideology. It also provoked a re-evaluation of the nun-lay woman relationship and the questioning of the former's dominance in charitable work. Gérin-Lajoie, Dandurand, and Barry couched their arguments against the status quo and in favour of an equal partnership between lay women and nuns in religious terms. Just as their arguments for women's rights were marked by an appeal to justice and to the Christian message of salvation, their claims to reform and voluntary benevolence invoked the virtue of charity. As charity was central to the Church's social mission, so were women. Both, feminists contended, were the bread and breath of life.[16] The idea that all women were naturally disposed to charitable work removed a barricade that in late nineteenth-century Quebec consigned lay women to a secondary place in philanthropic work. It also invalidated and erased the distinctions that had evolved between lay and religious work. Regardless of one's vocation, ministering to the spiritual and corporal needs of society derived from the single source of charity, which all women shared.

This notion of a united women's front had significant implications. Not only did it strengthen the lay woman's self-esteem and confidence in her ability as a social guardian, it also gave her a sense of identity, a history, and a feeling of belonging to a long tradition of activism. Marie Lacoste-Gérin-Lajoie was convinced of the necessity of uniting lay and religious benevolence under the single banner of "l'initiative féminine," the underpinning of which was charity, and warned of the negative effects of such divisions: "Nous nous nuirions singulièrement les femmes quand nous parlons de nos oeuvres, si nous en exclusions celles des religieuses, et si nous voulions échapper aux mérites que leurs institutions font rejaillir sur tout notre sexe."[17] She believed that defining women's work along "vocational lines" deprived French-Canadian women of a collective past and dulled their perception of their strengths and potentialities. Treating lay and religious women as separate entities, speaking of nuns and of their accomplishments in exclusively religious terms, negated the feminist impulse, that instinctive concern for, and identification with, the destitute and the needy, that united and led women to work for the betterment of humanity.

Women who shared Gérin-Lajoie's concerns and wanted to give women back their history searched the past, re-examining the lives of prominent religious women like Marguerite Bourgeoys, Marie de l'Incarnation, and Marguerite d'Youville from a feminist perspective. They used the achievements of Saints Gertrude, Roswintha, and Hilda, famous abbesses of the past, and of the renowned medieval scholar St. Catherine as double-edged swords to ward off the clerics' religious arguments for sexual discrimination and the self-styled experts on feminine psychology who depicted woman's nature as too delicate and too emotional to withstand the stress of political and professional life.[18] By the same token they situated their political concerns in a tradition of Catholic feminism.

The tendency to seek legitimacy for women's rights in religion and to ferret out names and incidents from the immediate and more distant past persisted well after lay women had established their hegemony in charitable work and social reform. The portrayal of nuns and holy women as fellow workers in the "secular city" and as exemplars of the as yet untapped potential of most women spilled into pro-suffrage propaganda. Feminists mocked the ludicrous yet perversely powerful argument that voting would corrupt women by reminding their opponents that nuns routinely elected their superiors. If history has proven that nuns had not thereby lost their "ressemblance à leur pur modèle, la très Ste. Vierge"[19] – a proposition no one dared question – then surely electing representatives to parliament and municipal governments would not debase lay women. Robertine Barry used a similar tactic when she wondered "ce que Nos Seigneurs les évêques auraient répondu à une députation féminine demandant à assister au concile qui s'est tenu dernièrement à Montréal"[20] in light of the fact that women had participated in the synods of the medieval Church. The implication of her musing was clear: women in the "Dark Ages" had been allowed a greater voice in the governing of the Church (and, in the medieval context, of society as well) than their lay counterparts in contemporary Quebec.

The feminists' interpretation of charity and women's history subverted the traditional norms denying lay women the right to a political and intellectual life while their organizational activity expanded the lay women's sphere of influence and over time integrated the religious women into a feminist praxis. In 1893 Dandurand, Gérin-Lajoie, and Barry, with a handful of other bourgeois francophone women, joined the National Council of Women of Canada (NCWC). In its Montreal local, they co-operated with anglophones on a number of fronts. The actual battles they waged to win political rights for women and the reforms they sought to introduce in the workplace provided francophone women with badly needed experience in social activism and apprenticeship in leadership. At the same time, wives and daughters of Quebec's leading politicians and financiers formed a women's section of the Association St-Jean-Baptiste de Montréal, a French-Canadian nationalist association. Although originally recruited to help raise funds for the building of a national monument, they soon expanded their mandate to educational matters.[21] In 1906 they founded the École Ménagère de Montréal. For two years, Antoinette Gérin-Lajoie and Jeanne Anctil, subsidized by the women's section of the association, studied domestic science in France and Switzerland. Upon their return, they became the school's first principals and trained many of the province's future domestic science teachers.[22]

A decade of participation in the NCWC brought francophone women to the realization that a Catholic and French association was necessary to build support for women's rights in Quebec. The council's brand of patriotism and such chauvinistic pronouncements by anglophone feminists as "I am English and Canadian, and as long as it is one and the same thing I will not have it separated," "it is because Canada is British that I am so full of patriotism"[23] discomforted the French-speaking minority. No doubt these and similar remarks were on Gérin-Lajoie's mind when, justifying her disagreement with the council's position that unity among women was the overriding priority, she noted that "nos moeurs, nos idées, notre langue, tout est différent; notre race a une vraie personnalité qui lui permet d'être bonne camarade mais lui défend de s'assimiler."[24] Despite its non-denominational orientation, the Protestant character of the NCWC presented another problem to francophones. Although Dandurand and Gérin-Lajoie had no qualms about co-operating with women of other denominations, they knew they could not expect Catholic philanthropic associations to link up with the council's organizational network. Indeed, the council drew no francophone association into its fold.

Although the formation in 1907 of the Fédération Nationale St-Jean-Baptiste created an alternative to the National Council of Women and to the women's section of the Association St-Jean-Baptiste, politically it remained close to them. Organized and directed by francophone women, the Fédération rested on a foundation that fused the diverse influence and traditions to which lay women as activists had been exposed. Naming the Fédération in honour of Quebec's patron saint situated the women's rights campaigns and social reform in a French and Catholic context. Similarly, it seemed to indicate that the preoccupations of the women's section of the Association St-Jean Baptiste were now those of the Fédération. A co-ordinating agency that consolidated and expanded ongoing efforts in charity, education, and social service, the Fédération was modelled on the National Council of Women's organizational structure. Moreover, like its antecedent, the Fédération deliberately avoided the contentious issue of suffrage before firmly establishing a connection between social reform and women's rights.[25] Finally, the Fédération formalized the nun-lay woman partnership as feminists had defined it and drew convents along with their ancillary institutions into its organizational structure. Over half of the twenty-two groups that affiliated with the Fédération were controlled by nuns. Although these groups, as all the others, retained their independence, they became eligible for, and over time dependent on, the monies the Fédération raised during its annual drives. The nuns who administered these charitable institutions automatically became members of the Fédération.[26]

Teaching nuns, accompanied by their older students, and nuns representing the affiliated charitable institutions attended the annual congresses of the Fédération. Their presence did not pass unnoticed:

> Parmi elles [participantes] figuraient un grand nombre de religieuses; leur présence faisait sentir les solides liens qui unissent dans des aspirations communes toutes les âmes de bonne volonté; il était touchant ce spectacle de laïques et de religieuses s'unissant dans des séances d'études pour se perfectionner dans la science de la charité et augmenter au sein de notre société la fécondité de leur apostolat.[27]

At the plenary sessions during the early years of the Fédération's existence, however, they remained silent and spoke only through lay intermediaries.

There are a few possible explanations for this apparent lack of participation. Caroline Béique, one of the Fédération's founding members, suggested it was the timidity of nuns that kept them from the platform.[28] It is also possible that within the framework of the Fédération nuns saw themselves as back-benchers whose role was merely to support and at times advise the lay leadership. Reluctance to speak could have been provoked in part as well by the "paternal" advice of the clergy. Given its conservatism, it is not unreasonable to assume that the clergy deemed it improper for a veiled woman to address a public gathering. If indeed clerical intervention put a damper on participation, this would help explain the persistent contradiction between the nuns' apparent silence and their frequent assurances to Gérin-Lajoie of willingness to play an active role during the congresses.[29]

Notwithstanding the behaviour of religious women at the congresses or their perceptions of their roles in the Fédération – important considerations but difficult to elaborate on the basis of available literature – communities did develop working relationships with its lay membership. The Grey Nuns, the Sisters of Providence, and the Sisters of Miséricorde are cases in point. Their crèches, half-way houses, and orphanages came under the Fédération's umbrella. Their members frequently attended the educational meetings on child care, hygiene, and prenatal care organized by lay women. Similarly, the Sisters of the Congregation of Notre Dame offered their premises for the Fédération's meetings and rallies and, as will be shown subsequently, worked closely and systematically with feminists and lay activists in creating new educational opportunities for women. When the Fédération launched a campaign in 1912 to reduce the staggering rate of infant mortality, the Grey Nuns helped in the distribution of pasteurized milk to poor families and operated milk stations in the neighbourhoods with the highest death rate. Individual nuns also supported the work of the Fédération by urging students and friends to join it, disseminating its literature, and soliciting funds and subscriptions for its journal, *La Bonne Parole*.[30]

Nuns and feminists combined forces on other issues of the day. The "domestic crisis," the shortage of properly trained domestics and the need for better and more efficient housekeeping, troubled both. Collectively they developed domestic science programs and through them proselytized on proper mothering and efficient household management. Whether training in domestic science produced dependable servants for the households of the bourgeoisie and for the mother houses of the prosperous religious communities remains unclear. Nor is it certain that it raised the standard of mothering. In the long run, however, such training limited the educational opportunity of lower-class women and directed them into domestic occupations and low-paying factory work.[31]

The most sustained and far-reaching effort to unite feminists and nuns was the founding in 1908 of the École d'enseignement supérieur pour les filles, renamed Le Collège Marguerite Bourgeoys in 1926. Its creation demanded the co-operation of all who were committed to extending higher education to upper- and middle-class francophone women, and pitted nuns and feminists against priests and politicians who feared the consequences of change. The program of the college and the study circle movement it spawned in turn provided the Fédération with a means of influencing and training the next generation of feminists.

Le Coin du Feu, the first women's magazine, and "Chroniques de lundi," Robertine Barry's weekly column in *La Patrie*, were the first to broach the issue of higher education for women. They monitored and reported the strides that women were making in the United States, Europe, and the neighbouring provinces in Canada and juxtaposed them to the lack of commensurate progress in Quebec.[32] Barry, Dandurand, and Gérin-Lajoie, the most ardent campaigners for greater educational and professional opportunity, used a variety of methods to prod the consciousness of men. Like feminists elsewhere, they tried to awaken a sense of justice and fair play and expressed disdain for those who protected privilege and acquiesced to injustice. They vowed to bring about change and mocked men who feared competition from women. "Si la terreur de se voir égalés ou surpassés les inspirent, qu'ils nous permettent encore une fois de calmer leurs larmes."[33] Occasionally they invoked nationalistic pride and enlisted it in their barrage of assaults against educational inequality. They argued that sexual discrimination in education inhibited the French-Canadian middle class in its quest for leadership and prestige in Canada. Raising the spectre of inferiority, suggesting that there might be some validity to the slur that Quebec was backward, Gérin-Lajoie reminded her opponents that "chaque année à l'étranger et plus près de nous chez nos soeurs anglo-saxonnes une élite de femmes se forme, qui entraine la race entière vers un idéal toujours plus élevé et des destinées plus hautes."[34] She assumed that, regardless of their opinions on female education, most of her contemporaries associated education with progress. With half of the nation chained by reason of gender to ignorance, her verdict was that the French race would not fare well in the international arena.

Besides engaging in polemics, feminists took matters into their own hands whenever the opportunity presented itself. As part of her effort to raise the level of feminine participation in intellectual life, Dandurand convinced lay and religious teachers to encourage students to submit their essays to literary contests sponsored by the NCWC. Winning essays were printed in *Le Coin du Feu*. Similarly, through Dandurand's initiative, a book-lending system giving rural women access to library materials was organized, women were granted the right to sit on the council of the National Library, and in 1904 they were given permission to audit literature courses at Laval University.[35]

Finally, feminists made overtures to nuns seeking their support and advice. Robertine Barry spoke to nuns first through her column in *La Patrie*, and after 1902 through *Le Journal de Françoise*, her bimonthly publication. Recalling the distant days when convents were "des pépinières de femmes érudites," she urged nuns to revive the golden past by establishing women's classical colleges and raising the standards in their schools to equip young women with the skills necessary for work and university. She also hoped that greater occupational opportunity would accompany educational reform and specifically requested that nuns make room for lay women professors in their academies and institutions of higher learning.[36] A plethora of suggestions coming from other women filled the pages of Barry's magazine as well. One contributor gave teaching communities the example of the innovative and avant-garde nun, Mme. Marie du Sacré Coeur, who had opened a women's Catholic college in France.[37] As the issue dragged on, Marie Lacoste-Gérin-Lajoie dispensed with subtle hints and asked bluntly:

> Pourquoi une de nos maisons religieuses ne remplirait-elle pas auprès de Laval les fonctions des soeurs de Notre-dame de Namur auprès de l'université de Washington? Pourquoi l'une d'entre elles ne consentirait-elle pas à suivre après le pensionnat le jeune fille studieuse que le monde ne prend pas toute entière? L'Église a toujours soutenu que l'éducation était sienne, dans ce pays d'ailleurs, que n'a-t-elle pas fait pour cette sainte cause?[38]

Besides goading nuns through the press, feminists also regularly discussed educational matters with them. The diary of Sister St. Anaclet, the assistant to the superior general in the 1890s and superior general from 1903 to 1912 of the Congregation of Notre Dame, indicates that Gérin-Lajoie had her community in mind when she asked embarrassing questions and published an outline of a tentative college curriculum in *Le Journal de Françoise*. In May, 1897, a delegation of lay women met with Sister St. Anaclet and her companion Sister St. Olivine to discuss higher education. The next day Sister St. Anaclet recorded that Ernestine Marchand, the convent's student and Dandurand's relative, "est venue et a répété de bonnes impressions que Mme. Dandurand a emportées de sa visite."[39] The favourable impression she and her colleague made on their visitors seemed to matter. Moreover, Ernestine Marchand's comment to Sister St. Anaclet suggests that no major differences on the question of female education divided the lay women and these two sisters. According to Sister St. Anaclet, Gérin-Lajoie also dropped in regularly on her own, at times to check on her daughter's progress in school as well as to remind teaching sisters of her intention to send her daughter to college, if not in Quebec then in the United States or Europe. Other visits were occasioned by Gérin-Lajoie's decision to write a handbook on civil law. Before publishing the text, she solicited Sister St. Anaclet's advice, and the two spent hours discussing the manuscript.[40] In 1902, when *Le Traité de Droit Usuel* came off the press, the community requested that Gérin-Lajoie teach law to its older students. Finally, when plans for the founding of the École Ménagère de Montréal were underway, Caroline Béique, Marie Thibodeau, and Marie de Beaujeu, who were instrumental in its establishment, met with Sister St. Anaclet on a regular basis.[41]

The extent to which Sister St. Anaclet supported the aspirations of her lay visitors is difficult to determine because of her discretion, which was part of a religious woman's ethos. But brief incidental remarks in the diary suggest that moments of unspoken rapport existed between the hostess and her guests. Hearing one of Gérin-Lajoie's lectures, she exclaimed: "quelle femme." Having read a text that degraded women, she simply wrote: "Toute réserve faite de notre [women's] dignité, n'est-ce pas ça l'histoire du chien?"[42] More important, during and a few years prior to her administration, a coterie of the Congregation's sisters headed by Sister St. Anne Marie were negotiating with Mgr. Bruchési, the archbishop of Montreal, for a women's college.

Sister St. Anne Marie, the oldest daughter of Guillaume Bengle and Philomène Pion-Lafontaine and the niece of Sister St. Luce, a powerful and highly regarded member of the community, joined the Congregation in 1879. After an inauspicious beginning as a teaching sister in Sherbrooke, she returned to the mother house in Montreal. There, as a teacher in Mont Ste. Marie, one of the most prestigious boarding schools offering a complete program in elementary and secondary education, she proved to be an exceptionally talented pedagogue and administrator. In 1897 she became the school's assistant principal and six years later its principal.[43] Sympathetic to feminist concerns, Sister St. Anne Marie began to lay the groundwork for a women's college in the 1890s. Quietly, with the moral support of abbé Henri Gauthier, the community's chaplain, and that of the Congregation's governing council, she introduced philosophy, chemistry, and law into Mont Ste. Marie's high school curriculum. In order to prepare teaching sisters for their future task as college teachers, she founded a chair of literary studies and asked Laval University professors to become its visiting lecturers. Corresponding with academics in Europe, she studied literature under their direction. In 1913, she passed the *licence en philosophie*, which qualified her as a college professor.[44]

Reactions in the community to Sister St. Anne Marie's initiative were mixed. Nuns with close ties to feminists were supportive and hoped that "son exemple ne reste pas stérile." Others were outraged by her "modernism" and applauded the efforts of the clergy to hold back the tide of change.[45] But, as in all major educational decisions involving religious communities, the fate of the college rested in the bishop's hands. Mgr. Bruchési, who had impressed Gérin-Lajoie as favourably disposed to women's concerns,[46] in this instance behaved most indecisively, one day agreeing with Sister St. Anne Marie's proposal and the next suggesting that implementing it was premature. For years the waltz continued. Bruchési's hesitation, however, ended abruptly. In April, 1908, *La Patrie* announced that two Montreal journalists, Eva Circé Côté and Gaëtane de Montreuil (Marie-Georgina Bélanger's pseudonym), were opening a *lycée* for girls on St. Denis Street.[47] The "audacity" of these women did not sit well with the clergy. Not only did it show that some women had the courage to take matters into their own hands, but it also drove a wedge into the clerical monopoly of secondary and higher education in the province. It created an alternative to the collegiate system of higher education in Quebec and opened the possibility of graduating women into English and American universities. Intending to sabotage the *lycée*, Mgr. Bruchési hastily approved Sister St. Anne Marie's long-standing proposal. In turn, Sister St. Anne Marie notified Montreal society through *La Semaine religieuse* that a women's college administered by the Sisters of the Congregation of Notre Dame and affiliated to Laval University would be opening in September, 1908. That fall, over forty students registered. Marie Lacoste-Gérin-Lajoie's daughter, Marie J., was one of them.[48]

Given the circumstances under which approval was granted, the right to equal educational opportunity and access to professions still had to be won. As higher education became a possibility for a privileged few, various attempts were made to introduce new discriminatory measures and to reinforce existing ones. In his keynote addres at the college's opening ceremony, Mgr. Dauth, the vice-rector of Laval University, stressed that limitations must be imposed on women's scholarly pursuits:

> Livrer trop largement les jeunes filles aux études abstraites, ne pas savoir leur doser prudemment la science selon la nature et la mesure de leur esprit, ne pas les immuniser contre le sot orgueil ou le vertige ... c'est les jeter en dehors de leur sphère et les engager dans une voie funeste,... c'est en faire non plus les compagnes généreuses et dévouées de l'homme, mais les rivales encombrantes et dans tous les cas incomprises.[49]

Women's greater susceptibility to pride and their preordained social roles as companions rather than men's rival dictated an approach to education that differed from the one employed in male colleges. While Dauth restricted his remarks on women's education to generalities, some of his colleagues entered into specifics. Appalled by Sister St. Anne Marie's decision to adopt intact the program used in male colleges, they questioned the validity of her choice and urged that she replace the masculine subjects of chemistry, physics, and even philosophy with "les matières féminines." Although Sister St. Anne Marie remained steadfast in her decision to give women a *bona fide* college education, she still had to compromise her stance by scheduling a series of extra-academic activities like piano recitals, poetry readings, and afternoon teas. These "feminine activities" were meant to placate her critics who insisted women could not withstand the strain of uninterrupted intellectual work.[50]

Further proof of discrimination was the lack of public support for the college. Its students were obliged to wage campaigns to convince French-Canadian society of the social merits of an educated female population, and Sister St. Anne Marie had to rely on her ingenuity, the community's financial backing, and students' fees to keep the college afloat. None of the politicians or members of the Church hierarchy, who attended the school's annual assemblies and spoke so eloquently and adamantly about restricting women's educational experience to what was relevant to marriage and mothering offered it financial support. In the final analysis, this miserly attitude compared to their generosity toward the developing domestic science programs underscored the lack of support for higher education for women.[51]

Sister St. Anne Marie's unfailing commitment may have guaranteed her students an equal education but like the more strident attempts by feminists, it was not enough to win women recognition for the fruits of their labour. A conspiracy of silence enveloped women's academic achievements. No mention was made of the fact that Marie J. Gérin-Lajoie, the first graduate of the École d'enseignement supérieur, came ahead of all her male competitors in provincial exams. In fact, Laval University hushed up this and similar "compromising incidents."[52] It was unacceptable to have women, whose right to higher education was still being contested, outsmarting those who were allegedly superior to them. Uncharacteristically, the press overlooked these peculiar developments. On the other hand, it reported in great detail harangues levelled at "les femmes savantes," to say nothing of its critical coverage of feminist activities. Instead of projecting a more accurate and nuanced image of the changing roles of women, newspaper discussions of the École d'enseignement supérieur persisted in defining educated women either as gentle, self-effacing, knowledgeable "sans prétension" and, thereby, conforming to the ideal, or as haughty, desexed imitators of men, representing its opposite.[53]

Finally and more significantly, there was the concerted and combined effort of clerical and political forces to keep women out of the professions. More successful than the attempts to restrict women's educational opportunity, it exploited the vulnerability of nuns and sought to create divisions between them and lay women. From the day the college opened its door to its many convocations, collegiate women were told that their degrees, regardless of merit, did not entitle them to the rights they bestowed on men. Women were not to undertake professional training in medicine, law, pharmacy, and accounting. In turn, Sister St. Anne Marie was instructed to keep her students in line and led to believe that, if they dared challenge the prescribed norms, she would lose her college. "Si vous voulez tuer le collège" was her answer to students who expressed interest in the forbidden professions.[54] In 1924, when Marthe Pellard, the first graduate to break with tradition, applied for medical training, Sister St. Anne Marie apologized and expressed regret to the Laval administrators: "Daignez me permettre de vous faire part du regret que j'ai éprouvé en apprenant que l'une de nos élèves de l'École d'enseignement supérieur avait été admis à suivre les cours du médecine."[55] Instead of applause, consternation greeted Marthe Pellard's academic success.

Although Sister St. Anne Marie had to tailor her response to the demands of feminists and to the ambitions of her students to accommodate the will of her male religious superiors, it is unlikely that she and the lay women who sought her support envisioned the consequences of educational and economic equality in the ways men did.[56] For feminists it meant giving women the opportunity to realize their intellectual and economic potential and a chance to contribute to society's welfare. In the minds of the male French-Canadian élite, women assuming "des fonctions lucratives jusqu'ici dévolues aux hommes"[57] conjured up images of women replacing men, patriarchal institutions crumbling, families disintegrating, and women postponing or rejecting marriage altogether. Many years later, abbé Lionel Groulx, who taught history at the École d'enseignement supérieur and who had questioned the wisdom of Sister St. Anne Marie's position on women's education, confessed that "on craignait que la femme n'acceptât plus le mariage et la famille une fois ses études universitaires terminées."[58] If for many men the elimination of sexual discrimination in the university and the workplace posed a threat to the social order, for the clergy in particular it spelled an added disaster, that of stemming the tide of religious vocations. Behind clerical confidence that Divine Providence was solely responsible for the many vocations in Quebec may well have lurked the suspicion that, with greater economic opportunities available to them, women might be less inclined to take the veil. Alphonse Pelletier, lawyer, senator, Lieutenant-Governor, and an adversary of women's rights, raised that very point to show the positive side of discrimination. In a letter to a sister of the Congregation of Notre Dame justifying his opposition to women practising law, he articulated the fears that the clergy might have been ashamed to admit openly:

Je crois plus que jamais que l'usage consacré, dans la province de Québec, au moins, de n'admettre que des hommes au Barreau est très sage, car s'il était permis à celles que l'on qualifie bien à tort de sexe faible, de pénétrer dans le temple de Themis, les communautés religieuses perdraient d'excellents sujets et ces

pauvres avocats auraient à lutter contre des rivales qui les éclip-
seraient très souvent, et il est fort probable que vous [his corres-
pondent] et ma chère Mère Pantaleon [his niece] auriez manqué
votre vocation à la vie religieuse pour entrer au Barreau.[59]

The "loss" of vocations among women would not only deplete the
ranks of religious communities; it would also undermine the
Church's dominance in social and educational affairs. A large female religious population was a pre-condition for clerical control
and influence in society. Nuns provided the services upon which the
hierarchy built a powerful Church. If the trend were reversed and
there were few or no nuns to mediate between the hierarchy and
the faithful, the Church would lose its control to lay voluntary or
state organizations.

Thus the history of the first women's college, the fate of its
graduates, and the reactions of Sister St. Anne Marie to her students' career choices unfolded within the parameters of a patriarchal
society whose protectors interpreted changes in women's economic
and political roles in apocalyptic terms. Yet ways were found to
circumvent the power of patriarchs. Their advice on the importance
of being "male's companions" went unheeded. Half of the École
d'enseignement supérieur's graduates never married. Many went
into religious communities, combining a vocation with professional
life. Others had taken Robertine Barry's requiem to yesterday's
spinster to heart and staked "a place in the sun" for themselves.
Few were as bold as Marthe Pellard, the first woman doctor certi-
fied in Quebec. The majority of graduates carved new niches for
themselves in the world of feminine occupations. They became
librarians, researchers, social workers, and full-time employees of
women's associations and governmental agencies.[60]

On another level the extracurricular activities of the college
brought feminists and collegiate women in close contact with one
another, opening yet another avenue to the co-operation between
nuns and feminists. The founding members of the Fédération were
interested in developing and expanding the organization's education
and social service components, as well as in finding an effective
method of recruitment into its ranks.[61] The program of the Cercle
Notre Dame satisfied both needs. Founded in 1909 by the students
of the École d'enseignement supérieur, its purpose was to enhance
women's intellectual and social development. Its members met
fortnightly to discuss and analyse selected topics in literature, history, and the arts or to study solutions to problems generated by

urbanization and industrialization. At times, books were abandoned in order to gain first-hand knowledge of poverty. Circle
members visited with, and offered their services to, the poor as
teachers, mothers' helpers, and counsellors.[62]

Encouragement from Sister St. Anne Marie, the group's honor-
ary president, and from the Fédération Nationale St-Jean-Baptiste
ensured the circle's survival, turning it into a permanent feature of
the college. Collegiate women assisted by the Fédération promoted
the creation of other study circles around which young women
could organize "à acquérir une formation intellectuelle et sociale."[63]
The idea of young women banding together to study and work
took hold, and within a span of five years ten study circles were in
operation. By 1916 nine of these circles federated into La Fédération
des cercles d'études canadiennes-françaises. Like the women of the
Fédération Nationale St-Jean-Baptiste, activists drawn to the circles
united to centralize and co-ordinate their work. Unity, it was hoped,
would facilitate growth and further the organizational movement.[64]

Between 1909 and 1925 the study circles stimulated a tremendous
amount of research and discussion about the working class, infant
mortality, poverty, education, and trade unionism. The findings
and the recommendations of the federated circles were reported in
La Bonne Parole. To combat the ills of capitalism and to help those
most affected by them, the study circles outlined a threefold approach: the promotion of popular education in the form of literacy
courses, home visits, and preaching of Catholic social doctrine
from the pulpit and the press; the organization of working women
into trade unions and professional organizations and the creation
of mutual aid societies; and, in the last resort, state intervention to
curb "les vices de notre organisation économique."[65] In other words,
the study circles proposed a combination of social reform, moral
regeneration, and self-help.

Through their involvement in popular education, women's associations and unions, the publication of La Bonne Parole, and participation in semaines sociales (annual meetings devoted to a study
of social problems), the study circles brought to bear on French-
Canadian society the full current of Catholic social doctrine. More
important perhaps, they, and particularly the Cercle Notre Dame,
prepared the second generation of lay activists for leadership roles
in the Fédération Nationale St-Jean-Baptiste. Like the preceding
one, this generation consisted primarily of upper- and middle-class
women[66] whose aim was to expand the role of lay women in society.
Some became full-time workers for the Fédération and sat on its

central committee, others edited *La Bonne Parole*; some joined the Comité de suffrage provincial in 1921 and, when it was disbanded, participated in the Ligue des droits de la femme, founded in 1928, others opened settlement houses for the poor and displaced.[67] The second generation altered the nature of social service in Quebec, transforming it from voluntary to professional work. While this evolution took years to complete, the recognition that charity alone would not overcome poverty and urban decay and a concomitant adoption of a scientific approach to social problems made it inevitable.[68]

A key figure in the professionalization of social work was Marie J. Gérin-Lajoie. Finishing her studies at the École d'enseignement supérieur, she travelled to France to study methods used there to organize and distribute relief. A few years later she moved to New York City to take an intensive course in social work at Columbia University. In the fall of 1919 she taught sociology and social work at the École d'enseignement supérieur, and in the years that followed she developed a full program of study that the School of Social Work, established in 1931, adopted.[69] In the early 1920s she founded an order known as the Institut de Notre-Dame-du-Bon-Conseil, once again reaffirming the strong links between Quebec social feminism and religious life.

Marie J. Gérin-Lajoie's vocation was inseparable from a commitment to feminism, particularly to that strand of the movement that connected activism to reform, education, and social work. Although her vocation took root during a retreat in 1911, it germinated slowly. Gérin-Lajoie studied, travelled, lectured, and worked on the central committee of the Fédération Nationale St-Jean-Baptiste. In the summers of 1919 and 1921 she retreated with a group of friends who shared her concerns into the country to live communally and to experiment with self-organized religious life. In the peace and quiet of the Laurentians, "la journée se passait à de petits travaux, à des lectures, à des promenades. Le Chapelet se disait en commun et la prière le soir."[70] In the meantime, she approached religious communities already involved in social service and missionary work with the hope that at least one would be flexible enough to accept women like her, desiring to take vows of chastity and poverty but reluctant to adhere to the strict and often restrictive rules of convent life. The purpose of this peculiar group of nuns would be to ensure the stability of the recently formulated feminist projects. "Et qu'y aurait-il de plus désirable que ces personnes fussent des religieuses?" Gérin-Lajoie asked. Bound by chastity, "les inévitables obligations familiales," the lot of most women, would not dampen their zeal and dedication. When all attempts to find a community "assez souple pour aider aux oeuvres nouvelles" failed, she requested the archbishop's permission to found a community of her own.[71] Papal approbation came in 1923, but enclosed was also the stipulation that Marie J. Gérin-Lajoie forfeit some of her unorthodox ideas about religious life. The notion of purging it of all its excessive paraphernalia was unacceptable to the Church hierarchy and, as a matter of fact, probably equally unpalatable to many religious women as well. All the externals of religious life, the fastidiously tailored habit, the daily routine, even the cloister, provided the added measure of control over the lives of religious women. Working on the assumption that "virtue" and "zeal" were sufficient to religious life, Marie J. Gérin-Lajoie had hoped to eliminate the cumbersome habit worn by nuns, to de-institutionalize the novitiate by allowing novices to spend part of the trial period at home, and to give professed nuns the option of residing in a traditional type of community or in a small collective near their places of work. Rome did permit minor modifications to religious convention: greater freedom of travel, the right to keep one's family name, and the adoption of a simple habit.[72]

Once the community was established, Mgr. Gauthier, Mgr. Bruchési's successor, tried imposing further restrictions. In 1927 the Institut de Notre-Dame-du-Bon-Conseil was told to cease collaborating with *La Bonne Parole*. Shortly afterward, presumably under pressure, Mgr. Gauthier modified his position, allowing nuns to assist anonymously in the publication of the journal. Caught in the middle of the rancorous debate on suffrage and women's rights, Gauthier felt uncomfortable with a community so closely affiliated to the pro-suffrage side. This at least was how Marie J. Gérin-Lajoie in a letter to her mother interpeted the archbishop's behaviour: "Ce qu'il veut avant tout c'est qu'il n'y ait ni fusion ni confusion aux yeux du public et que nous ne soyons pas engagés même de loin dans la question que tu sais."[73] Hence, Mgr. Gauthier defined the limits of co-operation between nuns and feminists: in social reform and charity it was acceptable, in suffrage absolutely inadmissible.

The Institut de Notre-Dame-du-Bon-Conseil grew out of the nun-lay woman relationship that feminists had forged in the early years of the movement and used to win for lay women a place in reform and the right to higher education. From the outset its founder declared her intention to reinforce that partnership and to use it to the advantage of lay women. Her insistence that the aim of the Institut was to support lay women, "non les remplacer, les aider et non les dispenser d'agir, les conseiller et non leur enlever toute initiative,"[74] described the type of relationship her mother, Marie Lacoste-Gérin-Lajoie, Joséphine Dandurand, and Robertine Barry had striven to create in the early days of the feminist movement. While the Grey Nuns, the Sisters of Providence, the Sisters of the Congregation of Notre Dame, and the other communities that participated in the social and educational programs of the Fédération Nationale St-Jean-Baptiste implicitly accepted the lay woman as a partner, the Institut de Notre-Dame-du-Bon-Conseil was the first explicitly created to enhance the work of lay women and to ensure that the programs the Fédération had undertaken would come to fruition. Marie J. Gérin-Lajoie and the young women who joined her in the 1920s and 1930s worked on the executive of the Fédération, ran the social service office of l'Hôpital Ste-Justine, founded by Marie Lacoste-Gérin-Lajoie's sister Justine Lacoste-Beaubien, contributed regularly to *La Bonne Parole*, promoted the study of sociology, and encouraged female participation in the study circles.[75]

Under the impetus of the feminist movement the nun-lay woman relationship travelled a considerable ideological distance. Throughout the nineteenth century and indeed as far back as New France, lay and religious women had been involved in a symbiotic relationship. The former relied on the nuns' educational and charitable services and beseeched their prayer and support at times of personal crisis. In turn, nuns depended on the lay women's recognition for survival and counted on their support and moral assistance. As Joséphine Dandurand put it, "en effet, que peuvent ces institutions sans le secours, les avis, et le concours des femmes du monde?"[76] But it was only in the late nineteenth century, when women throughout North America and Europe began demanding greater autonomy, that the social consequences of that relationship were grasped. Quebec's reliance on services nuns provided placed lay women at a political disadvantage. The work of nuns went "exclusivement au profit de l'idée religieuse,"[77] undercutting "l'initiative féminine" that underlay their activism. This blinded women to their own strength and deprived them of a sense of individual and collective accomplishment. Conversely, in a society ruled by men it served to enhance male prestige and perpetuated male tyranny. The underside of the battle for political and economic equality in late nineteenth century, therefore, had to be the burgeoning of lay charitable work, in essence, the conscious restructuring of the long-standing nun-lay woman relationship. In broad historical terms, this meant the undoing of the marginalization of lay women and the undermining of Mgr. Bourget's legacy in social service and education. The Fédération Nationale St-Jean-Baptiste, the École d'enseignement supérieur, and the Institut de Notre-Dame-du-Bon-Conseil were landmarks in that process, which terminated in the overt commitment of a small group of nuns to many of the goals of social feminism.

7

The Peacock and the Guinea Hen: Political Profiles of Dorothy Gretchen Steeves and Grace MacInnis

Susan Walsh

In the wake of suffrage victories, many early twentieth-century Canadian women worked hard to make that equality meaningful and to extend it to all areas of women's lives. For those who predicted great changes, however, too few took their hard-earned rights further than the polling station. Most expressed their concerns and goals within the more familiar world of women's organizations. Dorothy Steeves and Grace MacInnis were among the notable exceptions. While maintaining important ties with women's groups, they sought and won public office, pioneering important paths for generations of Canadian women to follow. These political trailblazers stand out for another important reason. They chose to establish their careers and test their political rights in a socialist party – the Cooperative Commonwealth Federation (CCF) – pledged to sexual emancipation and equal opportunities for women. They were, in short, dual rebels – as feminists and socialists – in a sex- and class-ordered world.

Canada's third party gave these two women a very warm reception. Both emerged as leaders within the British Columbia CCF after a relatively brief apprenticeship. But the championing of both causes was at the same time practically and theoretically arduous. In a fashion resembling socialist parties elsewhere, the CCF had difficulty living up to its promise of sexual egalitarianism. When class aspirations clashed with gender ones, the latter suffered. Nor did the majority of women within the party take the "great leap forward" that socialist theory forecast.

Party priorities clearly affected Steeves' and MacInnis's options and influenced the ways in which they investigated their loyalties to class and sex. A discussion of the CCF's position on class and sex issues, however, is beyond the scope of this essay. Rather, it focuses on personal attitudes and experiences that inspired their career paths and approach to socialist and feminist causes. The following political profiles should, nevertheless, be understood within the larger context of the CCF's half-hearted commitment to sexual equality.

When Grace MacInnis first met Gretchen Steeves, a Dutch immigrant, in 1932, she was impressed with Steeves' European *savoir-faire* and knowledge of a "great many things which didn't exist in Canada at the time."[1] Steeves' quick mind and strong public presence convinced MacInnis that this woman could win the respect of many. MacInnis's first impression proved correct. Upon the public platform, Steeves' sharp intellect, penetrating style, and broad education won considerable respect, including that of British Columbia's voters who in 1934 elected her to the provincial house. Steeves' political skill and flair proved most attractive to a young political party challenging the status quo. Francis Aldman of the *Vancouver Province* agreed, writing in 1936: "No other member of the legislature can match her brevity and forcefulness ... she is probably the most effective member in the present Provincial Parliament."[2]

Several years later, Aldman presented a similar assessment of another female MLA who likewise offered much to the young CCF. This time Grace MacInnis received the commendation. He noted: "She is an instinctive politician, a tower of strength to the opposition. ... Mrs. MacInnis is the equal of any and none are ever quite ready to engage in a battle of wits."[3]

As these observations suggest, Steeves and MacInnis were a good match. Although less aggressive in public approach, MacInnis possessed the very intellectual capacity, charismatic appeal, and political acumen she had so generously admired in Steeves. Equally important, she had the drive and courage necessary to exercise her talents. Indeed, like her CCF sister, once immersed in active politics she took to it, as she put it, "like a duck to water and never looked back."[4]

Colin Cameron, a close associate of both during the party's early history, once remarked to MacInnis: "You are like a guinea hen scratching around the Legislature, while Gretchen Steeves is like a peacock."[5] Thriving on public controversy and debate, Steeves particularly relished the limelight and shone on stage. MacInnis, on the other hand, enjoyed behind-the-scenes decision-making and, though a strong speaker, was a backroom politician *par excellence*. Still, as this brief portrait of their respective careers demonstrates through its delineation of their paths to power and its analysis of their socialist and feminist goals, the "peacock" and the "guinea hen" were fundamentally birds of the same feather.

Dorothy Gretchen Biersteker was born on May 26, 1891, in Amsterdam, The Netherlands, the first of three children and the only daughter of a Dutch physician and British school teacher. The Bierstekers enjoyed the traditions, prosperity, and comforts of Dutch professionals and were thus able to offer their new daughter a secure and intellectually rich home environment. Household servants attended to the family's domestic needs, leaving ample time for cultural, recreational, and, above all, academic pursuits. Gretchen took full advantage of her class privilege, developing a curious and critical intellect throughout her childhood and adolescence.[6]

Like most upper middle-class parents in Holland, the Bierstekers encouraged, indeed presumed, that all their children would receive post-secondary education. They made no distinction between their daughter and two sons. Gretchen thus followed the route of most wealthy and bright Dutch children, attending the classical "gymnasium" stream in high school and, upon graduation, entering university. Her particular aptitude for complex analysis guided her to professional training in law and economics and in 1916 she graduated *cum laude* from the University of Leiden.[7]

Shortly after receiving her law degree, she worked as a barrister for a law firm in Amsterdam. Her apprenticeship there, however, was short-lived. A family move, soon after, took her to Den Haag (The Hague), Holland's capital and centre of national government. But her work for a private law firm there was again brief. After only six months in the capital, she was appointed to the Dutch government's Wartime Prices and Trade Board, a position most appealing to a talented, ambitious, and increasingly politically conscious young lawyer.

Employment in the civil service during the war years was indeed challenging. Her energies were nevertheless spent on more than her professional responsibilities. A growing concern with social injustice and an increasing appetite for public affairs, whetted in university, led to membership in the Socialist Party of Holland as well as to two other fast-growing movements in the second decade of the twentieth century: the women's suffrage movement and the peace movement.

Gretchen's youthful enthusiasm for the socialist cause did not lead, however, to an especially profound commitment to the party. She focused greater attention on suffrage and pacifism. In fact, the Socialist Party's endorsement of female enfranchisement influenced her decision to join party ranks.[8] Yet, once again, her involvement in both, which was prominent enough to include public lectures, was not terribly systematic. Not until she was fully immersed in a more practical, less comfortable, and less affluent world did the young lawyer seriously commit herself to the collective process of social change, to the co-operative building of a new social order.

The event most immediately responsible for Gretchen's move to an environment that was to nurture a more profound political, social, and feminist consciousness was that which altered the lives of not a few young Dutch women at the end of the Great War: marriage to a Canadian POW, Rupert Steeves. Unsure of what to expect, like most young war brides, she was carried on a romantic cloud of excitement and new adventure. The adventure and challenge ahead, however, were not quite the kind the new Mrs. Steeves had anticipated. The "primitive cultural conditions"[9] she witnessed during her endless train trek across Canadian cities, mountains, farms, and wilderness disappointed the more sophisticated European. When she finally reached the coast in the winter of 1919, her enthusiasm was, at best, markedly circumscribed. Faced with tasks she had always counted on servants to perform, and appliances like a wood stove "with no clue how you lit the damn thing,"[10] romance dissipated and reality set in with a vengeance. One letter written to her mother shortly after her arrival encapsulates her dismay over the isolation and primitiveness of British Columbia culture. Particularly outstanding is her disdain for those women whom she considered slaves to a maternal and domestic identity.

After a brief but precise description of her tedious journey on the CNR, which included a stopover in Toronto at "the first civilized house I'd got to since I came to Canada ... where there were nice servants," she announced:

> I shall start housekeeping without a servant but have a Japanese woman if I can a couple of times a week to clean up ... if needs be myself to pay her. I'm not going to become a drudge like most Canadian women; they look either dowdy or flashy; there is not one simple aristocratic well-dressed English woman among them.[11]

Household management did take up much of Steeves' first few years in Canada. But, true to her vow, she did not become the household drudge she despised. She maintained an unusually active role in the community and for a brief time in the wage labour force as a legal adviser to the Dutch Consulate.

The birth of her son, Hughie, approximately a year after her arrival in Canada terminated her wage work. She continued her active interest in voluntary bodies, however, always with an eye to greater public activity once she was free of early child-care responsibilities. From 1926 to 1929, for example, she served on the Point Grey Town Planning Commission,[12] aware, perhaps, that such work would train her for larger community and social planning.

The opportunity to engage in larger community planning and more visible public activity arose during the second decade of Steeves' life in Canada. The devastation of the depression pushed Steeves into the public arena, in particular, into socialist politics. Her initial response was to help transform the informal left-wing study group to which she belonged into a more formal organization called the League for Social Reconstruction (LSR). Like similar groups forming across the country at the time, the LSR was composed of left-wing and progressive intellectuals and academics interested in a solution to the social and economic chaos of the 1930s. When the CCF was formed a short while later, it was evident, as Steeves recollected years later, that "it (the CCF) was the answer."[13] To prepare for affiliation, in 1932, the LSR transformed itself into the Reconstruction Party (RP). "Its platform was mildly socialist, but avoided the rigid Marxian terms of the Socialist Party."[14]

In 1933, the RP affiliated with the Socialist Party of Canada (SPC). Later that year, the RP further expanded its base through amalgamation with a loosely knit group of left-wing reform clubs collectively called the CCF Clubs. Together they formed the Associated CCF Clubs of British Columbia. Finally, in 1935, almost two years after affiliation, the Associated CCF Clubs and the SPC of British Columbia merged to become the British Columbia section of the CCF, a full-fledged member of the federal party.

As key contributor to the organization of the RP and to its affiliation with the SPC, Steeves, along with two other RP colleagues, Mildred Ousterhout and Frank MacKenzie, was invited to represent her group's interests at the first national convention in Regina in 1933. Her experience there was inspiring. From that point, there was no turning back. Challenged to help create a strong and viable third-party alternative for British Columbia and Canada's citizens, she returned to Vancouver convinced, as Ousterhout remembered, that "we were going to bring about great changes in our time."[15] Before long, she ran for provincial office and in a 1934 North Vancouver by-election, on a CCF slate, she was elected to the British Columbia Legislative Assembly.

In the provincial House, Steeves was an outspoken politician, respected and, to some extent, feared. As a socialist, she had no tolerance for class privilege. As a strong, fiercely independent woman she also had little time for discrimination on the basis of her sex. Evidence of either met with her wrath, and as Bruce Hutchison of the *Vancouver Sun* noted in his assessment of Steeves' first speech, her anger was not easily dismissed:

> Mrs. Steeves dispelled the boredom which threatens the house with a flash of wit, a certain feminine charm, a penetrating satire, sharp as a razor and a burst of indignation such as we have seldom heard ... What Mrs. Steeves said was a well-bred sneer at everything, a cry from the depths, for make no mistake about the sincerity of her protests, the bitterness of her hate.[16]

Most observers of Steeves' years in government and office remember her love for the platform – her passion for a stage to express her views and for an audience to absorb them. Many similarly often recall the sharp voice, at times filled with venom, which could easily intimidate those she challenged. Her friends and colleagues who knew her best, however, also remember her well-planned legislative contributions, the two most outstanding being her instrumental role in the introduction of housing co-operatives and credit union legislation. In 1937, for example, she introduced the first Credit Union Act, inspiring Harold Winch, the CCF's provincial leader, to call Steeves the "Mother of Credit Unions."[17] Nor can these contemporaries forget her fight for better employment, education, and social welfare or her ceaseless championing of women's rights. One of her favourite bills for this period in fact called for the inclusion of domestic servants, "the most exploited class of workers," in minimum wage laws.[18] She clearly had come a long way from the uppity war bride who first greeted Canadian shores.

Steeves' legislative activities were not restricted to home-based ills. She also shared her knowledge of and concern over international issues with the government and members of the House. Well-versed in international law and economics, she excelled when she addressed these matters. Yet her "radical" opinions and what, to many, were shocking proposals on foreign policy also roused the greatest opposition. Though Steeves could champion a fairly moderate approach to domestic issues, she largely rejected compromise on international matters. She could accept the need for immediate domestic reform, but to co-operate with capitalist parties on international policies would be to deny fundamental socialist principles. While others increasingly compromised, she steadily abandoned the Fabian socialism that inspired her early plunge into politics. As Jessie Mendels, CCF caucus secretary in the 1940s, aptly concluded, "with Gretchen it was a constant radicalization of her ideas."[19] Together with her colleague and close friend, Colin Cameron, Steeves emerged as the intellectual leader of the British Columbia CCF's left. Steeves' impatience with those adopting a more moderate stance was particularly evident in 1939 when, in the Legislative Assembly, she and Cameron lashed out at all those supporting Canada's participation in World War II, including her own party. It was not only the aggressor nations who were the enemy, she argued, but those who refused to abandon capitalist production practices and exploitive profit motives. To members of the House, caught in the fervour of a war to save democracy, her words were treasonous. In fact, according to Harold Winch, CCF House leader, she and Cameron came to within a hair of being charged with treason.

Nor did members of her party welcome her remarks. Some considered them treasonous, if not to the country, then certainly to the party. Grace MacInnis was among these critics and had this not uncommon reaction: "I believe that while Mrs. Steeves' speech was pleasing to many members of the CCF, it did considerable damage to our cause both within and outside the movement."[20]

In the interests of party unity, Steeves refrained from further public pronouncements on the war. Her co-operation, coupled with the otherwise high level of respect she had previously won from both provincial and federal members, eased somewhat the tension and division that had erupted. This awkward incident, however, marked the beginning of an uneasy relationship between Steeves and those who, like Grace MacInnis, held more moderate views.

The Liberal-Conservative coalition opposing the CCF in the 1945 provincial election defeated many CCF MLAs. Gretchen Steeves was among them. She never again sat in the legislature nor, with the exception of a year's membership on the Vancouver Parks Board, did she ever manage to sit in civic or national government. But her electoral setbacks did not weaken her commitment to socialist causes or the CCF. Refusing to retire, she turned her energy and attention to internal organizational work. She served, for instance, on the B.C. CCF's provincial council as vice-president in 1949 and president in 1950, sat on the national council, and devoted considerable amounts of time and attention to the editorship of the *CCF News*.

Within the narrower, yet still significant, arena of internal party politics, Steeves seized all opportunities to move party policy and practice in a leftward direction. To meet the demands of common people, the party needed forthright socialist policies. Her editorials frequently criticized doctrinal moderation while her public addresses barely hid the contempt she felt for those advancing gradualist policies. For, in Steeves' view, the CCF was becoming complacent when it needed to be stronger than ever. A letter written in October, 1955, clearly illustrates her deepening disillusionment. She wrote in part,

Did you hear on Saturday a week ago the play about Joe Hill, the IWW leader on CBC Focus . . . it was a shattering performance. I couldn't help weeping, thinking of the sacrificial and inspiring lives of the old working class leaders compared to our present stultification and complacence.[21]

Despite her growing frustration with party policy and stands, Steeves did not abandon ship. She continued to take an active role in the party until and after the CCF's transformation into the New Democratic Party in 1961. Until her death in 1978, at eighty-seven years of age, she appears to have retained a touch of optimism that democracy and peace would some day triumph.

The slow process of intellectual discovery Steeves underwent throughout the 1930s, 1940s, and 1950s deepened her commitment to socialism. It also helped her to discover the working class. Her support of workers, in fact, appears to have taken precedence over women's rights, the cause that initially attracted her to socialism. She did not, however, abandon feminist causes. Though her attention to class inequities overshadowed her attention to sexual discrimination, her legislative contribution, public addresses, and work within women's groups suggest that feminism found a significant place in her personal and public quest for a new social order.

Among the more straightforward illustrations of Steeves' commitment to women's emancipation were the many bills and resolutions she forwarded in the provincial legislature. She consistently championed such causes as access to birth control, adequate child-care support and facilities, equal pay for equal work, and fair employment practices.[22] She stressed changes especially beneficial to working-class women but also spoke as a determined feminist insisting on women's fundamental right to full equality. During one talk to the Vancouver Business and Professional Women's Club she argued that "Women have the same physical, mental, and spiritual desires as men and demand to be freed from the ancient taboos and superstitions being used against them. Among other things they are demanding ... to undertake any kind of work according to their ability."[23]

Of course, women's ability to undertake "any kind of work" was not simply a matter of social recognition of their skills. Ending her speech with "I doubt whether, logically speaking, the capitalist system can give women the opportunity they desire,"[24] she agreed with generations of socialist feminists that the liberation of women necessitated the restructuring of society. Socialism, by redistributing wealth and ensuring fair and equal economic opportunities for both men and women, would ensure economic independence and thus freedom from stifling dependence on men. "No longer would women's actions be governed by economic necessity."[25] It was thus crucial that women assist men to solve the social question.

Attitudinal changes naturally went hand in hand with practical steps to sexual equality. Without major ideological shifts, the introduction of socialist measures would hardly free women from second-class citizenship. "Women of today," Steeves posited, "[are] not only wage slaves but in a measure, slaves of men as well ... enslaved on all sides by social as well as economic conditions."[26] Women, therefore, had to challenge century-long myths and assumptions about the feminine mystique. "It is up to women if they want their future freedom – that emancipation which they have not – to make up their minds to solve the problem."[27]

Steeves' mind, of course, had long been made up. From young adulthood to senior citizenship, she individually and collectively challenged sexual stereotypes and discrimination. However, she found individual challenge to sexual injustice considerably easier than co-operative feminism. Although planting both feet in a number of women's organizations, with few exceptions she failed to develop strong intellectual or emotional ties with the middle-class women these groups housed. In short, she never felt at home in women's organizations.

This hesitant sisterhood stemmed in part from her strong identification with socialists wanting to advance the larger socialist goal. But it was also the intellectually superior woman or, in contemporary terms, the "Queen Bee," who found whole-hearted participation in the middle-class women's movement difficult. The comparatively narrow, inexperienced, and maternal views of many of its representatives then, endlessly, at times understandably, frustrated and irritated the intellectually advanced, sophisticated, and relatively undomestic politician.

Having made her own way to the top of the ladder, Steeves was unable to recognize the discrimination that made it difficult for many middle-class women to climb even the first few rungs[28] and she thus held serious reservations about her own sex. Her commitment to feminist causes was consequently circumscribed by an inability to identify with, or relate to, the majority of women she encountered. In fact, she never really lost her youthful disdain for women who lacked her sophistication and worldly experience. Her loyalty to the CCF and socialist causes was predictably deeper than that to a movement composed of women with whom she felt few intellectual and emotional bonds. The "peacock" of the British Columbia legislature was, first and foremost, a dynamic and confident spokeswoman for the working class. Her feminist identity, though significant, was pale beside her socialist one.

Socialism also came first for the "guinea hen" of the British Columbia legislature. Like the "peacock," she forged new paths for women, advanced women's rights, and assisted feminist campaigns. But her political activities and choices, to an even greater extent perhaps, reflected a preference for socialist fellowship and goals and a flight from a really profound identification with women's groups and women's causes. Grace Winona MacInnis's active political life, like that of Steeves', began during the depression with the birth of the CCF. While first finding formal expression during the 1930s, it was perhaps inevitable. Born on July 25, 1905, to James Shaver and Lucy Woodsworth, she spent the first twelve years of her life in North Winnipeg, a community that awakened her to the difficult lives of the city's unemployed and underemployed. She also found inspiration in the tireless assistance and support her parents gave to the otherwise forgotten poor who gathered at her father's Methodist All Peoples' Mission. Yet, throughout her high school, normal school, and university years, MacInnis shied away from really active political involvement. She concentrated instead on her primary goal at the time: the successful completion of her studies. MacInnis believed that if she divided her energies among several activities she would excel in none. If she was to give her all, choices had to be made!

When the eldest Woodsworth child finally did immerse herself in political life in 1932, it was with whole-hearted enthusiasm and single-minded drive. Her attention to the party and cause was undivided. At first she worked for her father in Ottawa, behind the scenes. She gradually assumed duties and responsibilities for the entire federal CCF caucus and before long stepped into front-line activity. According to MacInnis, her marriage in 1933 to Angus

MacInnis, popular MP from Vancouver South, accounted for this rapid move into the foreground and onto the speaker's podium.[29] Her natural talent, quick mind, and obvious compassion, however, ensured her presence there for many years to come.

MacInnis's first opportunity to speak came during a speaking tour she and her husband, of four days, made to promote the CCF in 1933. Her initiation was very thorough. During an arduous whistle-stop train journey from Ottawa to the Pacific, the Mac-Innises greeted forty-five different audiences in as many days. She had not originally intended to speak. When pressed to do so by members anxious to hear the daughter of the CCF's founder and "prophet," she was "scared to death and reluctant."[30] With Angus's encouragement, however, she ventured forth to afternoon meetings on her own and evening meetings in company with her spouse.

Afternoon gatherings, intended for housewives, were for Mac-Innis both informative and enjoyable. Her recollections of this first trip, however, dwell more on the mixed evenings. Their exchange of ideas, controversy, and debate finally held the greater appeal. This response foreshadowed her consistently stronger identification with mixed rather than predominantly female groups.

Since Vancouver was to be the MacInnis headquarters for at least half of the years Angus held federal office, MacInnis wasted little time in familiarizing herself with B.C.'s policy and concerns. It was soon clear that Angus's wife and J.S.'s daughter had, in her own right, much to offer the young CCF. Persistent requests to run for office followed. She did not consent, however, until almost a decade after she first entered the political realm. Finally, in the fall of 1941, she accepted the CCF nomination for Vancouver-Kingsway and shortly thereafter was elected to the British Columbia legislature, there joining Steeves and another female CCF MLA, Laura Jamieson.

Throughout her three-year term, which, as with Steeves and Jamieson, ended at the hands of the notorious Liberal-Conservative coalition of 1945, MacInnis concentrated on many of the same issues addressed by her two colleagues. Her ideas on socialist economics, human rights, living conditions, especially housing and nutrition, and women's rights joined theirs, echoing through the halls of the legislature.[31] Like her older CCF sisters, she also made clear her stand on international issues. There were, however, differences of opinion between MacInnis and Steeves. In fact, their clash over foreign policy brought to the fore different approaches to the process of political and social change, and as suggested earlier, ultimately placed them on opposite wings within the CCF. In turn, their considerable influence within each camp made them major antagonists in the battle. Needless to say, early intimacy between MacInnis and Steeves was destroyed in the process.[32]

MacInnis addressed, in her first speech of January, 1942, the issue that was perhaps the greatest, although not the single, source of controversy within the party and between MacInnis and Steeves: Canada's participation in international conflict. She emphasized the building of civilian morale through adequate social services, rather than through military and imperial affairs. Nonetheless, she did endorse Canada's involvement in World War II, arguing that Canadians were fighting the war so that democracy might be born.

To those who complained that her stance, like that of the National Council, fell short of the teachings of its leader, she replied:

> This is not a black and white world where we can say "this is so or that is right." It is a grey world. We can follow the teachings of those who have gone before us but we can change our own beliefs as we see them, if we are true to our own thinking in 1942.[33]

MacInnis's call for flexible thinking illuminated two significant characteristics of her political personality and socialist goals. This was her very pragmatic approach to CCF policy and her profound commitment to the survival and success of the party.

In Steeves' eyes, this pragmatism represented a fatal compromise with liberal thinking. Aware of her opponent's influence on policy, she saw MacInnis's endorsement of flexibility and gradualism as a threat to the realization of principles laid down in the Regina Manifesto. In turn, for MacInnis, Steeves' position reflected an "uncritical acceptance of Marxism."[34] With Steeves, she strongly objected to capitalist economics and values, arguing in 1939, for example, that these were responsible for "this story of human misery, degradation and waste,"[35] but like her father and husband, she believed that, given the conservative nature of the Canadian worker and general public, gradualism or evolutionary socialism was the only realistic route to the co-operative commonwealth.[36] Social-democratic countries such as those in Scandinavia were on the right track. Their pragmatic acceptance of a mixed economy prepared their citizens for the eventual transformation from capitalism to socialism. Thus, when Steeves editorialized in 1949 that the "right wing" was discrediting the spirit of J.S. Woodsworth through its abandonment of the basic principles of the Regina Manifesto, which was in her view "derived from Marxist theories," MacInnis retorted that the fundamental principles of the Manifesto varied considerably from Marxist theory. In particular, she pointed out that the Manifesto's insistence on democratic action directly opposed Marxist theories advocating the overthrow of the existing society. Returning to the response she gave to critics of the CCF's war policy, she argued:

> He or she who would follow the spirit of J.S. Woodsworth must be ready to break with past traditions and past beliefs, no matter how firmly held, when today's conditions call for new methods and new convictions.[37]

She concluded with the words her father spoke a decade earlier: "Is not the fear of breaking old beliefs the most insidious kind of belief? Faith is a confident adventuring into the unknown."[38]

MacInnis's approach to the route to socialism was clearly at odds with that of Steeves. Her strong links with the centre and support from moderates within the British Columbia section of the CCF ensured that her position triumphed. Ironically, while their ideas about the process differed significantly, their vision of the goal was remarkably similar. MacInnis's claim that in addition to economic equality "the central core of socialist philosophy lies in the idea that every human being is entitled to certain rights and is expected to assume certain responsibilities"[39] squared with Steeves' belief that the socialist ideal means more than economic rights: it also means equality of social rights.[40] Particularly striking about these two women is the extent to which, in their strategy, in their rallying of forces to their respective sides, in their indirect correspondence through the media, in short, in their tenacious battle for control, they were alike. They also shared one other characteristic, an understanding of which is critical to a complete portrait of MacInnis. Both were socialist feminists who resisted feminist sisterhood, preferring the fellowship of mixed, socialist circles. MacInnis, like Steeves, was finally more comfortable with class liberation and its socialist advocates than women's emancipation and the feminist champions of that cause.

Throughout her career, MacInnis emulated her older CCF sister by personally defying sex-typed conventions and publicly supporting women's rights, within the legislature, outside it, and within women's groups. Having grown up with parents who, according to MacInnis, did not distinguish between their sons and daughters when assigning household chores, discussing social questions, and encouraging career goals, she generally had little time for sexist attitudes and laws. She was taught independence at an early age particularly by her mother, who in her words "taught that there wasn't anything men could do in the world that women couldn't do if they wanted to."[41] Several speeches in the legislature reflected her strong critique of legal inequalities, especially those that victimized working-class women. Improved working conditions, equal pay for equal work, equal employment opportunities, and play-school co-operatives were among her demands.[42]

MacInnis's personal defiance of sex-ordered norms and her legislative demands reveal clear feminist aspirations. Indeed, writings and speeches that included such statements as "[Under the CCF] women could have just as much opportunity to work as men and receive equal remuneration for equal work"[43] and "only through having full employment can women find equality"[44] placed her squarely in the socialist feminist tradition. There was, however, a significant imbalance between her socialist and feminist aspirations. Unlike Steeves, she completely tied her feminist goals into her socialist ones, believing that one battle – the socialist one – was sufficient for a class- and gender-free society. She never admitted Steeves' sense of superiority over women and claimed respect for women who found it "necessary" to work in autonomous women's groups. But she considered such an approach "less mature" and preferred working in mixed groups.[45] "The first thing any man or woman needs in the line of liberation," MacInnis argued, "is to be liberated from the notion that they are just a man or just a woman ... there is something much better than being either and that's being a full human being."[46]

Underlying this insistence that men and women should be regarded as "people" struggling for the same ends was also a firm conviction that sexual exploitation was just another manifestation of the larger social problem: capitalist exploitation and the values accompanying it. In an article written for a German socialist publication, she cautioned:

> We as socialists know, however, that the differential treatment is not directed at women as such but against the majority of humans, men, women, and children, who could have a higher standard of living if the riches of this land would no longer be invested privately but used for the general welfare of the public. Our objective in the CCF is to convince men and women of the necessity for fundamental social changes.[47]

She clearly blamed capitalism, not patriarchy, for women's oppression. Socialism, then, satisfied both her objectives: equality between the sexes and a classless society. She was unwilling to admit the possibility that a dual battle had to be waged and thus directed almost all her energies within the CCF toward the class battle. Two closely related factors also appear to have reinforced her position.

The first and perhaps most significant explanation was Mac-Innis's very profound identification with and commitment to the CCF. Success for the party, which to her meant the emergence of a co-operative commonwealth, and, more personally, the realization of her father's dream, could only be achieved through the co-operative efforts of both men and women. To admit discrimination and differential treatment on the basis of sex within the CCF or socialist movement would logically demand a recognition that two struggles existed. For a party already in need of unity and support, such potential division both amongst party members and within members' homes was prohibitively expensive. Moreover, the party could little afford the time, energy, and funds a strong commitment to women's rights' issues required.

MacInnis's attitude toward the family offers a final explanation for her apparent unwillingness to recognize socialist vulnerability to sexual stereotyping and discrimination. Her socialism developed as a result of the sense of social responsibility her parents encouraged and lived. Using her own family as a model, she became convinced that the "family was the seedbed of citizenship."[48] Believing in its crucial role in the search for a better world, she was thus reluctant to criticize its sex-ordered and imbalanced power hierarchies. Too, while MacInnis promoted women's ability to succeed in time-honoured male domains, she could not entirely escape prevailing attitudes about women's critical role in the child-rearing process. She agreed that men could and should share in this activity. But she feared the ramifications of major changes to family structures, radical lifestyle alternatives, and institutional child care. The entry of large numbers of women in the political arena, though theoretically appealing, in practice threatened family stability, child welfare, and responsible citizenship.

MacInnis's claim that the "body politic should ideally consist of a working partnership between men and women,"[49] while liberating in intent, was, in practice, deficient. She refused to investigate the gaps between the theory and practice of sexual equality within the CCF. She largely rejected autonomous women's groups designed to facilitate women's assumption of equal partnership. She viewed the nuclear family and women's role in the child-rearing process through fairly conventional eyes. Her approach to the woman question did not match her approach to the social one. She made the class struggle a priority. The clarity of her feminist vision subsequently suffered.

In their strategies and attempts to steer the party in a direction each considered to be the most appropriate and in their approach to the "woman question," the "peacock" and the "guinea hen" were clearly two of a kind. Talented and tenacious, they helped engineer important gains for both workers and women. Personal, political, and party ambitions, however, worked against a whole-hearted campaign for sexual equality. Socialism came first. Their discovery of workers was considerably more profound than that of women. The emancipated womanhood of their dreams was not quite within reach.

8

"Weaving It Together": Life Cycle and the Industrial Experience of Female Cotton Workers in Quebec, 1910-1950

Gail Cuthbert Brandt

Valleyfield, 1908: One morning, at age fifteen, Hermina joins her father, three brothers, and an older sister on their daily journey to work. Their destination is the sprawling industrial complex of the Montreal Cottons Company, located in the heart of the town. There the young Hermina is engaged as a twister, joining together cotton threads, from 7 a.m. until 6 p.m. each day Monday to Friday, and for half a day on Saturdays. At the end of her first two weeks, she receives her pay envelope containing $6.50 for 110 hours of work. At age twenty-six, Hermina leaves the employ of the company to marry and to raise a family that will ultimately include eleven children. She will never return to the mills again.

Valleyfield, 1942: Jeanne's uncle, a loom fixer, persuades the foreman of the weave room at the Montreal Cottons to offer his niece a job. Jeanne is sixteen, and after a brief period as a shuttle threader, she is assigned her own set of looms. She works from 7 a.m. to 6 p.m. Monday to Friday, and at the end of two weeks she receives $32 for 100 hours of work. In 1947, at the age of twenty-one, she marries. From that time, until her final withdrawal from the company's ranks in 1966, her employment pattern is irregular since she quits and resumes work around each of her four pregnancies.

A careful consideration of the working lives of these women, who represent two different generations of Quebec's *travailleuses*, raises some important questions. What do these individuals have in common? How similar were their work experiences? What methodology is most appropriate for capturing the essence of the working woman's industrial situation? It is the underlying premise of this paper that feminist labour history is necessary and desirable, and that its achievement will require writers to emphasize different techniques from those they use when concentrating on male workers. As one feminist historian has pointed out:

> Women are members of families, citizens of different regions, economic producers, just as men are, but their emphasis on these various roles is different. The economic role of men predominates in their lives, but women shift readily from one role to another at different periods in their lives. It is in this that their function is different from men, and it is this which must form the basis for any conceptual framework.[1]

The most effective method for documenting the changes in the various roles women assume, and to relate their impact to women's paid employment, is through the study of the changing life situations of working women. This paper will attempt to show the potential of life-cycle analysis as a principal integrative technique in writing the history of working-class women. The study of age-related patterns helps to cast light not only on the lives of working women for whom there are few alternate historical sources, but also on the dynamics of the complex relationship between women, work, and the family.

What follows, then, is an attempt to use the life cycle as the framework in which to analyse women's role in the Quebec cotton industry. Since this work is but part of an ongoing research project, the conclusions are more tentative than definitive.[2] Much of the material has been extracted from thirty-five lengthy interviews conducted with female cotton workers in Valleyfield, Quebec. The information they provide has been supplemented by federal census data, government reports, archival sources, and newspaper accounts.

I

One of the largest employers of female labour in Quebec in the first half of the twentieth century was the textile industry, and in particular, the cotton industry. The establishment of this industry in the province dates from the early part of the preceding century, but the most significant expansion occurred between 1880 and 1900. Encouraged by the National Policy tariff, manufacturers were attracted to Quebec for it possessed two inexpensive and abundant resources: hydroelectricity and labourers. By 1911, 63 per cent of all Canadian cotton workers were located in Quebec.[3] As Table 1

Table 1
Distribution of the Quebec Cotton Industry Work Force, 1891-1951*

Year	Under 16		Over 16		Total	
	Male	Female	Male	Female	Male	Female
1891	454	335	1,262	1,741	1,716 (45%)	2,076 (55%)
1901	1,123 boys and girls		3,078	2,414		

	10-14		15-24		25-64		65+		Total	
	M.	F.	M.	F.	M.	F.	M.	F.	M.	F.
1911	140	189	1,120	2,212	1,435	578	28	7	2,723 (48%)	2,986 (52%)
1931	63	43	3,191	3,450	4,179	1,324	156	8	7,589 (61%)	4,825 (39%)
1941	10	4	4,155	3,515	7,692	2,409	214	4	12,071 (67%)	5,932 (33%)
1951	17	32	4,381	3,762	8,067	2,257	161	4	12,626 (68%)	6,055 (32%)

*Figures for 1921 are not available since analysis of the work force was provided by occupation rather than by industry.
SOURCES: *Census of Canada*, 1891, vol. 3, Table I, p. 120; 1901, vol. 3, Table II, pp. 34-35; 1911, vol. 3, Table V, pp. 216-17; 1931, vol. 7, Table 56, pp. 696-97; 1941, vol. 7, Table 18, pp. 572, 578; 1951, vol. 4, Table 19, pp. 19-79, 19-89.

indicates, between 1891 and 1951, women constituted a large proportion of the cotton mill workers, although by the latter date it had been substantially reduced.

There are several possible explanations for the replacement of women by men in the industry. First, technological change must be considered. In her early study of women workers in American cotton mills, Edith Abbott cited technological advancements, in the form of new machinery requiring more physical strength to operate, as the principal reason for the diminishing proportion of female workers.[4] This effect appears to have occurred somewhat later in Canada, for as late as 1938 it was reported that "the workers employed on the principal manufacturing machines are not required to furnish any considerable muscular effort, which explains in part, the employment of large numbers of young persons and women in factories."[5] Thus the full impact of the introduction of heavier machinery probably was felt after World War II, as a result of the large-scale modernization of Quebec mills. On the other hand, the Report of the Royal Commission of Enquiry into the Textile Industry did acknowledge that technology was altering employment prospects for women. It pointed out that "the increasing emphasis on finishing processes, such as dyeing and printing, may be factors in increasing the proportion of male workers."[6]

The principal reason for the decreasing proportion of female operatives, however, was economic. Many employers during the 1930s "gave preference to male employees and particularly those with dependants."[7] In their interviews, older women also frequently made reference to the difficulty married women encountered in obtaining or maintaining employment in the mills during the depression.

The increased production demands that resulted from Canadian participation in World War II most certainly effected a reversal in the trend toward a reduction in the female work force in the cotton mills. Unfortunately, the 1941 census figures do not record this change since it occurred subsequently. Beginning in 1942, the federal government campaigned vigorously to recruit women into the labour force. One of the areas where women were needed was textiles, for many male workers had been attracted to the higher-paying jobs in direct war industry. The success of the campaign to enlist women in industry is attested to by the repeated denunciations of this trend by clerical and nationalist groups throughout Quebec.[8] The employment of married women in particular was condemned for it was tantamount to destroying the family, the cornerstone in the fortress of French-Canadian survival. It is therefore interesting to note in Table 2 that, although the proportion of female workers had declined even further by 1951, the percentage of married women had significantly increased.

All of these reasons for the replacement of women by men – technological change, fluctuating labour demands, societal attitudes toward working women – were closely related to another basic factor: the demographic behaviour of female cotton workers. An examination of the life cycle of the female wage-earner is essential to comprehend her participation in the labour force and her industrial experience.

II

For many young women who lived in the textile centre of Valleyfield, located forty-five kilometres southwest of Montreal, adolescence heralded their entry into the Montreal Cotton Company

Table 2
Age and Marital Status of Women Working in the Quebec Cotton Industry, 1931-1951

	Age								
	Under 15	*15-19*	*20-24*	*25-34*	*35-44*	*45-54*	*55-64*	*65*	*Total*
1931	43	1,812	1,638	952	248	93	31	8	4,825
	(.5%)	(37.6%)	(34.0%)	(19.7%)	(5.1%)	(1.9%)	(.6%)	(.2%)	(100%)
1941	4	1,777	1,738	1,597	588	168	56	4	5,932
	(.0%)	(30.0%)	(29.3%)	(26.9%)	(10.0%)	(2.8%)	(.9%)	(.1%)	(100%)
1951	32	2,009	1,753	1,224	637	288	108	4	6,055
	(.5%)	(33.3%)	(29.0%)	(20.2%)	(10.5%)	(4.7%)	(1.7%)	(.0%)	(100%)

	*Marital Status**				
	Single	*Married*	*Widowed*	*Separated/ Divorced*	*Total*
1941	5,158	589	111	74	5,932
	(87%)	(10%)	(2%)	(1%)	(100%)
1951	4,870	1,050	127	9	6,056
	(81%)	(17%)	(2%)	(—)	(100%)

*Marital Status was not indicated in 1931.

SOURCES: *Census of Canada*, 1931, vol. 7, Table 56, pp. 696-97; 1941, vol. 7, Table 18, pp. 578-79; 1951, vol. 4, Table 19, pp. 19-89, 19-90.

mills. The company began operations in Valleyfield in 1875, and by 1900, with over 1,500 employees, it dominated the local economy. For women with little formal education, there were few alternate sources of employment. One woman interviewed put it succinctly: "Il y avait que cela quand on n'avait pas d'instruction, on allait à la manufacture de coton."[9]

From their early teens, at least until marriage, these women would be "au coton."[10] In spite of the existence of provincial factory and school legislation, prior to 1930 it was not unusual for parents to send their daughters into the industry at thirteen and fourteen years of age. After 1930, it was much more rare to find fourteen-year-old girls at the mills, but this change was undoubtedly more the result of the difficulty in finding employment during the depression than of the stricter observance of provincial legislation.

Although there was a slight increase in the starting ages of those women interviewed who entered the industry after 1930, they were still very young. Seventy per cent were between the ages of fifteen and nineteen, and most had ended their education at primary school.

Among the women interviewed, no matter when they began working, the reason for seeking employment at the mill remained constant. Nearly all cited the need to contribute to the family's economy as the primary factor in their becoming employees of the Montreal Cotton Company. Few exercised any personal influence over the decision: it was made for them by their parents. As one woman explained:

> Ce n'est pas moi qui a décidé cela, dans notre temps c'était notre mère qui décide pour nous autres. Une journée ma mère a dit "Demain tu commences à travailler." Quelqu'un m'avait trouvé un ouvrage, alors je suis allée travailler. On avait pas le choix, c'était comme cela pour nous autres.[11]

As in this woman's case, most of the young women who became mill operatives had close relatives or friends already working in the mills. Frequently, it was these individuals who subsequently aided in their adaptation to industrial life. In some cases, familiarity with the mill and with the work the woman would eventually perform was acquired before she was officially hired. Children were often assigned the task of carrying lunch to other members of the family working at the mill, and during the lunch hour they were initiated into the skills of spinning and weaving under the watchful eye of an experienced family member. Consequently, they were able to secure employment more readily and to avoid a prolonged period as lowly paid apprentice or learner.

While family ties facilitated the entry of young women into the cotton industry, they also impeded the development of personal independence. The young woman frequently was placed in a department where another family member could keep her under protective surveillance. Not only did parents decide when and where their daughters could work, they could also influence their subsequent attitudes toward work. One woman recalled, "Je ne me suis jamais plainte, s'il y avait eu des problèmes je serais demeurée ici, c'est simple hein! Mon père aurait dit 'Reste donc ici ma petite.' "[12]

Nearly all of the women interviewed stated that they lived at home prior to marriage, and in most cases they handed over their entire earnings to their parents. As one woman vividly recounted,

"On arrivait le midi de notre paie et on plaçait notre salaire dans l'assiette de maman. Notre cachet c'était que l'enveloppe ne soit pas ouverte. Maman ouvrait notre enveloppe et nous donnait parfois le change de notre paie."[13] Almost without exception, this handing over of their salaries to the family economy was considered normal by the women interviewed, at least in their first years of working. By her mid-twenties, if the young worker was still single, in most families she was no longer expected to surrender all her wages, but only a portion to cover her room and board.

In view of their economic importance to the family one would expect parents to encourage their daughters to defer marriage so that the family could benefit from their earnings for as long as possible. Late marriages appear to have been common for female cotton workers in Valleyfield prior to 1940. The median marriage age for women who began working before that date was twenty-five years; for women who began working between 1940 and 1950, it was twenty-one years. It is not surprising that the age of first marriage among cotton workers would decline in the 1940s. A return to prosperity enabled young men to achieve economic security, a prerequisite for establishing their own households at an earlier age; as a result, their brides were younger also. The greater ease that household heads experienced in securing and maintaining employment may also have lessened the family's reliance on the earnings of single daughters.

For women working at the mill before 1930, not only was employment there likely to influence their age at marriage but also their choice of a marriage partner. Sixty per cent of the women interviewed who were working at that time reported that, at the time of their marriage, their husbands were also employed at the Montreal Cotton Company. By contrast, only 44 per cent of the husbands of women who began work in the 1930s and 1940s were so employed. This change may have been due to two factors: an increase in employment opportunities for young men in the community, and more frequent contact between young women and young men outside the place of work. The operation of the first factor is easily documented, for World War II witnessed a significant diversification in the town's industrial base.[14]

Once married, few of the female cotton workers continued to work outside the home. The low proportion of married women generally in the Valleyfield mill prior to World War II was repeatedly mentioned in the interviews. As Table 2 indicates, the proportion of married women in the female work force in the Quebec cotton industry was small as late as 1951. This situation presents a marked contrast with that observed by Tamara Hareven in her study of French-Canadian workers in Manchester, New Hampshire. She found that two-thirds of the women who married continued to work in the mills, and a large proportion worked between pregnancies.[15] One possible explanation for this difference in behaviour between the Valleyfield workers and those in Manchester is a dissimilarity in the availability of labour. According to Hareven, the Amoskeag Cotton Company found it difficult especially before 1920 to obtain a full complement of workers. Therefore the company was forced to tolerate greater flexibility in the individual worker's employment pattern. Married women, if they were skilled spinners or weavers, found it relatively easy to leave and re-enter the work force as dictated by their child-bearing experience. Only one woman among those interviewed in Valleyfield felt this same flexibility existed for the married woman at the Montreal Cotton Company, and she was referring to the late 1940s and early 1950s.

In the 1930s the lessened demand for women workers coincided with an intensification of the campaign against married women working outside the home. The principal arguments of this school of thought were assimilated to a great extent by working-class males. Nearly all of the women interviewed who quit working after their marriages cited societal attitudes toward working wives and mothers and their husbands' opposition to their employment outside the home as the main reasons for their decision. Most men clearly believed that it was their responsibility to provide for the family; for the wife to go out to work was an indicator of their failure to fulfil this basic responsibility. A typical statement of this attitude was provided by one interviewee: "Mon mari m'avait dit 'Tu ne retravailleras plus,' il n'était pas d'accord. En ce temps-là ce n'était pas de mode autant que la femme travaille. Si j'aurais voulu travailler je crois que ça aurait été bien difficile."[16] As Philippe Garigue pointed out in his study of the French-Canadian family, there was a definite link between the father's role as economic provider and his authority within the family. Being the primary or sole wage-earner endowed him with special status and power in his relationship with his wife and children.[17]

Although it is not possible at this time to draw definite conclusions concerning variations in family size among different cohorts of female cotton workers, there do appear to have been some interesting and important changes in their reproductive patterns that will require further analysis. For example, none of the women who married before 1940 practised any form of birth control; however, one-third of those who married after this date did. All utilized the Ogino-Knauss (rhythm) method of contraception. Thus, one might conclude that the 1940s and 1950s were significant decades, for they marked the transition from the two-stage life cycle, characterized by a period of gainful employment prior to marriage and withdrawal from the work force after marriage, to a three-stage cycle. The latter consisted of the first two phases, but the duration of the second phase was markedly reduced since the woman was now having fewer children and having them earlier. As a result, a third phase, which often included a return to work once the children reached a certain age, was discernible by the late 1940s.

This change in life cycle for the Valleyfield workers during the 1940s appears to reflect changes occurring for all female cotton workers in Quebec, and for Quebec women in general. An examination of Table 2 reveals that there was a significant decline between 1941 and 1951 in the percentage of workers aged 25-34 years, and a 40 per cent increase in the proportion of women over the age of forty-five. The first change could be attributed to earlier age at marriage and the second to a return of married women to work. In his study of the participation of married women in the Quebec labour force, Nicolas Zay noted similar trends for all Quebec women, and in particular a striking increase in the participation of women aged 45-64 in the work force.[18]

III

A study of the life cycle of women cotton workers can add significantly to our understanding of their industrial experience. The presence of large numbers of female workers, the vast majority of whom were young and single, was bound to have important consequences. For one thing, it meant that there would be relatively rapid turnover among employees. The result was that the companies regarded all women, regardless of their individual circumstances, as temporary workers and provided no occupational mobility for them. "Promotions" consisted of moving from the rank of cleaner or doffer to that of spinner, or from shuttle threader to weaver. For French-Canadian male workers, mobility was limited but it did exist; for example, weaving was sometimes only a preliminary stage for a man, necessary for him to know if he was to become a loom fixer or a foreman. Most of the women interviewed spent all their working years, in some cases half a century, performing the same tasks day after day.

If the high rate of turnover among female employees created certain difficulties for employers, it also posed problems for unions. It has often been claimed that the youth of women workers made it difficult to organize them since they did not view themselves as permanent members of the work force and therefore sought to improve their lot through marriage rather than through union activity.[19] Given this argument, it is important to examine the participation of female cotton workers in various union movements, their attitudes toward the unions, and to assess what influence changes in the life cycle may have had for women's militancy.

Women figured prominently in the first successful union movement in the cotton industry, the Federation of Textile Workers of Canada. This organization was particularly active between 1906 and 1908, and according to its president, Wilfrid Paquette, women accounted for two-thirds of the members and were among the most active.[20] Women held the position of vice-president in several of the locals, and in Valleyfield they had their own local, No. 7, Les Dames et Demoiselles de Valleyfield.[21]

Throughout the early part of the century, women were also actively involved in industrial disputes in the Quebec cotton industry. An examination of the files of the Royal Commission of 1908 and of the federal Ministry of Labour reveals that several work stoppages directly involved women.[22] In 1900, to give but one example, female spoolers in Valleyfield walked off the job when the foreman began to employ apprentices to perform their work. As a result of their action, the mill was forced to close for two weeks, and the spoolers only returned to work when the manager resolved the dispute in their favour. This strike was known locally as "la grève des jeunes filles."[23]

Female cotton workers were much less conspicuous in subsequent union efforts, at least in Valleyfield. Later unions were the National Catholic Textile Federation and the United Textile Workers of America.[24] The women also appear to have been less militant in terms of their work stoppages after 1920.[25] In the case of the Catholic unions, the anti-feminist attitudes of the principal leaders may have been a factor in reducing female militancy. Throughout the depression, the Canadian and Catholic Confederation of Labour, with which the National Catholic Textile Federation was affiliated, called repeatedly upon the provincial government to restrict the use of female labour and recommended the dismissal of married women.[26] The preamble to a 1939 resolution provides an excellent summary of the CCCL's views on the dangers of female employment:

Ce régime facilite une trop grande émancipation de la jeune fille de telle sorte qu'un bon nombre se dégagent de la tutelle de leurs parents pour aller vivre en toute liberté d'action et souvent de conduite, ce qui entraîne une foule de conséquences graves relativement à la morale. Le Travail Féminin contribue à retarder les mariages, ce qui occuperait ces jeunes filles dans leur foyer respectif, milieu naturel de l'exercice de leurs activités. Ces jeunes filles et femmes remplacent les jeunes gens et les hommes et entretiennent l'ère des bas salaires obligeant les patrons consciencieux à engager une main d'oeuvre féminine pour concurrencer avec les compétiteurs. Et le cercle vicieux recommence. Le travail féminin désorganise le marché de l'emploiement et cet état de chose appelle encore plus de main d'oeuvre féminine.[27]

In the case of the United Textile Workers of America under whose banner Kent Rowley and Madeleine Parent began to organize in 1942, there was no anti-feminist bias evident at an official level. Not only did Parent serve as the secretary-treasurer of the national council from 1946 to 1951, but also during these years female representation at the annual conventions increased.[28] At the local level, the union sought to gain equal treatment of male and female workers; for example, in Valleyfield it proposed the abolition of a difference in benefits paid to male and female workers.[29] In spite of the more favourable attitudes enunciated by the UTWA toward women wage-earners, it appears that women were underrepresented in the Valleyfield local. According to a list dated November, 1944, 26 per cent (19 out of 74) of the signed members were women. Another list from August, 1945, indicated that only 8 per cent (7 out of 88) were women.[30]

Among those interviewees employed between 1930 and 1950, most (20 of 24) were indifferent or even hostile to the textile unions, whether they were Catholic or international. It is beyond the scope of this paper to provide a detailed analysis of all the forces contributing to these attitudes. One of the most striking aspects of the discussion with all the women interviewed was the absence of a sense of having been exploited; an examination of the interplay of subjective and objective factors that resulted in this belief merits its own special treatment. Nevertheless, there is another recurrent theme in the women's comments about unions that relates directly to structural changes occurring in the industry, and these changes must be considered, along with transformations in the life cycle of the workers, in any analysis of the female workers' militancy.

Almost without exception, the interviewees believed that conditions worsened as the years progressed. Each decade witnessed increased demands on the worker's productive capacity as production quotas increased, and the number of employees frequently decreased. Most of the women stated that they felt less oppressed by the factory system in the 1920s and 1930s than they subsequently did. In spite of the often deplorable conditions existing then, there was some time to fraternize with other workers, and consequently there existed a certain camaraderie among the employees. As one woman explained:

On travaillait mais je veux dire il y avait de joie entre nous autres, on ne travaillait pas revolté. Il y avait une fraternité qui régnait parce qu'on ne changeait pas d'employés à tous les jours. On vivait en famille.[31]

With the increased emphasis on speed, particularly in the postwar period, the workers were reduced to mere automata. Another woman recalled:

Quand tu avais ta paie tu étais bien contente, tu vas travailler, tu ne te plaignais pas parce que les premiers temps on travaillait moins fort que quand après ils ont mis le bonus [après la guerre]. Après qu'il y a le bonus là, on travaillait plus fort. Il y avait plus de vitesse, plus de machines.[32]

The UTWA recognized the importance of this problem, as indicated by the following comments of their research officer:

This question of "speed-up" is particularly acute at this period in the larger textile mills where the companies are attempting to maintain the higher level attained during the war, while at the same time, cutting down the hours of work and subsequently reducing the worker's weekly take-home pay.[33]

The unions, however, appeared helpless to prevent this practice, and this failure on their part explains the low level of interest in the union movement among some of the Valleyfield women. They accounted for their lack of involvement in union activities thus:

Parce que ça [le syndicat] m'intéressait pas plus que cela. Ce n'était pas assez fort.[34]

J'étais contre le bonus. J'avais pas de confiance dans le syndicat.[35]

Le syndicat n'était pas assez fort.[36]

De ma part les femmes n'avaient pas une grande autorité envers les unions.[37]

Although the unions were able to improve wages and some working conditions, they were unable to attain significant progress in an area deemed extremely important by female operatives: the worker's ability to maintain a reasonable rate of production.

Furthermore, there is no indication that the unions were sensitive to another change occurring in the employment of women in the cotton industry: the increased sexual division of labour and the relegation of women to unskilled positions. According to testimony given before the Royal Commission of 1908, large numbers of women were employed in the carding, spinning, and weaving departments. It was estimated by one witness that between one-half and two-thirds of all weavers at the Hochelaga factory were women.[38] Another document presented to the same commission indicated the importance of female operatives at Dominion Textile's Merchants plant in Montreal: 63.7 per cent of the workers in the card rooms, 66.6 per cent of the frame spinners, 85 per cent of the spoolers, 54 per cent of the slashers, and 50 per cent of the weavers were women.[39]

By 1940 a dramatic shift in employment opportunities for women inside the cotton manufactures had occurred. In 1931, only 39 per cent of the carders, 64 per cent of the spinners, and 46 per cent of the weavers in Quebec were women.[40] In 1941, only 49 per cent of the spinners and 32 per cent of the weavers were women.[41] Increasingly, members of the female work force were performing tasks that required few job skills, as cloth inspectors, folders, pressers, and packers. The result was that women no longer held key jobs that permitted them to occupy a strategic position in the industry and therefore in militant activities, whether these consisted of active involvement in unions or participation in strikes and lockouts.

The reduction in the level of female participation in these activities in Valleyfield would also seem related to changes in the life cycle noted earlier. By the 1940s women were entering the mills later and leaving them earlier to marry than had their mothers and grandmothers. While it was not unusual for women who began working in the pre-1930 period to work for fifteen years before they married, by the 1940s it was much more common for them to work five years before marriage. It would seem logical to assume that the psychology of impermanence would have been substantially reinforced among the latter group and would have impeded the development of a strong interest in the union movement.

IV

This initial attempt to analyse the life cycle of female cotton workers in Quebec between 1910 and 1950 reveals that there were both consistency and change in the prevalent patterns. First it should be noted that although single young women played an important economic role, they experienced little increase in personal independence as a result of their employment outside the home. They remained closely tied to the family for they continued to live at home and to work alongside relatives or family friends. Many of these women gave all their wages to their parents. This lack of personal autonomy characterized women who began working in the 1940s as well as those who began working much earlier in the century.

Prior to World War II, employment in the cotton mills resulted in fairly late marriages among women. This tendency may well have been due to the single woman's significant financial role within the family. Given the fact that a large proportion of the female operatives married men who were also employed at the mills, the age at marriage may also have been influenced by the degree of difficulty the men experienced in setting up their own households. Once married, only a small percentage of the women continued to work.

The 1940s appear to have been a transitional decade that laid the groundwork for a new life cycle consisting of three rather than two phases. Previously there had been a pre-marital employment phase, followed by a period given over to the bearing and rearing of children. After 1940, more of the workers were making an effort to limit the size of their families and were beginning to experience a third stage during which they returned to paid employment.

These changes in life cycle were inextricably linked to women's participation in the cotton industry. As a result of technological change that began on a significant scale in the 1920s and the discriminatory practices against female workers in the 1930s, a more distinct sexual division of labour was created. Women were less likely to hold skilled positions than they had in the past. It would appear that they were marrying younger and withdrawing at least temporarily from the work force. The net result was an erosion of the female cotton worker's militancy.

Selected Bibliography: 1980-

In the proliferation of materials in Canadian women's history published since the first *Neglected Majority* appeared in 1977, there is great variety. While Canadian production is marked by a noticeable lack of monographs, the periodical literature displays a range in quality that is typical of historical writing everywhere. Students of the subject will do well to read scholarly as well as more popular works critically and be aware that the contrast often drawn between them can be misleading. It is a mistake to treat the so-called academic study as gospel; nor are all studies intended for non-academic markets completely lacking in historical sophistication or insight. Caution on the part of the reader is called for in both cases. Readers should also note that not all studies containing the word "women" in the title are actually about women and that many on supposedly gender-neutral topics may have much to say about women. For example, articles on the family or education may contain insights or information of great interest to the historian of women. The materials itemized below, although by no means a definitive list, were selected with these points in mind. In the listing, we have favoured more substantial studies over research reports and very brief essays. We have excluded all but the most useful of the materials that appeared before the publication in 1980 of *True Daughters of the North*, the annotated bibliography by Beth Light and Veronica Strong-Boag, the first book students in Canadian women's history should turn to when searching for bibliographical information. In all categories we have listed books first and then articles and shorter studies.

Historiographical and Bibliographical Studies

In addition to the Light/Strong-Boag bibliography, interesting historiographical analyses and guides to the literature may be found in article form as well as in most of the essay and documentary collections. Students of women's history should also search the following periodicals for articles and bibliography: *Atlantis*, *Canadian Women's Studies*, *Canadian Historical Review*, *Histoire sociale/Social History*, *Labour/Le Travail*, *Resources for Feminist Research*, and *Revue d'histoire de l'Amérique française*, as well as regional history journals such as *Acadiensis*, *Ontario History*, and *B.C. Studies*.

Light, Beth, and Veronica Strong-Boag. *True Daughters of the North. Canadian Women's History: An Annotated Bibliography*. Toronto: OISE Press, 1980.

Cohen, Yolande. *Les thèses québécoises sur les femmes*. Québec: Institut québécois de recherche sur la culture, 1983.

Cohen, Yolande. "L'histoire des femmes au Québec 1900-1950," *Recherches sociographiques*, 21, 3 (September-December, 1980), 339-45.

Cohen, Yolande. "La Recherche universitaire sur les femmes au Québec, 1929-1980," *Resources for Feminist Research*, 10, 4 (December 1981-January 1982), 5-24.

Conrad, Margaret. "The Re-Birth of Canada's Past: A Decade of Women's History," *Acadiensis*, 12 (Spring, 1983), 140-62.

Pierson, Ruth. "Women's History: The State of the Art in Atlantic Canada," *Acadiensis*, 7 (Autumn, 1977), 121-31.

Silverman, Elaine Leslau. "Writing Canadian Women's History, 1970-1982: An Historiographical Analysis," *Canadian Historical Review*, 63, 4 (December, 1982), 513-33.

Strong-Boag, Veronica. "Mapping Women's Studies in Canada: Some Signposts," *Journal of Educational Thought*, 17, 2 (August, 1983), 94-111.

Strong-Boag, Veronica. "Raising Clio's Consciousness: Women's History and Archives in Canada," *Archivaria*, 6 (Summer, 1978), 70-82.

Trofimenkoff, Susan Mann. "Nationalism, Feminism and Canadian Intellectual History," *Canadian Literature*, 83 (Winter, 1979), 7-20.

Van Kirk, Sylvia, ed. "Canadian Women's History: Teaching and Research," *Resources for Feminist Research*, 7 (July, 1979), 5-71.

Documentary Studies

Here we list book-length studies only but call attention to the fact that *Atlantis* frequently publishes documents of great interest to historians in its "archives" section, as does *The Beaver*. Researchers looking for primary source material on particular aspects of Canadian women's history should also be aware of the existence of guides to archival holdings and the possibility of requesting copies of particular documents by mail or obtaining microfilm on interlibrary loan. A number of archival guides have been published in *Resources for Feminist Research*; the Women's History Committee of the Canadian Historical Association has sponsored the creation of others; and several archives have published their own.

Binnie-Clark, Georgina. *Wheat and Woman*. Introduction by Susan Jackel. Toronto: University of Toronto Press, 1979.

Blom, Margaret Howard, and Thomas Blom, eds. *Canada Home: Juliana Horatia Ewing's Fredericton Letters, 1867-1869*. Vancouver: University of British Columbia Press, 1983.

Coulter, John, ed. *Prelude to a Marriage: Letters and Diaries of John Coulter and Olive Clare Primrose*. Montreal: Oberon Press, 1979.

Gillett, Margaret, and K. Sibbald, eds. *A Fair Shake: Autobiographical Essays by McGill Women*. Montreal: Eden Press, 1984.

Groarke, Charlotte. *Letters from Doug*. Winnipeg: Queenston House, 1983.

Hayden, Michael, ed. *So Much To Do, So Little Time: The Writings of Hilda Neatby*. Vancouver: University of British Columbia Press, 1983.

Hopkins, Monica. *Letters from a Lady Rancher*. Calgary: Glenbow Museum, 1982.

Hubbard, Mrs. L. *A Woman's Way Through Unknown Labrador*. St. John's: Breakwater Books, 1981.

Jackel, Susan, ed. *A Flannel Shirt and Liberty: Emigrant British Gentlewomen in the Canadian West 1880-1914*. Vancouver: University of British Columbia Press, 1982.

Light, Beth, and Joy Parr, eds. *Canadian Women on the Move, 1867-1920*. Toronto: New Hogtown Press and OISE Press, 1983.

Light, Beth, and Alison Prentice, eds. *Pioneer and Gentlewomen of British North America*. Toronto: New Hogtown Press, 1980.

Mitchell, Elizabeth B. *In Western Canada Before the War*. Introduction by Susan Jackel. Saskatoon: Western Producer Prairie Books, 1981.

Morton, W.L., with Vera Fast, ed. *God's Galloping Girl: The Peace*

River Diaries of Monica Storrs, 1929-1931. Vancouver: University of British Columbia Press, 1979.

Salverson, Laura. *Confessions of an Immigrant's Daughter*. Toronto: University of Toronto Press, 1981.

Smith, Elizabeth. *A Woman with a Purpose: The Diaries of Elizabeth Smith, 1872-1884*. Introduction by V. Strong-Boag. Toronto: University of Toronto Press, 1980.

Tausky, Thomas E., ed. *Sara Jeanette Duncan: Selected Journalism*. Ottawa: Tecumseh Press, 1978.

Biographies

We list book-length studies only. Booklets for school-aged readers, such as the Fitzhenry and Whiteside series, and biographical collections also frequently contain much of interest, as do articles on individual women or groups of women. Look for the latter under "Topical Studies" below.

Blackman, Margaret B. *During My Time: Florence Edensaw Davidson, a Haida Woman*. Vancouver: Douglas and MacIntyre/Seattle: University of Washington Press, 1982.

Campbell, Marjorie Wilkins. *The Silent Song of Mary Eleanor*. Saskatoon: Western Producer Prairie Books, 1983.

Doyle, James. *Annie Howells and Achille Frechette*. Toronto: University of Toronto Press, 1979.

Duncan, Helen. *Kate Rice, Prospector*. Toronto: Simon and Pierre, 1983.

Reynolds, Louise. *Agnes: The Life of Lady Macdonald*. Toronto: Samuel-Stevens, 1979.

MacGill, Elsie G. *My Mother the Judge*. Introduction by Naomi Black. Toronto: Peter Martin, 1981.

McMullen, Lorraine. *An Odd Attempt in a Woman: The Literary Life of Frances Brooke*. Vancouver: University of British Columbia Press, 1983.

Savage, Candace. *Our Nell. A Scrapbook Biography of Nellie L. McClung*. Saskatoon: Western Producer Prairie Books, 1980.

Tippett, Maria. *Emily Carr*. Toronto: Oxford University Press, 1979.

General Studies and Essay Collections

Acton, Janice, *et al.*, eds. *Women at Work: Ontario 1850-1920*. Toronto: Canadian Women's Educational Press, 1974.

Le Collectif Clio. *L'Histoire des femmes au Québec depuis quatre siècles*. Montréal: Les Quinze, 1982.

Hammerton, A.J. *English Gentlewomen: Genteel Poverty and Female Emigration 1830-1914*. London: Croom Helm, 1978.

Kealey, Linda, ed. *A Not Unreasonable Claim: Women and Reform in Canada 1880s-1920s*. Toronto: Canadian Women's Educational Press, 1979.

Latham, Barbara, and Cathy Kess. *In Her Own Right: Selected Essays on Women's History in B.C.* Victoria: Camosun College, 1980.

Latham, Barbara, and Roberta Pazdro, eds. *Not Just Pin Money: Selected Essays on the History of Women's Work in British Columbia*. Victoria: Camosun College, 1984.

Lavigne, Marie, and Yolande Pinard, eds. *Les Femmes dans la Société Québécoise: Aspects historiques*. Montréal: Boréal Express, 1977.

Lavigne, Marie, and Yolande Pinard, eds. *Travailleuses et féministes: Aspects historiques*. Montréal: Boréal Express, 1983.

Silverman, Elaine Leslau. *Last Best West: Women on the Alberta Frontier, 1880-1930*. Montreal: Eden Press, 1984.

Trofimenkoff, Susan Mann, and Alison Prentice, eds. *The Neglected Majority: Essays in Canadian Women's History*. Toronto: McClelland and Stewart, 1977.

Topical Studies

By grouping studies topically we run the risk of oversimplifying; many of the works listed below belong under more than one heading and the choice of categories itself is problematic. We do it nevertheless to alert readers to the major areas that have recently interested writers of Canadian women's history and to assist searchers with particular interests or questions in mind. The listings should be taken as suggestive rather than complete or definitive.

Politics and Organizations

Bacchi, Carol Lee. *Liberation Deferred? The Ideas of the English-Canadian Suffragists, 1877-1918*. Toronto: University of Toronto Press, 1982.

Cohen, Yolande, ed. *Femmes et politique*. Montréal: Le Jour, 1981.

Strong-Boag, Veronica. *The Parliament of Women: The National Council of Women of Canada, 1893-1929.* History Division Paper no. 18. Ottawa: National Museums of Canada, 1976.

Baskevin, Sylvia. "Social Change and Political Partisanship, The Development of Women's Attitudes in Quebec, 1965-1979," *Comparative Political Studies*, 16, 2 (July, 1983), 147-72.

Beeby, Dean. "Women in the Ontario C.C.F. 1940-1950," *Ontario History*, 74, 4 (December, 1982), 258-83.

Black, Jerome H., and Nancy E. McGlen. "Male-Female Political Involvement Differentials in Canada, 1965-1974," *Canadian Journal of Political Science*, 12, 3 (September, 1979), 471-97.

Brandt, Gail Cuthbert. " 'Pigeon-Holed and Forgotten': The Work of the Subcommittee on the Post-War Problems of Women, 1943," *Histoire sociale/Social History*, 15, 29 (May, 1982), 239-59.

Buckley, Suzann. "British Female Emigration and Imperial Development: Experiments in Canada, 1885-1931," *Hecate*, 3, 2 (July, 1977), 26-40.

Crowley, Terry. "Ada Mary Brown Courtice: Pacifist, Feminist and Educational Reformer in Early Twentieth Century Canada," *Studies in History and Politics*, 1, 1 (Fall, 1980), 76-114.

Desilets, Andrée. "Un élan missionnaire à Gaspé: Les Soeurs Missionnaires du Christ-Roi (1928-1972)," Canadian Catholic Historical Association, *Sessions d'études*, 46 (1979), 65-85.

Dumont-Johnson, Micheline. "Les communautés religieuses et la condition féminine," *Recherches sociographiques*, 9, 1 (janvier-avril, 1978), 79-102.

Jean, Michele. "Histoire des luttes féministes au Québec," *Possibles*, 4, 1 (Autumn, 1979), 17-32.

Kealey, Linda. "Canadian Socialism and the Woman Question, 1900-1914," *Labour/Le Travail*, 13 (Spring, 1984), 77-100.

Lauer, Bernarda. "Russian Germans and the Ursulines of Prelate, Sask., 1919-1934," Canadian Catholic Historical Association, *Study Sessions*, 46 (1979), 83-98.

Manley, John. "Women and the Left in the 1930s: The Case of the Toronto C.C.F. Women's Joint Committee," *Atlantis*, 5, 2 (Spring, 1980), 100-19.

Marchildon, Rudy G. "The 'Persons' Controversy: The Legal Aspects of the Fight for Women Senators," *Atlantis*, 6, 2 (Spring, 1981), 99-113.

Mitchinson, W. "The Women's Christian Temperance Union: A

Study in Organization," *International Journal of Women's Studies*, 4, 2 (1981), 143-56.

Mitchinson, Wendy. "The YWCA and Reform in the Nineteenth Century," *Histoire sociale/Social History*, 12, 24 (November, 1979), 368-84.

Morris, Cerise. " 'Determination and Thoroughness': The Movement for a Royal Commission on the Status of Women in Canada," *Atlantis*, 5, 2 (Spring, 1980), 1-21.

O'Gallagher, Marianna. "The Sisters of Charity of Halifax – The Early and Middle Years," Canadian Catholic Historical Association, *Study Sessions*, 47 (1980), 57-68.

Roberts, Barbara. "Sex, Politics and Religion: Controversies in Female Immigration Reform Work in Montreal, 1881-1919," *Atlantis*, 6, 1 (Autumn, 1980), 25-38.

Rooke, Patricia T., and R.L. Schnell. "The Rise and Decline of British North American Protestant Orphans' Homes as Woman's Domain, 1850-1930," *Atlantis*, 7, 2 (Spring, 1982), 21-35.

Sheehan, Nancy M. "The WCTU on the Prairies, 1886-1930: An Alberta-Saskatchewan Comparison," *Prairie Forum*, 6, 1 (Spring, 1981), 17-33.

Stoddart, Jennifer. "Quebec's Legal Elite Looks at Women's Rights: The Dorion Commission 1929-1931," in D.H. Flaherty, ed., *Essays in the History of Canadian Law*, vol. I (Toronto: The Osgoode Society, 1981), 323-57.

Stone, Olive M. "Canadian Women as Legal Persons: How Alberta Combined Judicial, Executive and Legislative Powers to Win Full Legal Personality For All Canadian Women," *Alberta Law Review*, 17, 3 (1979), 331-71.

Thomas, John D. "Servants of the Church: Canadian Methodist Deaconess Work, 1890-1926," *Canadian Historical Review*, 65, 3 (September, 1984), 371-95.

Work

Armstrong, Pat, and Hugh Armstrong. *The Double Ghetto: Canadian Women and their Segregated Work*, 2nd ed. Toronto: McClelland and Stewart, 1984.

Acton, Janice, *et al.*, eds. *Women at Work: Ontario 1850-1920*. Toronto: Canadian Women's Educational Press, 1974.

Briskin, Linda, and Lynda Yanz, eds. *Union Sisters: Women in the Labour Movement*. Toronto: Women's Press, 1983.

Johnson, Laura C., and Robert E. Johnson. *The Seam Allowance: Industrial Home Sewing in Canada*. Toronto: Women's Press, 1982.

Latham, Barbara, and Roberta Pazdro, eds. *Not Just Pin Money: Selected Essays on the History of Women's Work in British Columbia*. Victoria: Camosun College, 1984.

Luxton, Meg. *More Than a Labour of Love: Three Generations of Women's Work in the Home*. Toronto: Women's Educational Press, 1980.

Phillips, Paul, and Erin Phillips. *Women and Work: Inequality in the Labour Market*. Toronto: James Lorimer, 1983.

Van Kirk, Sylvia. *"Many Tender Ties": Women in Fur Trade Society in Western Canada, 1700-1850*. Winnipeg: Watson and Dwyer, 1980.

Bedford, Judy. "Prostitution in Calgary, 1905-1914," *Alberta History*, 29, 2 (Spring, 1981), 1-11.

Biggs, C. Lesley. "The Case of the Missing Midwives: A History of Midwifery in Ontario from 1795-1900," *Ontario History*, 75 (March, 1983).

Bird, Patricia. "Hamilton Working Women in the Period of the Great Depression," *Atlantis*, 8, 2 (Spring, 1983), 125-36.

Bradbury, Bettina. "Women and Wage Labour in a Period of Transition: Montreal, 1861-1881," *Histoire sociale/Social History*, 17 (May, 1984), 115-31.

Danylewycz, Marta, Beth Light, and Alison Prentice. "The Evolution of the Sexual Division of Labour in Teaching: A Nineteenth Century Ontario and Quebec Case Study," *Histoire sociale/Social History*, 16, 31 (May, 1983), 81-109.

Danylewycz, Marta, and Alison Prentice. "Teachers, Gender and Bureaucratizing School Systems in Nineteenth Century Montreal and Toronto," *History of Education Quarterly*, 24 (Spring, 1984), 75-100.

Denis, Ann B. "Femmes: ethnie et occupation au Québec et en Ontario, 1913-1917," *Canadian Ethnic Studies*, 13, 1 (1981), 75-90.

Dumont-Johnson, Micheline. "Les garderies au XIXe siècle: Les salles d'asile des Soeurs Grises à Montréal," *Revue d'histoire de l'Amérique française*, 34, 1 (June, 1980), 27-55.

Groulx, Lionel, et Charlotte Poirier. "Les pionnieres en service social: Nouveau métier féminin dans le champ philanthropique," in *Women's Culture: Selected Papers from the Halifax Conference*, CRIAW Papers No. 3 (Ottawa: The Canadian

Research Institute for the Advancement of Women, 1982), 34-46.

Heap, Ruby. "La Ligue de l'enseignement (1902-1904): héritage du passe et nouveaux défis," *Revue d'histoire de l'Amérique française*, 36, 3 (December, 1982), 339-73.

Lacelle, Claudette. "Les domestiques dans les villes canadiennes au XIXe siècle: effectifs et conditions de vie," *Histoire sociale/ Social History*, 15, 29 (May, 1982), 181-207.

Lapointe, Michelle. "Le syndicat catholique des allumetieres de Hull, 1919-1924," *Revue d'histoire de l'Amérique française*, 32, 4 (March, 1979), 603-28.

Lowe, Graham S. "The Administrative Revolution in the Canadian Office: An Overview," in Katherine L.P. Lundy and Barbara D. Warme, eds., *Work in the Canadian Context* (Toronto: Butterworth's, 1981), 153-73.

Lowe, Graham S. "Class, Job and Gender in the Canadian Office," *Labour/Le Travail*, 10 (Autumn, 1982), 11-37.

Lowe, Graham S. "Women, Work and the Office: The Feminization of Clerical Occupations in Canada, 1901-1931," *Canadian Journal of Sociology*, 5, 4 (1980), 361-81.

Pierson, Ruth Roach. "Canadian Women and Canadian Mobilization during the Second World War," *Revue Internationale d'Histoire Militaire*, 51 (1982), 181-207.

Pierson, Ruth. "'Jill Canuck': CWAC of All Trades, But No 'Pistol Packing Momma,'" Canadian Historical Association, *Historical Papers* (1978), 106-33.

Ramirez, Bruno. "French Canadian Immigrants in the New England Cotton Industry: A Socioeconomic Profile," *Labour/Le Travail*, 11 (Spring, 1983), 125-42.

Robinson, Gertrude. "The Media and Social Change: 30 Years of Magazine Coverage of Women and Work (1950-1977)," *Atlantis*, 8, 2 (Spring, 1983), 87-112.

Sangster, Joan. "Women and Unions in Canada: A Review of Historical Research," *Resources for Feminist Research*, 10, 2 (July, 1981), 2-6.

Schulz, Pat V. "Day Care in Canada: 1850-1962," in Kathleen Gallagher Ross, *Good Day Care* (Toronto: The Women's Press, 1978), 137-58.

Strong-Boag, Veronica. "Working Women and the State: The Case of Canada, 1889-1945," *Atlantis*, 6, 2 (Spring, 1981), 1-10.

Struthers, James. "A Profession in Crisis: Charlotte Whitton and

Canadian Social Work in the 1930s," *Canadian Historical Review*, 62, 2 (June, 1981), 169-85.

Ideology, Education, and Culture

Cobb, Myrna, and Sher Morgan. *Eight Women Photographers of B.C., 1860-1968*. Victoria: Camosun College, 1979.

Collard, Eileen. *Women's Dress in the 1920's: An Outline of Women's Clothing in Canada During the Roaring Twenties*. Burlington, Ontario: E. Collard, 1981.

Fahmy-Eid, Nadia, and Micheline Dumont, eds. *Maîtresses de maison, maîtresses d'école: Femmes, famille et éducation dans l'histoire du Québec*. Montréal: Boréal Express, 1983.

Gillet, Margaret. *We Walked Very Warily: A History of Women at McGill*. Montreal: Eden Press, 1981.

Reid, John Graham. *Mount Allison University: A History to 1963*. Toronto: University of Toronto Press, 1984.

Séguin, Robert-Lionel. *La sorcellerie au Québec du XVIIe au XIXe siècle*. Montréal: Leméac, 1978.

Thivierge, Nicole. *L'enseignement ménager au Québec 1880-1910*. Québec: Institut québécois de recherche sur la culture, 1982.

Ballstadt, Carl, Michael Peterman, and Elizabeth Hopkins. "'A Glorious Madness': Susanna Moodie and the Spiritualist Movement," *Journal of Canadian Studies*, 17, 4 (Winter, 1982-83), 88-101.

Bland, Sue. "Henrietta the Homemaker and Rosie the Riveter: Images of Women in Advertising 1939-1950," *Atlantis*, 8, 2 (Spring, 1983), 61-86.

Brouwer, Ruth Compton. "The 'Between-Age' Christianity of Agnes Machar," *Canadian Historical Review*, 65 (September, 1984).

Danylewycz, Marta, Nadia Fahmy-Eid, and Nicole Thivierge. "L'enseignement ménager et les 'home economics' au Québec et en Ontario au début du 20e siècle: une analyse comparée," in J. Donald Wilson, ed., *An Imperfect Past: Education and Society in Canadian History* (London: Althouse Press, 1984), 67-119.

Fox, John, and Timothy F. Hartnagel. "Changing Social Roles and Female Crime in Canada: A Time Series Analysis," *Canadian Review of Sociology and Anthropology*, XVI, 1 (1979), 96-104.

Giltrow, Janet. "Painful Experience in a Distant Land: Mrs. Moodie in Canada and Mrs. Trollope in America," *Mosaic*, 14, 2 (Spring, 1981), 131-44.

Indra, Doreen Marie. "The Invisible Mosaic: Women, Ethnicity and the Vancouver Press, 1900-1976," *Canadian Ethnic Studies*, 13, 1 (1981), 63-74.

Labonte, René. "Gabrielle Roy, Journaliste, Au Fil de Ses Reportages (1939-1945)," *Studies in Canadian Literature*, 7, 1 (1982), 90-109.

Matters, Diane L. "Public Welfare Vancouver Style, 1910-1920," *Journal of Canadian Studies*, 14, 1 (Spring, 1979), 3-15.

McConnachie, Kathleen. "Methodology in the Study of Women's History: A Case Study of Helen MacMurchy, M.D.," *Ontario History*, 75 (March, 1983).

Pearl, Jonathan L. "Witchcraft in New France in the Seventeenth Century: The Social Aspects," *Historical Reflections*, 4, 2 (Winter, 1977), 191-206.

Reid, John G. "The Education of Women at Mount Allison, 1854-1914," *Acadiensis*, 12 (Spring, 1983), 3-33.

Rooke, Patricia T., and R.L. Schnell. "'An Idiot's Flowerbed': A Study of Charlotte Whitton's Feminist Thought, 1941-1950," *International Journal of Women's Studies*, 5, 1 (January-February, 1982), 29-46.

Rooke, Patricia T., and R.L. Schnell. "Charlotte Whitton meets 'the Last Best West': The Politics of Child Welfare in Alberta, 1929-1949," *Prairie Forum*, 6, 2 (Fall, 1981), 143-62.

Sheehan, Nancy M. "Temperance, Education and the WCTU in Alberta, 1905-1930," *Journal of Educational Thought*, 14, 2 (August, 1980), 108-24.

Sheehan, Nancy M. "The WCTU and Educational Strategies on the Canadian Prairie," *History of Education Quarterly*, 24 (Spring, 1984), 101-20.

Silverman, Elaine L. "Women and the Victorian Work Ethic on the Alberta Frontier: Prescription and Description," in Howard Palmer and Donald Smith, eds., *The New Provinces: Alberta and Saskatchewan, 1905-1980* (Vancouver: Tantalus Research Limited, 1973), 91-99.

Tavill, A.A. "Early Medical Co-Education and Women's Medical College, Kingston, Ontario 1880-1894," *Historic Kingston*, 30 (January, 1982), 68-89.

Wilson, L.J. "Educational Role of the United Farm Women of Alberta," in David C. Jones, Nancy M. Sheehan, and Robert

A. Stamp, eds., *Shaping the Schools of the Canadian West* (Calgary: Detselig, 1979), 124-35.

Family

Brown, Jennifer S.H. *Strangers in Blood: Fur Trade Company Families in Indian Country*. Vancouver: University of British Columbia Press, 1980.

Parr, Joy, ed. *Childhood and Family in Canadian History*. Toronto: McClelland and Stewart, 1982.

Rooke, Patricia T., and R.L. Schnell, eds. *Studies in Childhood History: A Canadian Perspective*. Calgary: Detselig, 1982.

Angus, Margaret. "A Gentlewoman in Early Kingston," *Historic Kingston*, 24 (1976), 73-85.

Bradbury, Bettina. "The Family Economy and Work in an Industrializing City: Montreal in the 1870s," Canadian Historical Association, *Historical Papers* (1979), 71-96.

Charbonneau, Hubert. "Jeunes femmes et vieux maris: la fécondité des marriages précoces," *Population*, 35, 6 (November-December, 1980), 1101-22.

Collet, Paulette. "Les romancières québécoises des annees 60 face a la maternité," *Atlantis*, 5, 2 (Spring, 1980), 131-41.

Dahlie, Jorgen. "Scandinavian Experiences on the Prairies, 1890-1920: The Frederiksens of Nokomis," in Howard Palmer, ed., *The Settlement of the West* (Calgary: Comprint Publishing Co., 1977), 102-13.

Davis, Dona. "The Family and Social Change in the Newfoundland Outport," *Culture*, 3, 1 (1983), 19-32.

Dumais, Monique. *La mère dans la société québécoise*. CRIAW Papers 5. Ottawa: Canadian Research Institute for the Advancement of Women, 1983.

Gee, Ellen M.T. "Female Marriage Patterns in Canada: Changes and Differentials," *Journal of Comparative Family Studies*, 11, 4 (Autumn, 1980), 457-73.

Gee, Ellen M. Thomas. "Marriage in Nineteenth Century Canada," *Canadian Review of Sociology and Anthropology*, 19, 3 (August, 1982), 311-25.

Kernaghan, Lois D. "A Man and His Mistress: J.F.W. DesBarres and Mary Cannon," *Acadiensis*, 11, 1 (Autumn, 1981), 23-42.

Lewis, Norah L. "Creating the Little Machine: Child Rearing in British Columbia, 1919 to 1939," *B.C. Studies*, 56 (Winter, 1982-1983), 44-60.

Mathieu, Jacques, *et al.* "Les alliances matrimonial exogames dans le gouvernement de Québec, 1700-1760," *Revue d'histoire de l'Amérique française*, 35, 1 (June, 1981), 3-32.

McConnachie, Kathleen. "A Note on Fertility Roles Among Married Women in Toronto, 1871," *Ontario History*, 75 (March, 1983).

Medjuck, Sheva. "Family and Household Composition in the Nineteenth Century: The Case of Moncton, New Brunswick, 1851 to 1871," *Canadian Journal of Sociology*, 4, 3 (Summer, 1979), 275-86.

Snell, James G. "'The White Life for Two': The Defense of Marriage and Sexual Morality in Canada, 1890-1914," *Histoire sociale/Social History*, 16, 31 (May, 1983), 111-28.

Van Kirk, Sylvia. "'What If Mama is an Indian?'" in John E. Foster, ed., *The Developing West* (Edmonton: University of Alberta Press, 1983), 123-36.

Sexuality and Health

Backhouse, Constance. "Involuntary Motherhood: Abortion, Birth Control and the Law in 19th Century Canada," *Windsor Yearbook of Access to Justice*, 3 (1983), 61-130.

Bishop, Mary F. "The Early Birth Controllers of B.C.," *B.C. Studies*, 61 (Spring, 1984), 64-84.

Buckley, Suzann, and Janice Dickin McGinnis. "Venereal Disease and Public Health Reform in Canada," *Canadian Historical Review*, 63, 3 (September, 1982), 337-54.

Dodd, Diane. "The Hamilton Birth Control Clinic of the 1930s," *Ontario History*, 75 (March, 1983), 71-86.

Kennedy, Joan E. "Jane Soley Hamilton, Midwife," *Nova Scotia Historical Review*, 2, 1 (1982), 6-29.

Lenskyi, Helen. "Femininity First: Sport and Physical Education for Ontario Girls, 1890-1930," *Canadian Journal of the History of Sport*, 13, 2 (December, 1982), 4-17.

Lévesque, Andrée. "Mères ou malades: les Québécoises de l'entre-deux-guerres vues par les médicins," *Revue d'histoire de l'Amérique française*, 38, 1 (Summer, 1984), 23-37.

MacDougall, Heather. "Researching Public Health Services in Ontario, 1882-1930," *Archivaria*, 10 (Summer, 1980), 157-72.

McLaren, Angus. "'What Has This to do With Working Class Women?': Birth Control and the Canadian Left, 1900-1939," *Histoire sociale/Social History*, 14, 28 (November, 1981), 435-54.

Mitchinson, Wendy. "A Medical Debate in Nineteenth-Century English Canada: Ovariotomies," *Histoire sociale/Social History*, 17 (May, 1984), 133-47.

Mitchinson, Wendy. "Gynecological Operations on Insane Women: London, Ontario, 1895-1901," *Journal of Social History*, 15, 3 (Spring, 1982), 467-84.

Oppenheimer, Jo. "Childbirth in Ontario: The Transition from Home to Hospital in the Early Twentieth Century," *Ontario History*, 75 (March, 1983), 36-60.

Paradis, Roger. "Henriette, *la capuche*: The Portrait of a Frontier Midwife," *Canadian Folklore*, 3, 2 (1981), 10-26.

Pierre-Deschênes, Claudine. "Santé publique et organisation de la profession médicale au Québec, 1870-1918," *Revue d'histoire de l'Amérique française*, 35, 3 (December, 1981), 355-75.

Pierson, Ruth. "The Double Bind of the Double Standard: VD Control and the CWAC in World War II," *Canadian Historical Review*, 62, 1 (March, 1981), 31-58.

Sutherland, Neil. "Social Policy, Deviant Children, and the Public Health Apparatus in British Columbia between the Wars," *Journal of Educational Thought*, 14, 2 (August, 1980), 80-91.

Ward, W. Peter. "Unwed Motherhood in Nineteenth Century English Canada," *Canadian Historical Association, Historical Papers* (1981), 34-56.

Notes

Prentice and Trofimenkoff, Introduction

1. Susan Mann Trofimenkoff and Alison Prentice, eds., *The Neglected Majority: Essays in Canadian Women's History* (Toronto, 1977). The introduction to this volume draws heavily on the editors' own overviews of women's history: Susan Trofimenkoff's lecture, "An introduction to women's history," given to senior-level undergraduates in history and women's studies at the University of Ottawa and Alison Prentice's paper, "Women's History in Canada: A Project in Process," presented to the Colloquium on Social History organized by the journal *Histoire sociale/Social History* during the sessions of the Learned Societies in Ottawa in June, 1982.
2. See the bibliography in this volume.
3. Susan Mosher Stuard, "The Annales School and Feminist History: Opening Dialogue with the American Stepchild," *Signs*, 7, 1 (Autumn, 1981), pp. 135-43, and, in the same issue (pp. 71-80), the translation of Christine Faure's essay "Absent from History," first published in *Temps Moderne* 410 (septembre, 1980).
4. The recently inaugurated *Women and History* from Haworth Press (1982-   ) is not a standard periodical containing several articles in each issue but rather a monograph series. Each quarterly edition contains a book-length study of a single topic.
5. Carol Bacchi's *Liberation Deferred* (Toronto, 1983) traces the pattern.
6. Numerous articles in the *Canadian Monthly* during the 1870s and in *The Week* in the 1880s raise these issues.
7. Most evident in British Columbia. See the report in the *Globe and Mail*, 26 July 1983.
8. See Pat and Hugh Armstrong, *The Double Ghetto: Canadian Women and Their Segregated Work*, 2nd ed. (Toronto, 1984).
9. See the article by M. Barber in this collection.
10. See the article by G. Cuthbert Brandt in this collection.
11. Meg Luxton, *More than a Labour of Love* (Toronto, 1980).
12. Ruth Schwartz Cowan, *More Work for Mother* (New York, 1983).
13. A quick way into the area is Alison Prentice, "Towards a Feminist History

of Women and Education," in David Jones *et al.*, eds., *Approaches to Educational History* (Winnipeg, 1981), pp. 39-64.

14.   A. Prentice, "The Feminization of Teaching," in Trofimenkoff and Prentice, eds., *The Neglected Majority*, pp. 49-65.

15.   Sylvia Van Kirk, *"Many Tender Ties": Women in Fur Trade Society, 1670-1870* (Winnipeg, [1981]), esp. Ch. 9.

16.   See the article by A. McLaren in this collection.

17.   The article by S. Walsh in this collection just opens the door to this question.

Noel, New France

1.   F.-X. Charlevoix, *History and General Description of New France* (New York, 1900), vol. 23, p. 28.

2.   Cited in R.-L. Séguin, "La Canadienne aux XVIIe et XVIIIe siècles," *Revue d'histoire de l'Amérique français* (hereafter *RHAF*), 13 (mars, 1960), p. 492.

3.   Séguin, "La Canadienne," p. 500.

4.   *Ibid.*

5.   L. Franquet, *Voyages et mémoires sur le Canada* (Montréal, 1974), p. 57, recording a tour in 1752-53.

6.   *Ibid.*, p. 31.

7.   Séguin, "La Canadienne," pp. 492, 505.

8.   G. Fagniez, *La Femme et la société française dans la première moitié du XVIIe siècle* (Paris, 1929), p. 154.

9.   Marcel Trudel, *Montréal, la formation d'une société* (Montréal, 1976), pp. 216-17.

10.   John F. Bosher, "The Family in New France," in Barry Gough, ed., *In Search of the Visible Past* (Waterloo, Ont., 1976), p. 7.

11.   Fagniez, *Femme et société française*, p. 121.

12.   *Ibid.*, pp. 149, 104, 193.

13.   Philippe Ariès, *Centuries of Childhood* (New York, 1962), pp. 392-406.

14.   *Ibid.*, pp. 365-66.

15.   Peter Laslett, "Characteristics of the Western Family Considered over Time," *Journal of Family History*, 2 (Summer, 1977), pp. 89-115.

16.   Richard Vann, "Women in Preindustrial Capitalism," in R. Bridenthal, ed., *Becoming Visible: Women in European History* (Boston, 1977), p. 206.

17.   *Ibid.*, pp. 206-08; Ariès, *Centuries of Childhood*, pp. 397-406.

18.   Fagniez, *Femme et société française*, pp. 122-23, 179.

19.   Vann, "Women in Preindustrial Capitalism," p. 206.

20.   Franquet, *Voyages*, pp. 135, 61.

21.   Séguin, "La Canadienne," p. 499; R. Boyer, *Les Crimes et châtiments au Canada française du XVIIIe au XXe siècle* (Montréal, 1966), p. 391.

22.   Séguin, "La Canadienne," p. 506.

23.   Boyer, *Crimes et châtiments*, p. 351.

24.   *Ibid.*, pp. 344-46.

25. Laslett, "Western Family," p. 95.

26. I. Foulché-Delbosc, "Women of Three Rivers, 1651-1663," in A. Prentice and S. Trofimenkoff, eds., *The Neglected Majority* (Toronto, 1977), p. 26.

27. Bosher ("The Family," p. 3) found the marriage rate in New France to be about three times that of modern-day Quebec.

28. This information is taken from a study of Normandy, which was the birthplace of many of the Canadian colonists. J.M. Gouesse, "La Formation du couple en Basse-Normandie," *XVIIᵉ Siècle*, nos. 102-3 (1974), p. 56.

29. Laslett, "Western Family," p. 106.

30. Fagniez, *Femme et société française*, pp. 99-104, 108, 111, 114-16.

31. Louise Dechêne, *Habitants et marchands de Montréal au XVIIᵉ siècle* (Paris, 1974), p. 393.

32. Fagniez, *Femme et société française*, p. 101; Séguin, "La Canadienne," p. 503; also G. Lanctôt, *Filles de joie ou filles du roi* (Montréal, 1952), pp. 210-13.

33. Cf. Paul Butel, "Comportements familiaux dans le négoce bordelais au XVIIIᵉ siècle," *Annales du Midi*, 88 (1976), pp. 139-57.

34. M.E. Chabot, "Marie Guyart de L'Incarnation, 1599-1672," in M. Innis, ed., *The Clear Spirit* (Toronto, 1966), p. 28.

35. Bosher, "The Family," p. 7; H. Neatby, *Quebec, The Revolutionary Age* (Toronto, 1966), p. 46.

36. Foulché-Delbosc, "Women of Three Rivers," p. 15.

37. Bosher, "The Family," p. 3. I have rounded his figures.

38. Dechêne, *Habitants et marchands*, p. 434; Bosher, "The Family," p. 5.

39. Vann, "Women in Preindustrial Capitalism," p. 205; cf. also Alice Clark, *Working Life of Women in the Seventeenth Century* (London, 1968), Chs. V, VI; and Fagniez, *Femme et société française*, for the scarcity of women's guilds by the seventeenth century.

40. *Ibid.*, pp. 168ff.

41. Y. Zoltvany, "Esquisse de la Coutume de Paris," *RHAF* (décembre, 1971).

42. Foulché-Delbosc, "Women of Three Rivers," p. 19.

43. Neatby, *Quebec*, p. 46.

44. Fagniez, *Femme et société française*, p. 147.

45. Dechêne, *Habitants et marchands*, pp. 423-24.

46. A. Morel, "Réflexions sur la justice criminelle canadienne au 18ᵉ siècle," *RHAF*, 29 (septembre, 1975), pp. 241-53.

47. Lanctôt, *Filles de joie*, p. 219.

48. Boyer, *Crimes et Châtiments*, pp. 128-29.

49. W.J. Eccles, "Social Welfare Measures and Policies in New France," *Congreso Internacional de Americanistas*, IV (1966), Seville, pp. 9-19.

50. J. Bosher, "Government and Private Interests in New France," in J.M. Bumsted, ed., *Canadian History Before Confederation* (Georgetown, Ontario, 1972), p. 122.

51. Bosher, "The Family," pp. 5-7; Fagniez, *Femme et société française*, p. 182.

52. Franquet, *Voyages*, p. 148; cf., also Frégault, *Le XVIIIe siècle canadien* (Montréal, 1968), pp. 292-93.
53. W.J. Eccles, "The Social, Economic and Political Significance of the Military Establishment in New France," *Canadian Historical Review*, LII (March, 1971), pp. 8-10.
54. Franquet, *Voyages*, pp. 129-30. For another, similar trip, see pp. 140-42.
55. Frégault, *Le XVIIIe siècle*, pp. 208-09, 216-21.
56. *Ibid.*, pp. 229-30.
57. Y. Zoltvany, *Philippe de Rigaud de Vaudreuil* (Toronto, 1974), pp. 110, 217.
58. Frégault, *Le XVIIIe siècle*, pp. 228-30.
59. W.J. Eccles, *Frontenac: The Courtier Governor* (Toronto, 1959), p. 29.
60. *Rapport de l'archiviste de la province de Québec*, 1922-23, p. 151.
61. For example, George Rudé, *The Crowd in the French Revolution* (New York, 1959).
62. Superbly described in E.P. Thompson, *The Making of the English Working Class* (London, 1976), Ch. Three.
63. Cited in T. Crowley, "'Thunder Gusts': Popular Disturbances in Early French Canada," *CHA R* (1979), pp. 19-20.
64. Jean Hamelin, "What Middle Class?" *Society and Conquest*, Miquelon, ed. (Toronto, 1977), pp. 109-10); and Dechêne, *Habitants et marchands*, p. 44, who concludes that the largest contingents of male immigrants arriving in seventeenth-century Montreal were *engagés* and soldiers.
65. H. Charbonneau, *Vie et mort de nos ancêtres* (Montréal, 1975), p. 38; A. Burguière, "Le Rituel du mariage en France: Pratiques ecclésiastiques et pratiques populaires, (XVIe-XVIIIe siècle)," *Annales E.S.C.*, 33e année (mai-juin, 1978), p. 640; R. Mousnier, *La famille, l'enfant et l'éducation en France et en Grande-Bretagne du XVIe au XVIIIe siècle* (Paris, 1975); Fagniez, *Femme et société française*, p. 97. Commercial activities, however, also prevailed among the women of Bordeaux, an important port in the Canada trade. *Ibid.*, p. 196.
66. Fagniez, *Femme et société française*, pp. 267, 273-74, 311-12, 360-61.
67. Claude Lessard, "L'Aide financière de l'Eglise de France à l'Eglise naissante du Canada," in Pierre Savard, ed., *Mélanges d'histoire du Canada français offerts au professeur Marcel Trudel* (Ottawa, 1978), p. 175.
68. Fagniez, *Femme et société française*, pp. 311-21.
69. Marcel Trudel, *The Beginnings of New France* (Toronto, 1973), for a gloomy assessment of the neglected colony during this period.
70. G. Brown *et al.*, eds., *Dictionary of Canadian Biography* (hereafter *DCB*) (Toronto, 1966-), vol. 1, p. 118; J. Marshall, ed., *Word from New France* (Toronto, 1967), p. 2.
71. Fagniez, *Femme et société française*, pp. 320-33, 358. Of course, not all *religieuses* were competent as leaders. Madame de la Peltrie, for example, patron of the Ursuline convent, appears to have been a rather unreliable benefactress. Despite her first-hand knowledge of the difficulties under which the Ursulines laboured, her "charity" was quixotic. In 1642, she

suddenly withdrew her support from the Ursulines in order to join the colonists setting off to found Montreal. Later she again held back her funds in favour of a cherished chapel project, even though the Ursulines' lodgings had just burned to the ground.

72. Chabot, "Marie Guyart de l'Incarnation," pp. 27, 37; *DCB*, 1, p. 353; Lessard, "Aide financière," pp. 169-70.

73. *DCB*, 1, pp. 483-87; also Lessard, "Aide financière," p. 175.

74. This is the interpretation given by G. Lanctôt in *Montreal under Maisonneuve* (Toronto, 1969), pp. 20-24, 170.

75. *Ibid.*, p. 188.

76. Lanctôt, *Filles de joie*, p. 81; Trudel, *Montréal*, p. 21. The Hôtel-Dieu de Montréal also sponsored immigrants from 1655 to 1662 (Lanctôt, *Filles de joie*, p. 81.).

77. Trudel, *Montréal*, p. 84.

78. Eccles, "Social Welfare Measures," p. 19; F. Rousseau, "Hôpital et société en Nouvelle-France: l'Hôtel-Dieu de Québec à la fin du XVIIe siècle," *RHAF*, 31 (juin, 1977), p. 47.

79. Mousnier, *La famille l'enfant et l'éducation*, pp. 319-31.

80. Vann, "Women in Preindustrial Capitalism," p. 208.

81. Trudel, *Montréal*, pp. 276, 87; P. Goubert, *The Ancien Régime* (New York, 1974), p. 262.

82. Neatby, *Quebec*, p. 237; French soldiers had a literacy rate of three to four per cent. A. Corvisier, *L'Armée française de la fin du XVIIe siècle ou ministère de Choiseul* (Paris, 1964), p. 862.

83. Fagniez, *Femme et société canadienne*, p. 191.

84. Séguin, "La Canadienne," p. 501, lists nine of these schools in addition to the original one in Montreal.

85. Franquet, *Voyages*, pp. 31-32.

86. According to Lanctôt (*Filles de joie*, pp. 121-30), there were 961. Silvio Dumas counts only 774 (*Les Filles du roi en Nouvelle France* [Québec, 1972], p. 164). Other estimates have ranged between 713 and 857.

87. J.-N. Fauteux, *Essai sur l'industrie au Canada sous le Régime Français* (Québec, 1927), "Introduction."

88. For the record, it now seems fairly well established that the females sent to New France, unlike those sent to the West Indies, were carefully screened, and any of questionable morality were returned by the authorities to France. Lanctôt (*Filles de joie*) and Dumas (*Filles du roi*) agree on this. See also Foulché-Delbosc, "Women of Three Rivers," pp. 22-23.

89. Dechêne finds a majority of *Parisiennes* among the Montréal filles (*Habitants et marchands*, p. 96). Lanctôt states that one-half of the 1634-63 emigrants were urbanites and that two-thirds of the *filles* were from Ile-de-France (*Filles de joie*, pp. 76-79, 124). On education in France, see Mousnier, *La famille, l'enfant et l'éducation*, pp. 319-25.

90. Lanctôt, *Filles de joie*, pp. 110-30, 202.

91. Dumas, *Filles du roi*, pp. 39, 41, 51-54, 56, 59.

92. Séguin, "La Canadienne," p. 492; Franquet, *Voyages*, p. 57.

93. J. Henripin, *La Population canadienne au début du XVIIIe Siècle* (Paris, 1954), p. 120. The overall population was 63 per cent male in 1663 (Trudel, *Beginnings*, p. 261), an imbalance that gradually declined.

94. Trudel, *Montréal*, pp. 45-47, 108, 113.

95. Foulché-Delbosc, "Women of Three Rivers," p. 19.

96. Cole Harris, *The Seigneurial System in Early Canada* (Québec, 1968), p. 163.

97. The richest single source for evidence along these lines is Dechêne's *Habitants et marchands*.

98. Boyer, *Crimes et châtiments*, p. 326.

99. Toronto *Globe and Mail*, 29 October 1979, p. 1; Boyer, *Crimes et châtiments*, pp. 329, 340. Cf. also N. Hawthorne's novel, *The Scarlet Letter*, based on an actual occurrence.

100. Boyer, *Crimes et châtiments*, pp. 329, 350, 361-62; also Morel, "Justice criminelle canadienne." See also the more recent discussion of women and crime by A. LaChance, "Women and Crime in Canada in the Early Eighteenth Century," in L. Knafla, ed., *Crime and Criminal Justice in Canada* (Calgary, 1981), pp. 157-78.

101. Dechêne, *Habitants et marchands*, p. 464.

102. Séguin, "La Canadienne," pp. 497-99.

103. Jean Lunn, "The Illegal Fur Trade Out of New France 1713-60," *Canadian Historical Association Report* (1939), pp. 61-62.

104. Boyer, *Crimes et châtiments*, pp. 286-87.

105. Marshall, *Word from New France*, pp. 287-95.

106. Boyer, *Crimes et châtiments*, p. 306.

107. Eccles, "The Social, Economic and Political Significance of the Military."

108. Charlevoix, *New France*, vol. 3, p. 35.

109. Ethel Bennett, "Madame de La Tour, 1602-1645," in M. Innis, ed., *The Clear Spirit* (Toronto, 1966), p. 21.

110. *DCB*, 3, pp. 308-13.

111. *Ibid.*; Boyer, *Crimes et châtiments*, pp. 338-39.

112. For a splendid description of the attitudes and lifestyle of this class in France, see P. de Vaissière, *Gentilhommes campagnards de l'ancienne France* (Paris, 1903).

113. G. Frégault, *Le Grand Marquis* (Montréal, 1952), pp. 74-75; Corvisier, *L'Armée française*, p. 777.

114. *Ibid.*, pp. 762-63, 826.

115. Franquet, *Voyages*, pp. 56, 67-68, 200.

116. *Ibid.*, pp. 35, 76, 88.

117. Dechêne, *Habitants et marchands*, p. 398; Franquet, *Voyages*, p. 16.

118. *DCB*, 2, p. 491.

119. Marshall, *Word from New France*, pp. 27, 213, 222-23, 233.

120. Dechêne, *Habitants et marchands*, p. 393; Franquet, *Voyages*, p. 199; Foulché-Delbosc, "Women of Three Rivers," p. 25; Corvisier, *L'Armée française*, p. 760.

121. Boyer, *Crimes et châtiments*, pp. 349-51; Dechêne, *Habitants et mar-*

chands, p. 41. Dechêne concludes that, considering Montreal was a garrison town with a shortage of marriageable women, the degree of prostitution was normal or, to use her term, *conformiste* (pp. 437-38).

122.   Eccles, "The Social Economic and Political Significance of the Military," pp. 11-17; Dechêne, *Habitants et marchands*, p. 121.

123.   J. Henripin, *Trends and Factors of Fertility in Canada* (Ottawa, 1972), p. 2; Séguin, "La Canadienne," pp. 495, 503.

124.   Trudel, *Montréal*, pp. 30-33; Charbonneau, *Vie et mort*, p. 135.

125.   Foulché-Delbosc, "Women of Three Rivers," p. 25.

126.   Trudel, *Montréal*, p. 163.

127.   Bennett, "Madame de la Tour," p. 16; Madame Joybert was the mother of the future Madame de Vaudreuil. *DCB*, 1, p. 399. For E. de Grandmaison, see *DCB*, 1, p. 345.

128.   Lunn, "Illegal Fur Trade," p. 62.

129.   Eccles, *Canadian Society*, p. 61.

130.   Lunn, "Illegal Fur Trade," pp. 61-75.

131.   Franquet, *Voyages*, pp. 120-21.

132.   Lilianne Plamondon, "Une femme d'affaires en Nouvelle-France: Marie-Anne Barbel, Veuve Fornel," *RHAF*, 31 (septembre, 1977).

133.   Franquet, *Voyages*, pp. 156-58.

134.   For example, Hamelin in "What Middle Class?" The absence of an indigenous bourgeoisie is also central to the interpretation of Dechêne in *Habitants et marchands*.

135.   Séguin, "La Canadienne," p. 494.

136.   For accounts of Agathe de Saint-Père, see *DCB*, 3, pp. 580-81; Fauteux, *Industrie au Canada*, pp. 464-69; Massicote, *Bulletin des Recherches historiques* (hereafter *BRH*) (1944), pp. 202-07.

137.   Neatby refers to this activity in the early post-Conquest era (*Quebec*, pp. 72-73); Franquet encountered Madame Benoist in 1753 (*Voyages*, p. 150).

138.   For discussion of the De Ramezays' business affairs, see Massicote, *BRH* (1931), p. 530; Fauteux, *Industrie au Canada*, pp. 158-59, 204-15, 442.

139.   *DCB*, 2, p. 548.

140.   Fauteux, *Industrie au Canada*, pp. 158, 297, 420-21, 522; P. Moogk, *Building a House in New France* (Toronto, 1977), pp. 60-64.

141.   Lunn, *Illegal Fur Trade*, p. 61.

142.   See Moogk (*Building a House*, p. 8) for one case of a husband's transfer of these powers.

143.   Franquet, *Voyages*, p. 17.

144.   Dechêne, *Habitants et marchands*, pp. 151-53, 187, 391; Séguin, "La Canadienne," p. 494.

145.   Charbonneau, *Vie et mort*, p. 184; Fagniez, *Femme et société française*, pp. 111, 182-84. A recent study by Butel ("Comportements familiaux") has documented the phenomenon of widows taking over the family business in eighteenth-century Bordeaux.

146.   Trudel, *Beginnings*, p. 250. This was largely due to the enormous holdings of Jean Lauzon's widow. Dechêne, *Habitants et marchands*, pp. 209, 204-

05, 393; Plamandon, "Femme d'affaires." W.S. MacNutt, *The Atlantic Provinces* (Toronto, 1965), p. 25.

147. This happened on seigneuries as well as in town, as in the case M. de Lanouguère, "a soldier by preference," whose wife, Marguerite-Renée Denys, directed their seigneury (*DCB*, 1, p. 418).

148. The original version of this paper was written as the result of a stimulating graduate seminar conducted by Professor William J. Eccles at the University of Toronto. My thanks to him, and to others who have offered helpful comments and criticisms, particularly Professors Sylvia Van Kirk and Allan Greer at the University of Toronto. The revised version printed here has benefited from the detailed response of Professor Micheline Dumont to the original version published in the Spring, 1981, volume of *Atlantis*. For Professor Dumont's critique of the article, and my reply, see *Atlantis*, 8, 1 (Spring, 1982), pp. 118-30.

Conrad, Recording Angels

1. *The Woman Suffrage Movement in Canada* (reprint, Toronto, 1974), Ch. 6. For a sharp critique of Cleverdon and Ramsay Cook's introduction to the 1974 edition, see E.R. Forbes, "In Search of a Post-Confederation Maritime Historiography, 1900-1967," *Acadiensis*, VIII (Autumn, 1978), pp. 3-21. The exceptions include Alison Prentice and Beth Light, *Pioneer and Gentlewomen* (Toronto, 1980); Ramsay Cook and Wendy Mitchinson, eds., *The Proper Sphere* (Toronto, 1976). The soon-to-be published work by Ernest R. Forbes on the suffrage movement in Nova Scotia will challenge Cleverdon's stereotype: "Carol Bacchi and the Suffragists of Halifax," *Atlantis*, X, 2 (Spring, 1985).

2. The diaries and correspondence discussed in this essay have been gathered by the Maritime Women's Archives Project. A co-operative venture co-ordinated by Toni Laidlaw, Donna Smyth, and the author, the project was sponsored in part by a research grant from the Canadian Research Institute for the Advancement of Women / Institut canadien de recherches sur les femmes.

3. *Census of Canada*, 1890-91, vol. II, Table XIII, pp. 194-216.

4. Robert A. Fothergill, *Private Chronicles: A Study of English Diaries* (London, 1974), pp. 31-34.

5. Estelle C. Jelinek, ed., *Women's Autobiography* (Bloomington, Indiana, 1980), pp. 13-15.

6. Fothergill, *Private Chronicles*, p. 50.

7. Laura June Slauenwhite diary, 1911-1960 (private possession.

8. Eliza Chipman, *Memoir of Mrs. Eliza Anne Chipman, wife of Rev. William Chipman of Pleasant Valley, Cornwallis* (Halifax, 1855).

9. Carrie Best, *That Lonesome Road* (New Glasgow, 1977); Edith Tufts, *Acadian Women* (privately published, 1972).

10. Rebecca Byles Almon correspondence, 1777-1829, Public Archives of Nova Scotia. See also the reminiscences of Mary Fisher, published as "The

Grandmother's Story," in Peter Fisher, *The First History of New Brunswick*, ed. W.O. Raymond (reprint, Woodstock, 1980), pp. 126-30; Sarah Frost, Diary, 1783, published in Walter Bates, *Kingston and the Loyalists of 1783*, ed. W.O. Raymond (Saint John, 1889), pp. 26-30; Hannah Ingraham, memoir, typescript, University of New Brunswick Archives; Elizabeth Lichtenstein Johnston, *Recollections of a Georgia Loyalist* (New York, 1901). For a discussion of general population movements, see W.S. MacNutt, *The Atlantic Provinces: The Emergence of Colonial Society, 1712-1857* (Toronto, 1965).

11.   Vénérande Robichaud Correspondence, Centre d'études acadiennes, University of Moncton. On Acadian demography, see Jean Daigle, ed., *The Acadians of the Maritimes* (Moncton, 1982).

12.   Unpublished manuscript, Mary Bradley, New England Historic Genealogical Society.

13.   *A Narrative of the Life and Christian Experience of Mrs. Mary Bradley* (Boston, 1849), pp. 101-10.

14.   *Ibid.*, p. 80.

15.   *Ibid.*, p. 83.

16.   *Ibid.*, p. 42.

17.   New Brunswick Museum, Archives Division, Saint John Probate Records, vol. (i), 1855-61.

18.   Chipman, *Memoir of Mrs. Eliza Anne Chipman*.

19.   Robert V. Wells, "Women's Lives Transformed: Demography and Family Patterns in America, 1600-1970," in Carol Ruth Berkin and Mary Beth Norton, eds., *Women in America: A History* (Boston, 1979), p. 17; see also Lorne Tepperman, "Ethnic Variations in Marriage and Fertility: Canada 1871," *Canadian Review of Sociology and Anthropology*, II (1974), pp. 324-43.

20.   James Doyle Davison, *Alice of Grand Pré* (Wolfville, N.S., 1981).

21.   The Baptists published *The Christian Messenger* and the Methodists *The Provincial Wesleyan*.

22.   Margaret Gillett, *We Walked Very Warily* (Montreal, 1981), pp. 11, 39.

23.   R. Pierce Beaver, *American Protestant Women in World Mission: A History of the First Feminist Movement in North America* (Grand Rapids, 1980); Wendy Mitchinson, "Canadian Women and Church Missionary Societies in the Nineteenth Century: A Step Towards Independence," *Atlantis*, 2, 2, Part 2 (Spring, 1977), pp. 57-75.

24.   For a discussion of Maritime Baptist women, see Denise Hansen, "Sisters Unite – the United Baptist Women's Missionary Movement, 1867-1914" (B.A. honours thesis, Acadia University, 1979).

25.   Mrs. George Churchill, *Letters from My Home in India* (New York, 1916).

26.   Sheila Rothman, *Women's Proper Place* (New York, 1978), Ch. 2.

27.   *Atlantis*, 6, 1 (Fall, 1980), pp. 65-82.

28.   Karen Sanders, "Margaret Marshall Saunders" (M.A. thesis, Dalhousie University, 1978). See also Saunders diary for 1906-07, which offers an excellent insight into her preoccupations and prejudices (Acadia University Library).

29. This seems to be as true for Maritime college women as for those elsewhere. At Acadia University, for example, one in three women taking degrees prior to 1900 remained single. See Watson Kirkconnell, *The Acadia Record* (Kentville, N.S., 1953).

30. Teresa McDonald letters, Beaton Institute, College of Cape Breton.

31. Alan A. Brookes, "The Exodus: Migration from the Maritime Provinces to Boston During the Second Half of the Nineteenth Century" (Ph.D. thesis, University of New Brunswick, 1978), p. 127.

32. *The Maritime Provinces in Their Relation to the National Economy of Canada* (Ottawa, 1934), p. 27; see also Alan A. Brookes, "Out-migration from the Maritimes, 1860-1900: Some Preliminary Considerations," *Acadensis*, V, 2 (Spring, 1976), pp. 25-55; "The Golden Age and the Exodus: The Case of Canning, Kings County," *Acadensis*, XI, 1 (Autumn, 1981), pp. 57-82.

33. Hannah Richardson diary, 1872 (private possession). Margaret Connell letters, Hector Centre, Pictou, N.S.

34. Letters supplied courtesy of Alan A. Brookes.

35. Clifford A. Roe, *The Great War on White Slavery or Fighting for the Protection of Our Girls* (New York, 1911), p. 238. See also the story of "Cora Lee" in the St. John *Progress*, 24 November 1888, 1 December 1888.

36. Mary Smith diary, Beaton Centre, College of Cape Breton.

37. Rebecca Chase Ells diary (private possession).

38. See also Christopher Clark, "Household Economy, Market Exchange and the Rise of Capitalism in the Connecticut Valley, 1800-1860," *Journal of Social History*, 13, 2 (Winter, 1979), pp. 169-89; James A. Herretta, "Families and Farms: Mentalité in Pre-Industrial America," *William and Mary Quarterly*, 3rd series, 35, 1 (January, 1978), pp. 3-32; Michael Merrill, "Cash is Good to Eat: Self-sufficiency and Exchange in the Rural Economy of the United States," *Radical History Review* (Winter, 1977), pp. 42-71.

39. Fothergill, *Private Chronicles*, p. 57; Sophia Mary Carman diary, Ganong Collection, New Brunswick Museum.

40. Barbara Welter, "The Cult of True Womanhood, 1820-1860," *American Quarterly*, 18 (1966), pp. 151-74.

41. Veronica Burrill Ross, *Moments Make a Year* (Sackville, N.B., 1958).

42. Basil Greenhill and Anne Giffard, *Women Under Sail* (Newton Abbot, 1970).

43. Amelia Holder diary, 1867-73, Provincial Archives of New Brunswick.

44. Alice Coalfleet diary, 1886-92 (private possession).

45. Slauenwhite diary.

46. Mary Killian MacQuarrie, memoir, Beaton Institute, College of Cape Breton.

47. Ella Liscomb diary, Beaton Institute; D.S. Morrison Collection, Beaton Institute.

48. Graham S. Lowe, "Women, work and the office: the feminization of clerical occupations in Canada, 1901-1931," *Canadian Journal of Sociology*, 5, 4 (1980), pp. 361-81.

49.   Ruth Roach Pierson, "'Jill Canuck': CWAC of All Trades, But No 'Pistol-Packing Momma," Canadian Historical Association, *Historical Papers* (1978), pp. 106-33.
50.   Nancy Cott, *The Bonds of Womanhood* (New Haven, 1977), Ch. 4.
51.   Barbara Berg, *The Remembered Gate: Origins of American Feminist: The Women and the City, 1800-1860* (New York, 1978), Ch. 4.
52.   Olive Banks, *Faces of Feminism* (Oxford, 1981), Ch. 2.
53.   *Census of Canada*, 1921-1951.
54.   Cleverdon, *The Woman Suffrage Movement.* This statement may need explanation because of the importance of prairie rural women in the suffrage movement, but recent research makes it clear that in the West suffrage had an urban base and leadership, and the weight of colonialism was less deeply rooted. See Carol Bacchi, "Divided Allegiances: The Response of Farm and Labour Women to Suffrage," in Linda Kealey, ed., *A Not Unreasonable Claim* (Toronto, 1979), pp. 89-107.
55.   Kirkconnell, *Acadia Record*, p. 49; Rosalind Rosenberg, *Beyond Separate Spheres* (New Haven, 1982), p. 34.
56.   Elizabeth Hall papers, 1911-1924, Public Archives of Nova Scotia.
57.   Ann Douglas, *The Feminization of American Culture* (New York, 1980), p. 10.

Cohen, Women in Canadian Dairying

1.   J.A. Ruddick, "The Development of the Dairy Industry in Canada," in Harold A. Innis, ed., *The Dairy Industry in Canada* (Toronto, 1937), p. 44.
2.   Robert Leslie Jones, *History of Agriculture in Ontario, 1613-1880* (Toronto, 1946), p. 102. Vernon Fowke, *Canadian Agricultural Policy: The Historical Pattern* (Toronto, 1946), p. 213.
3.   This invisibility of women in accounts of Canadian dairying has been noted by feminist historians. See Beth Light and Veronica Strong-Boag, *True Daughters of the North* (Toronto, 1980), p. 2; Susan Trofimenkoff and Alison Prentice, eds., *The Neglected Majority: Essays in Canadian Women's History* (Toronto, 1977), p. 153.
4.   W.J. Eccles, *Canadian Society During the French Regime* (Montreal, 1968), p. 74.
5.   *Nova Scotia Gazette and Weekly Chronicle*, 23 May 1776, reprinted in Beth Light and Alison Prentice, eds., *Pioneer and Gentlewomen of British North America, 1713-1867* (Toronto, 1980), p. 42.
6.   John Young, *The Letters of Agricola* (Halifax, 1822), p. ix.
7.   By 1871 Nova Scotia had a substantial dairy industry. It produced about 10 per cent of Canada's butter and about 18 per cent of the country's homemade cheese. *Census of Canada*, 1871, vol. III, p. 20.
8.   James Croil, *Dundas or A Sketch of Canadian History* (Montreal, 1861), p. 211.
9.   *Ibid.*
10.   Georgina Binnie-Clark, *Wheat and Woman* (Toronto, [1914] 1979), p. 128.

11. Georgina Binnie-Clark, address given to members of the Royal Colonial Institute, 8 April 1913, in Susan Jackel, ed., *A Flannel Shirt and Liberty: British Emigrant Gentlewomen in the Canadian West, 1880-1914* (Vancouver, 1982), p. 184.

12. For discussions of the instability of staple production, see H. Clare Pentland, *Labour and Capital in Canada, 1650-1860* (Toronto, 1981), pp. 177-78; Harold A. Innis, "Unused Capacity as a Factor in Canadian Economic History," in Mary Q. Innis, ed., *Essays in Canadian Economic History* (Toronto, 1956), pp. 141-55; Daniel Drache, "Harold Innis and Canadian Capitalist Development," *Canadian Journal of Political and Social Theory*, 6 (Winter/Spring, 1982), pp. 36-38.

13. For a discussion of the importance of diversity in farm production in the Canadian West, see Max Hedley, "Independent commodity production and the dynamics of tradition," *Canadian Review of Sociology and Anthropology*, 13 (1976), pp. 413-21, in particular, p. 417, where he says, "the diversity of operations, in conjunction with virtual self-sufficiency in domestic consumption, offered some protection against unpredictable price fluctuations and the vulnerability of a single commodity to the effects of natural hazards."

14. In 1861 only one farmer in Dundas County specialized in dairying. See Croil, *Dundas*, p. 202. Earlier, Anna Jameson had remarked that in many parts of Upper Canada a dairy farm was so rare it was a curiosity. Cited in Jones, *Agriculture in Ontario*, p. 250.

15. See Innis, *The Dairy Industry*, p. 4, for a discussion of the effect of staple production on the slow growth of dairying in Canada.

16. Eric E. Lampard, *The Rise of the Dairy Industry in Wisconsin: A Study in Agricultural Change, 1820-1920* (Madison, 1962), p. 23.

17. While little is known about the organization of women's farm dairying in the United States, it is clear that early markets in northeastern states were more integrated and larger than in more sparsely settled areas. Joan M. Jensen shows that by 1840 from 14 to 23 per cent of the agricultural income of New England came from dairy production. The effect that this had on the structure of women's labour is still to be discovered. Joan M. Jensen, "Cloth, Butter and Boarders: Women's Household Production for the Market," *Review of Radical Political Economics*, 12 (Summer, 1980), p. 17. Many books on U.S. dairying refer to women as the producers of cheese and butter on farms but do not examine the specific nature of the work. See, for example, Edward Wiest, *The Butter Industry in the United States* (New York, [1916] 1968), p. 16; Robert Leslie Jones, *History of Agriculture in Ohio to 1880* (Kent, Ohio, 1983), Ch. 9; Lampard, *The Dairy Industry in Wisconsin*.

18. For accounts of women's work in dairying in England from the Middle Ages to the end of the nineteenth century, see Eileen Power, *Medieval Women*, ed. M.M. Postan (London, 1975); Alice Clark, *Working Life of Women in the Seventeenth Century* (London, [1919] 1982); Ivy Pinchbeck, *Women Workers and the Industrial Revolution, 1750-1850* (London, [1930] 1981); Jane Kitteringham, "Country Work Girls in Nineteenth-Century

England," in Raphael Samuel, ed., *Village Life and Labour* (London, 1975), pp. 73-138.

19. Pinchbeck, *Women Workers*, pp. 10ff. Pinchbeck notes, however, that as dairy farms became larger and the principal work of the farm, women's labour was more restricted to butter- and cheese-making (p. 42). Nevertheless, she explains women's disappearance from outdoor work on dairy farms as a result of competition for their labour in more attractive occupations (p. 110).

20. Kitteringham, "Country Work Girls," pp. 95-96.

21. Ella G. Sykes pointed out the differences between English and Canadian domestic servants: "British servants are usually specialist, and do not grasp that in Canada they must turn their hands to anything, and be cook, house-parlourmaid, washerwoman, and perhaps baker and dairymaid all in one." Sykes, *A Home-Help in Canada* (London, 1912), pp. 24-25. In 1886 Henrietta McGill wrote of the high demand for the labour of "young girls that understand milking and doing general housework." McGill, *What Women Say of the Canadian Northwest* (London, 1886), p. 34.

22. Canada, Department of Agriculture, *First Annual Report of the Dairy Commissioner of Canada for 1890* (Ottawa, 1891), p. 138.

23. Steward St. John, "Mrs. St. John's Diary, January 2, 1903 to March 30, 1904," *Saskatchewan History*, II (Autumn, 1949), pp. 25-30.

24. Cited by Virginia Watson Rouslin, "The Intelligent Woman's Guide to Pioneering in Canada," *Dalhousie Review*, 56 (Summer, 1976), p. 328.

25. Isabel Skelton, *The Backwoodswoman: A Chronicle of Pioneer Home Life in Upper and Lower Canada* (Toronto, 1924), p. 221.

26. W.M. Drummond, "Problems of the Canadian Dairy Industry," in Innis, ed., *The Dairy Industry* p. 139.

27. Laura Rose, *Farm Dairying* (London, 1911), p. 143.

28. See Ruddick, "Development of the Dairy Industry," p. 26, for a description of the difficulty in churning butter when temperature conditions are not exactly right.

29. *Report of the Dairy Commissioner for 1890*, p. 138.

30. *Ibid.* Unfortunately, the dairy commissioner felt compelled to make his argument stronger by conjuring up the trivial and competitive nature of women: "I believe if one woman gets a nice, attractive, cheap dress, 20 more women want to get the same or something better; and if one woman gets a nice new milk house and churn, 20 more women give their husbands no peace, day or night, until they get that new milk house and churn also. This would bring very much good to the dairy business."

31. Eliza M. Jones, *Laiterie payante ou la vache du pauvre* (Trois-Rivières, 1894), p. 40. Emphasis in the original.

32. The term "family farm" obscures the ownership issue of the farm and its technology. For an interesting discussion of this problem, see Max H. Hedley, " 'Normal expectations': Rural Women without Property," *Resources for Feminist Research*, 11 (March, 1982), pp. 15-17.

33. John Macdougall, *Rural Life in Canada: Its Trends and Tasks* (Toronto, [1917] 1973), p. 128.

34. Ruddick, "Development of the Dairy Industry," p. 26; Binnie-Clark, *Wheat and Women*, p. 128; "Mrs. St. John's Diary," p. 26.

35. For example, Louise Tivy, *Your Loving Anna: Letters from the Ontario Frontier* (Toronto, 1972), pp. 72-73.

36. "The trading of dairy goods for dry goods and groceries is one of the greatest hindrances to the development of dairying in Canada, as it places little or no premium upon brains and skill, which are necessary factors in the making of a fine quality of dairy goods." Henry H. Dean, *Canadian Dairying* (Toronto, 1903), pp. 64-65.

37. Binnie-Clark, *Wheat and Women*, p. 128; Jensen, "Cloth, Butter and Boarders," p. 18. It is clear from the comments of women about their dairying that many regarded the income they received from it as belonging to them, even though the proceeds were to be applied to the family's keep. See, for example, *What Women Say of the Canadian Northwest*; and "Mrs. St. John's Dairy," p. 26.

38. For an illustration of the amount of work involved in cloth-making in a family whose primary income came from butter, see Susan Dunlap's diary written in Nova Scotia in the middle of the nineteenth century. G.G. Campbell, "Susan Dunlap: Her Diary," *Dalhousie Review*, 46 (Summer, 1966), p. 218.

39. Jones, *Agriculture in Ontario*, p. 286.

40. Hilda Murray, *More than 50%* (St. John's, 1980), describes women's work in fishing and family subsistence activities in Newfoundland.

41. Mrs. George Cran, *A Woman in Canada* (London, 1910), pp. 118-19.

42. "Good Cooking," *The Grain Growers' Guide*, 4 (8 April 1910), reprinted in Ramsay Cook and Wendy Mitchinson, eds., *The Proper Sphere: Woman's Place in Canadian Society* (Toronto, 1976), pp. 189-91.

43. Sykes, *A Home-Help*, p. 34.

44. Cran, *A Woman in Canada*, p. 101.

45. *Ibid.*, p. 135. The problem of finding farm servants was serious, particularly in the western parts of the country. According to "The Manitoba Women's Burden," an article published in *The Virden Advance*, 4 July 1904, "One of the most urgent problems before the farming community in Manitoba is the securing of help in the house and in such branches of the industry as dairying and poultry raising, so essentially feminine. . . . Many men have to abandon farming as a profession because their wives are unequal to the physical strain which the endless duties of a farm house imposes on them." Cited by Genevieve Leslie, "Domestic Service in Canada, 1880-1920," in Janice Acton, Penny Goldsmith, and Bonnie Shepard, eds., *Women at Work: Ontario, 1850-1930* (Toronto, 1974), p. 109.

46. Ruddick, "Development of the Dairy Industry," p. 25.

47. *Ibid.* Butter-making in itself was difficult and time-consuming, particularly if done by hand. See H.A. Innis and A.R.M. Lower, eds., *Select Documents in Canadian Economic History, 1783-1885* (Toronto, 1933), p. 558. Even when done with a churn, butter-making was hard work. The barrel churn was often extremely primitive, merely being four planks of wood nailed together on a bottom. A great deal of labour was involved in keeping this

202 THE NEGLECTED MAJORITY

type of churn clean. See Skelton, *The Backwoodswoman*, p. 222. But even though the wooden coopermade dash churn, which was in common use on farms until the 1880s, was a considerable improvement on the cruder homemade one, it was "an instrument of torture, still remembered by those who, as boys, had to operate them." Ruddick, "Development of the Dairy Industry," p. 25. (This remark, which stresses the suffering of males rather than females, is interesting in particular because it comes from one of the few dairy historians who recognizes the feminine nature of farm dairying.) For an excellent description of the complexities of making farm butter, see Rose, *Farm Dairying*, Ch. 33.

Early cheese-making was particularly time-consuming. Until cheese factories sold rennet, the farm women had to make this essential ingredient themselves. This was done by cleaning thoroughly and salting, drying, and preserving the stomach of a suckling calf. With a solution of this, the curds and whey could be separated. See Skelton, *The Backwoodswoman*, p. 223. The heaviest work involved the pressing and turning of the cheese: "The clumsy press and its huge stone weights, the bulky cheeses themselves which had to be fitted and rubbed so many times before being properly dried and seasoned, constituted very heavy labour which the worker had no appliances to lighten." (*Ibid.*) For a description of later methods of farm cheese-making, see Ruddick, "Development of the Dairy Industry," p. 57; Rose, *Farm Dairying*, Ch. 42.

48. Jones, *Agriculture in Ontario*, p. 252.
49. John McCallum, *Unequal Beginnings: Agriculture and Economic Development in Quebec and Ontario until 1870* (Toronto, 1980), p. 37.
50. Jones, *Agriculture in Ontario*, p. 253.
51. Early in the nineteenth century the prohibition of free trade and its effect on women received particularly scathing comments from Harriet Martineau. She tells of meeting a woman in Canada who gave an account of how it was necessary to smuggle butter and eggs into Buffalo from her neighbourhood. Harriet Martineau, *Retrospect of Western Travel*, vol. 1 (London, 1838), p. 142.
52. The Reciprocity Treaty of 1854-66 established free trade between Canada and the U.S. in all raw materials. Foodstuffs were included in this classification. On the effects of reciprocity, see Robert E. Ankli, "The Reciprocity Treaty of 1854," *Canadian Journal of Economics*, IV, 1 (1971), pp. 1-20; L. Officer and L. Smith, "The Canadian-American Reciprocity Treaty of 1855-1866," *Journal of Economic History*, 28, 4 (1968), pp. 598-623.
53. Calculated from William J. Patterson, *Home and Foreign Trade of the Dominion of Canada: Also, Annual Report of the Commerce of Montreal 1871* (Montreal, 1872), p. 89.
54. Jones, *Agriculture in Ontario*, p. 253.
55. Innis, *The Dairy Industry*, p. 5.
56. In 1870-71 butter exports were valued at over $3 million while the value of cheese exports was $670,000. William J. Patterson, *Report 1876*, p. 3.
57. Patterson, *Report 1883-85*, p. 113.

58.	Early cheese factories were generally small local operations, employing one or two people, which did not operate either full-time or the whole year. The production methods and the technology used were not much different from those used in farm dairies. Ruddick, "Development of the Dairy Industry," p. 57. Usually the cheese factories consisted of two buildings, one a "make" room and the other a curing room. According to the first head of the dairy school at Guelph, Ontario, in 1888 the cost of establishing a cheese factory with the capacity to handle milk from 200 cows was about $1,000. Public Archives of Ontario, Acc. 10058, "History of Cheesemaking in Ontario," annual meeting of Western Ontario Cheesemakers Association, Ontario Agricultural College, Guelph, 12 March 1964, mimeo.

59.	Of these factories, 323 were in Ontario, twenty-five in Quebec, three in New Brunswick, and two in Nova Scotia. Patterson, *Report 1876*, p. 38.

60.	*Report of the Dairy Commissioner for 1890*, p. 6. By this time there were 1,565 cheese factories in Canada, with 892 in Ontario and 618 in Quebec. *Census of Canada*, 1891, bulletin no. 8, pp. 30, 36.

61.	Butter factories were commonly called creameries.

62.	Rosemary R. Ball, "The Perfect Farmer's Wife: Women in 19th Century Rural Ontario," *Canada: An Historical Magazine*, 3 (December, 1975), p. 11. Nellie McClung wrote of a wealthy farmer who owned three farms and left one to each of his three sons. "To his daughter Martha, a woman of forty years of age, the eldest of the family, who had always stayed at home, and worked for the whole family – he left a cow and one hundred dollars. The wording of the will ran: 'To my dear daughter, Martha, I leave the sum of one hundred dollars, and one cow named Bella.'" Nellie McClung, *In Times Like These* (Toronto, [1915] 1972), p. 91.

63.	An immigrant woman, writing in 1901 with advice for pre-immigration training for British women, counselled that while skills in butter-making were essential, learning to milk was not necessary. "She will find she has quite enough to do without this, if she attend properly to the house, poultry and probably the garden." Elizabeth Lewthwaite, "Women's Work in Western Canada," *Fortnightly Review* (October, 1901), reprinted in Jackel, ed., *A Flannel Shirt and Liberty*, p. 119.

64.	Rose, *Farm Dairying*, pp. 121-22.

65.	Milking continued to be done by hand for a long time after factory production of cheese was commonplace. Although milking machines were available, most farmers found the milk yield was likely to be greater with hand milking. By the time Laura Rose wrote her textbook in 1911, the use of milking machines was clearly the way of the future. However, even then their use tended to be restricted to farms with herds of fifty or more. *Ibid.*, pp. 132-33.

66.	Jones, *Agriculture in Ontario*, p. 251.

67.	By 1911 homemade cheese accounted for less than one per cent of total cheese production in Canada. Canada, Dominion Bureau of Statistics, *Dairy Factories 1920*, p. iv. Women's rapid exit from cheese-making in Canada was probably accentuated because of the adoption of the English,

204   THE NEGLECTED MAJORITY

rather than the French, taste for cheese. Where local, regional differences in cheese are important to consumers (as in France), farm production and women's work as cheesemakers tend to remain longer than where the product has a more homogeneous nature. I am grateful to Griff Cunningham for pointing this out to me.

68. In the nineteenth century there was a trend toward producing particularly large cheeses. The biggest, "The Canadian Mite," was made for the Chicago World Fair in 1893. It weighed 22,000 pounds, was 28 feet in circumference, 6 feet high, and was made from 207,000 pounds of milk. Virginia McCormick, *A Hundred Years in the Dairy Industry* (Ottawa, 1968), pp. 72-73.

69. One commentator felt women tended to overestimate the amount of labour involved in cheese-making. "There is no reason why farm dairy cheese should not be made in about four hours, or in such time that the farmer's wife or daughter may get through before noon, as most women object to work of this kind after dinner – and rightly so." Dean, *Canadian Dairying*, p. 97.

70. *Census of Canada*, 1921, vol. V, p. vii.

71. *Dairy Factories 1920*. The first successful creamery in Ontario was begun by two storekeepers in Teeswater in 1876. But very little butter was made in factories before 1880. Jones, *Agriculture in Ontario*, p. 263. By 1890 there were 112 creameries in Quebec and forty-five in Ontario. *Census of Canada*, 1891, bulletin no. 8, pp. 30, 36.

72. It is important to note that farm production was probably considerably higher than statistics indicated. The census of 1911 in particular noted that farmers rarely kept adequate records, "and as a consequence are apt either to ignore altogether or greatly underestimate the quantities of vegetables, fruit, milk, cream, butter, cheese, eggs and honey consumed on the farm during the seasons when these are produced in greatest abundance." *Census of Canada*, 1911, vol. IV, p. vi.

73. Wiest, *The Butter Industry*, p. 40.

74. Calculated from *Census of Canada*, 1891, bulletin no. 8, pp. 19-39; *Census of Canada*, 1901, vol. II, p. liii.

75. Jones, *Agriculture in Ontario*, pp. 263-64.

76. Laura Rose describes the gravity method in use before the centrifugal separator was widely used. This involved letting milk set in shallow pans for twenty-four hours. The cream would rise to the top and then could be skimmed off into a pan. She says the disadvantages of this method were serious, including: "a great surface of the milk exposed to atmospheric contamination; the milk liable to become too rancid for domestic and feeding purposes; the cream clotted and over-ripe; the creaming incomplete; a large space necessary for the pans, and much labour involved." Rose, *Farm Dairying*, p. 144. Another method was the deep can method, where cans from eight to twenty inches deep were set in tanks of cold water for twelve to thirty-six hours. This procedure involved considerable amounts of ice and much heavy lifting. Ruddick, "Development of the Dairy Industry," p. 27.

77.   *Report of the Dairy Commissioner for 1890*, p. 12.

78.   Dean, *Canadian Dairying*, p. 64; Jones, *Agriculture in Ontario*, p. 261; Mrs. Edward Copleston, *Canada: Why we live in it and why we like it* (London, 1861), p. 73.

79.   Innis and Lower, *Select Documents*, pp. 558-59.

80.   *Ibid.*

81.   *Journal of the House of Commons*, 1877, 11, p. 162. The problem of poor-quality dairy products was not peculiar to Canada. Early in the twentieth century an English dairying analyst referred to "ill-made and evil-flavoured" cheese in Britain. John Prince Sheldon, *Dairying* (Toronto, 1912), p. v; also see Sutherland Thomson, *British and Colonial Dairying* (London, 1913), p. 152.

82.   Ruddick, "Development of the Dairy Industry," p. 33.

83.   Skelton, *The Backwoodswoman*, pp. 221-22; Patterson, *Report 1872*, p. 119.

84.   *Ibid.*, p. 120.

85.   Ruddick, "Development of the Dairy Industry," p. 42.

86.   *Dairy Factories 1920*, p. 1.

87.   Rose, *Farm Dairying*, p. 148.

88.   Dean, *Canadian Dairying*, p. 65.

89.   Separators were often a luxury that many farm households could not afford. A separator for a farm dairy with a herd of four to eight cows could cost between $55 and $75. Rose, *Farm Dairying*, p. 174. Considering that the produce from a cow could be expected to bring in from $30 to $60 a year, the relative cost of a separator was high. *Ibid.*, p. 45. A price list of dairy supplies at the turn of the century shows Danish hand- and foot-powered separators selling for $120 to $135 while power separators cost $200-$500. John S. Pearce, *Price List of Dairy Supplies* (London, Ont., 1900), pp. 12-13.

90.   Unless otherwise noted the information on government assistance to the dairy industry comes from Ruddick, "Development of the Dairy Industry," and Fowke, *Canadian Agricultural Policy*, pp. 215-18.

91.   For an excellent study of how development planners deal with women today, see Barbara Roberts, *The Domestication of Women: Discrimination in Developing Societies* (London, 1980).

92.   Jones, *Agriculture in Ontario*, pp. 260-63; Fowke, *Canadian Agricultural Policy*, pp. 213-14.

93.   Ruddick, "Development of the Dairy Industry," p. 98.

94.   For example, on Prince Edward Island in 1893 eleven new cheese factories were started with government agents as managers. By 1895 twenty-eight cheese and two butter factories in the province were operated for farmers by the government. In some parts of the country, government management of operations lasted for a long time. In Saskatchewan individual co-operative creameries continued "under what was practically general management by the government until the end of 1917." *Ibid.*, pp. 113-14.

95.   See Ester Boserup, *Women's Role in Economic Development* (London,

1970), for a discussion of the adverse effect of male-centred education programs in agricultural societies. Because of the discriminatory education policies of most colonial administrators, a productivity gap between male and female farmers is created, a gap that subsequently seems to justify their prejudice against women in agriculture.

96. Laura Rose is one of the few well-known women's names in Canadian dairying. In addition to operating her travelling dairy, she also lectured at the Farm Dairy School of the Ontario Agricultural College in Guelph and for the Ontario Department of Agriculture. In B.C. and Ontario she was an active organizer of the Women's Institutes. For information on Laura Rose, see Alexandra Zacharias, "British Columbia Women's Institutes in the Early Years: Time to Remember," in Barbara Latham and Cathy Kess, eds., *In Her Own Right: Selected Essays on Women's History in B.C.* (Victoria, 1980), p. 57; also see James Morgan, ed., *The Canadian: Men and Women of the Time* (Toronto, 1912), for a short biography and reference to Rose's much-admired address on "The Womanly Sphere of Women."

97. National Council of Women, *Women of Canada: Their Life and Work* (Ottawa, [1900] 1975), p. 87.

98. Sheldon, *Dairying*, pp. 330-31.

99. Rose, *Farm Dairying*, pp. 15-16.

100. Elizabeth B. Mitchell, *In Western Canada Before the War: Impressions of Early Twentieth Century Prairie Communities* (Saskatoon, [1915] 1981), p. 160.

101. *Ibid.*, pp. 117-18.

102. *Labour Gazette* (December, 1904), p. 651; Mitchell, *In Western Canada Before the War*, p. 161; Zacharias, "British Columbia Women's Institutes," p. 60.

103. Many farm women were exasperated by the nature of the programs of the Women's Institutes. Mary Nicolaeff complained about the narrowness of their program: "Always suggestions about housework, knitting, and the main woman's destination: 'preparing of dainty side-dishes and salads', Kitchen, kitchen, and again kitchen!" The reply to her letter pointed out that the program also included a study of parliamentary procedure, the history of great women, and social settlement work in great cities. Mary Nicolaeff, *Grain Growers' Guide*, 6 September 1915, reprinted in Linda Rasmussen, Candace Savage, and Anne Wheeler, eds., *A Harvest Yet to Reap: A History of Prairie Women* (Toronto, 1976), p. 132.

104. By 1911 there were no cheese factories and only eight creameries in British Columbia. Of the more than 2,000 people employed in creameries in Canada, less than one-tenth were west of Ontario. And of more than 2,000 cheese factories in Canada, only seventeen were in the western provinces. *Census of Canada*, 1911, vol. III.

105. Linda Graff, "The Changing Nature of Farm Women's Work Roles Under the Industrialization of Agricultural Production" (M.A. thesis, McMaster University, 1979), p. 184.

106. *Ibid.*, pp. 149-53.

McLaren, Birth Control and Abortion

I would like to thank Alan Brookes, Michael Bliss, Michael and Anita Fellman, Phyllis Sherrin, Edward Shorter, and Veronica Strong-Boag for their comments and suggestions, and Basil Stubbs, chief librarian of the University of British Columbia, for making available to me his private collection of late nineteenth-century medical and marriage manuals.

1. Toronto *Evening Telegram*, 26 March 1908, p. 9.
2. Sylvanus Stall, *What a Young Man Ought to Know* (Toronto, 1897), p. 198.
3. Toronto *Globe*, 17 December 1901, p. 8.
4. *Manitoba Free Press*, 30 August 1909, p. 3.
5. "Childless Marriages," *Canadian Churchman*, 29 November 1900, p. 724. In 1908 the Lambeth Conference of the Anglican Church officially condemned "the practice of resorting to artificial means for the avoidance or prevention of child bearing." E.R. Norman, *Church and Society in England, 1770-1970* (Oxford, 1976), p. 270. See also *Canadian Churchman*, July-August, 1908.
6. M.C. Urquhart and K.A.H. Buckley, *Historical Statistics of Canada* (Cambridge, 1965), pp. 14-18, 38-42; Terry Copp, *The Anatomy of Poverty: The Condition of the Working Class in Montreal, 1897-1929* (Toronto, 1974), pp. 29, 44-45.
7. W.S. Wallace, "The Canadian Immigration Policy," *Canadian Magazine*, XXX (1907-08), p. 360.
8. Lydia Kingsmill Commander, *The American Idea: Does the National Tendency Toward a Small Family Point to Race Suicide or Race Degeneration?* (New York, 1907), cited in O.C. Beall, *Racial Decay: A Compilation of Evidence from World Sources* (London, 1911), p. 89. *Canadian Churchman*, 29 November 1900, p. 724; see also *ibid.*, 17 January 1901, p. 37. On French-Canadian pressure in the Eastern Townships, see Robert Sellar, *The Tragedy of Quebec: The Expulsion of its Protestant Farmers* (Toronto, 1907; reprint 1974 with introduction by Robert Hill); Henry Lemay, "The Future of the French Canadian Race," *Canadian Magazine*, XXXVII (1911), pp. 11-17; P. Louis Lalande, "La revanche des berceaux," *Action française*, II (1918), p. 98. For fears expressed by the Québécois about their own birth rate, see R.P. Henri Martin, OP, "La dépopulation," in *Semaine Sociale du Canada, IVe Session* (Montréal, 1923); "La Famille," *Compte rendu des cours et conférences* (Montréal, 1924); and Susan Trofimenkoff, *Action Française: French Canadian Nationalism in the Twenties* (Toronto, 1975), pp. 74-75.
9. Jacques Henripin, *Trends and Factors of Fertility in Canada* (Ottawa, 1972), p. 21; also see John Davidson, "The Census of Canada," *Economic Journal*, XI (1901), pp. 595-602; W.J.A. Donald, "The Growth and Distribution of Canadian Population," *Journal of Political Economy*, XXI (1913), pp. 296-312.
10. On statistical evidence that such controls were employed by the upper middle class from the 1850s, see Michael Katz, *The People of Hamilton,*

Canada West: Family and Class in a Mid-Nineteenth Century City (Cambridge, Mass., 1975), p. 35; see also Lorne Tepperman, "Ethnic Variations in Marriage and Fertility: Canada in 1871," *Canadian Review of Sociology and Anthropology*, XI (1974), pp. 287-307.

11. See L.F. Bouvier, "The Spacing of Births Among French Canadian Families: An Historical Approach," *Canadian Review of Sociology and Anthropology*, V (1968), pp. 17-26; Jacques Henripin, *La population canadienne au début du XVIIIᵉ siècle* (Paris, 1954), pp. 86-87.

12. On the prevalence of coitus interruptus, see E. Lewis Faning, *Report on an Enquiry into Family Limitation and its Influence on Human Fertility During the Past Fifty Years*, Papers on the Royal Commission on Population, vol. 1 (London, 1949), pp. 7-10; Earl Lomon Koos, "Class Differences in Employment of Contraceptive Measures," *Human Fertility*, XII (1947), pp. 97-101.

13. On the attempt to use section 207 against Dorothea Palmer of the Parents' Information Bureau of Kitchener, Ontario, see R. vs. Palmer (1937), *Ontario Weekly Notes*, p. 371; R. vs. Palmer (1937), *Canadian Criminal Cases*, p. 20. On the American experience, see Linda Gordon, *Women's Body, Women's Right: A Social History of Birth Control in America* (New York, 1976).

14. With a taboo subject such as artificial limitation of family size the historian is faced with the inherent limitations of public sources and the fact that such sources deal primarily with urban conditions. On the problem of such sources and in particular the use of American tracts that circulated in Canada, see Michael Bliss, "Pure Books on Avoided Subjects: Pre-Freudian Sexual Ideas in Canada," *Historical Papers* (1970), pp. 89-108. For a specific example of the way in which information on "sex hygiene" was brought from America to Canada, see Beatrice Brigden, "One Woman's Campaign for Social Purity and Social Reform," in Richard Allen, ed., *The Social Gospel in Canada*, National Museum of Man Mercury Series (Ottawa, 1975), pp. 36-62. The full story of birth control in Canada can only be known after the completion of the number of women's oral history projects currently under way. For work done elsewhere, see "Family History Issue," *Oral History*, III (1975), pp. 1-64; and Sherna Gluck, "Recovering Our Past Through Oral History Interviews," cited in Susan J. Kleinberg, "The Systematic Study of Urban Women," in Milton Cantor and Bruce Laurie, eds., *Class, Sex and the Woman Worker* (Westport, Conn., 1977), p. 35.

15. Emma F. Angell Drake, *What a Young Wife Ought to Know* (Toronto, 1908), pp. 131ff.

16. Augustus K. Gardner, *Conjugal Sins Against the Law of Life and Health* (New York, 1874), pp. 182-83. An additional reason for doctors' enthusiasm for the "safe period" was the Vatican's tacit acceptance from the 1880s of this "natural" form of control. See John T. Noonan, *Contraception: A History of its Treatment by Catholic Theologians and Canonists* (Cambridge, Mass., 1965), pp. 441-42.

17. John Cowan, *The Science of New Life* (New York, 1869), pp. 110ff; George

H. Napheys, *The Physical Life of Women* (Toronto, n.d.), pp. 92-96; Winfield Scott Hall, *Sexual Knowledge* (Toronto, 1916), p. 215.

18. H.W. Long, *Sane Sex Life and Sane Sex Living* (New York, 1919); B.G. Jefferis and J.L. Nichols, *Searchlights on Health: Light on Dark Corners* (Toronto, 1897), p. 248. See also Anon., *Nature's Secrets Revealed* (Marietta, Ohio, 1917), pp. 197ff.

19. There were Canadian editions of both *Karezza* and *Tokology*. For Stockham, see Bliss, "Pure Books on Avoided Subjects," p. 104. On coitus reservatus, see also Long, *Sane Sex*, p. 128.

20. For the development of contraceptives in the nineteenth century, see the notes in Angus McLaren, "Contraception and the Working Classes: The Social Ideology of the English Birth Control Movement in its Early Years," *Comparative Studies in Society and History*, XVIII (1976), pp. 236-51.

21. *T. Eaton Co. Catalogue* – Spring and Summer, no. 46 (Toronto, 1901), p. 1920; Toronto *Daily Mail and Empire*, 21 March 1908, p. 21; *Dominion Medical Monthly* (July, 1916). Also see *Woodward Catalogue* (Vancouver, 1912), p. 143.

22. Linda Rasmussen *et al.*, *A Harvest Yet to Reap* (Toronto, 1976), p. 72. See also G. Kolischer, "The Prevention of Conception," *Dominion Medical Monthly*, XIX (1902), pp. 116-19.

23. C.S. Clark, *Of Toronto the Good* (Montreal, 1898), p. 127. As examples of what Clark was talking about, see the advertisements of "rubber goods" placed by F.E. Karn Ltd., "The People's Popular Drug Store," in the *Toronto Daily Star* and by Cyrus H. Bowes in the *Victoria Daily Colonist* of 1906.

24. For attacks on withdrawal, see Napheys, *Physical Life*, p. 97; Jefferis and Nichols, *Searchlights*, pp. 244ff; J.H. Kellogg, *Man, the Masterpiece* (London, 1903), p. 426. That medical warnings against coitus interruptus were not taken seriously, at least by Canadians of Scottish ancestry, is suggested by the fact that the practice was jocularly referred to as "Getting off at Kilmarnock," that is, the last train stop before Glasgow (personal communication).

25. See C. Tietze, "The Use-Effectiveness of Contraceptive Methods," in C.V. Kiser, ed., *Research in Family Planning* (Princeton, 1962), p. 367.

26. Gardner, *Conjugal Sins*, pp. 180-81. The readers of the *Canada Lancet*, XXVII (1895), p. 337, were informed: "Married men and women are either refusing [to bear children] or limiting their output to two or three. This is the fruitful source of prostitutionism, abortionism, onanism and mental and moral degeneracy." See also the warnings in Jefferis and Nichols, *Searchlights*, p. 244.

27. On the practice in England, see Angus McLaren, "Abortion in England, 1890-1914," *Victorian Studies*, XX (1977), pp. 379-400; and "Women's Work and Regulation of Family Size: The Question of Abortion in the Nineteenth Century," *History Workshop Journal*, IV (1977), pp. 70-81. For New Zealand, see Andrée Lévesque, "Grandmother Took Ergot: An Historical Perspective on Abortion in New Zealand, 1897-1937," *Broadsheet*, XLIV (1976), pp. 18-31.

28. In the United States, where the birth-rate decline had preceded that of Canada, the first surge of protests against abortion came in the 1860s and 1870s. See Horatio Storer, *On Criminal Abortion* (Boston, 1860); John Todd, *Serpents in the Dove's Nest* (Boston, 1867); R. Sauer, "Attitudes Towards Abortion in America 1800-1973," *Population Studies*, XXVIII (1974), pp. 53-67; also James C. Mohr, *Abortion in America* (New York, 1978).

29. *Daily Mail and Empire*, 21 March 1908, p. 21. "Kit," the pioneer woman journalist Kathleen Blake Watkins, knew more than most about the medical profession as she was married to a physician, Dr. Theodore Coleman.

30. *Ibid.*, 16 March 1908, p. 4. An equally prominent physician, Dr. Archibald Lawson, lecturer on the principles and practices of medicine at Halifax, had been implicated in a similar affair in 1883. See *Canada Medical and Surgical Journal*, XII (1883-84), p. 252.

31. *Daily Mail and Empire*, 4 April 1908, p. 21; see also the *Evening Telegram*, 18, 20 March 1908.

32. Advertisements taken at random from the Toronto *Globe*, November, 1901; *Daily Mail and Empire*, October, 1892; Toronto *World*, November, 1900; *Dominion Illustrated Monthly*, September, 1898. Cook's Cotton Root Compound appears to have been the most widely advertised product, being puffed as early as 1892 and as late as 1906 in papers as far apart as the Vancouver *Semi-Weekly World*, December, 1900, and the Halifax *Herald*, January, 1906. On the use of cotton root as a popular abortifacient in the southern U.S., see Herbert Gutman, *The Black Family in Slavery and Freedom, 1750-1925* (New York, 1976), pp. 80-82.

33. On the Karn case, see R. vs. Karn (1903) 5 *Ontario Law Reports*, p. 704 (CA); R. vs. Karn 5 *Canadian Criminal Cases*, p. 479; R. vs. Karn 6 *Canadian Criminal Cases*, p. 543. On other abortives, see R. vs. Scott (1912) 3, *Ontario Weekly Notes*, p. 1167 (CA). Some women might have taken such pills simply to ease menstrual pains but there is little doubt that the intent of the advertisers was to suggest that their products could be put to less innocent uses.

34. William Alcott, *Physiology of Marriage* (Boston, 1856), p. 185.

35. See R. vs. Stitt (1879) 30, *Upper Canada Common Pleas*, p. 30.

36. Pennyroyal and tansy are irritant drugs with a toxic action; ergot of rye, cottonroot, and quinine are oxytocic agents that stimulate the mobility of the uterus. On home remedies, see *Canadian Practitioner and Review*, XXXIX (1914), p. 668; C.J. Polson and R.N. Tattersall, *Clinical Toxicology* (London, 1959), pp. 545-49.

37. *Daily Mail and Empire*, 21 March 1908.

38. *Manitoba Free Press*, 30 August 1909.

39. Canadian papers also carried the advertisements of American druggists and physicians, and some Canadian women, to protect their anonymity, sought abortions in nearby American cities such as Chicago, Rochester, and Detroit. See, for example, R. vs. Backrack (1913) 28, *Ontario Law Reports*, p. 32 (CA), in which the question was posed if the crime committed by Canadians while in the U.S. could be prosecuted in Canadian courts.

40. *Daily Mail and Empire*, 6 April 1908, p. 4.

41. *Canadian Practitioner and Review*, XXXIII (1908), p. 253.

42. *Dominion Medical Monthly*, XXXII (1909), p. 121.

43. Alfred A. Andrews, "On Abortion," *Canada Lancet*, VII (1875), p. 289.

44. On therapeutic abortions, see *Canada Lancet*, XIII (1881), pp. 342-43; XXXII (1899), p. 113; *Canadian Practitioner and Review*, XXV (1900), pp. 331, 334-36, 401.

45. Andrews, "On Abortion," p. 291.

46. "Abortionists," *Canada Lancet*, XXI (1889), p. 217. See also "Does Abortion Pay?" *ibid.*, XLII (1908-09), pp. 648-49; John T. Winter, "Criminal Abortion," *American Journal of Obstetrics*, XXXVIII (1898), pp. 85-92.

47. See, for example, *Canada Lancet*, XXVI (1894), p. 76; XXXVIII (1905), pp. 88-89. A few sex reformers asserted that men, because of their lack of self-control, so burdened women with pregnancies that their seeking abortion was really the fault of males. See Kellogg, *Man*, p. 423; James C. Jackson, *American Womanhood: Its Peculiarities and Necessities* (Dansville, N.Y., 1870), pp. 89-90.

48. *Canada Lancet*, XXI (1889), p. 217. On the problem of registration, see R.E. Mill, "Birth Registration and Public Health," *Canadian Journal of Public Health*, VI (1915), pp. 135-36.

49. Andrews, "On Abortion," p. 291.

50. *Canadian Practitioner and Review*, XXXIII (1908), p. 253.

51. Mrs. Mary Wood-Allen, *What a Young Woman Ought to Know* (Toronto, 1898), p. 241.

52. Drake, *Young Wife*, pp. 125, 129, 130.

53. Bernarr McFadden, *Womanhood and Marriage* (New York, 1918), p. 139.

54. Hugh L. Hodge, *Foeticide or Criminal Abortion* (Philadelphia, 1869), pp. 32-33; see also Ely van de Warker, *The Detection of Criminal Abortion* (Boston, 1872), p. 42.

55. *American Journal of Obstetrics*, XXXIII (1896), pp. 130-31.

56. *Ibid.*, XLV (1902), p. 237.

57. Hodge, *Foeticide*, pp. 21-22. See also Andrew Nebinger, *Criminal Abortion: Its Extent and Prevention* (Philadelphia, 1870), p. 16; "A physician," *Satan in Society* (New York, 1872), p. 119.

58. See L.A. Parry, *Criminal Abortion* (London, 1931).

59. O.A. Cannon, "Septic Abortion," *Canadian Medical Association Journal*, XII (1922), p. 166.

60. See R. vs. Cook (1909) 19, *Ontario Law Reports*, 174 (CA); R. vs. Garrow and Creech (1896) 5, *British Columbia Reports*, 61; R. vs. Pettibone (1918) 2, *Western Weekly Reports*, 806.

61. Gardener was in fact purposely murdered by Dr. Thomas Neill Cream, a madman who, claiming to provide abortifacients, administered poison to and killed at least two Canadian and four English women. On the career of this Canadian "Jack the Ripper," see W. Teighnmouth Shore, *The Trial of Thomas Neill* (London, 1923).

62. Dr. Edward A. Ballock, in *American Journal of Obstetrics*, XLV (1902), p. 238.

63. Scott estimated that 75 to 90 per cent of all abortions were carried out by

married women: "Criminal Abortions," *American Journal of Obstetrics*, XXXIII (1896), p. 80.

64. *Canadian Practitioner and Review*, XLI (1916), pp. 120-21; and see J.H. Kellogg, *The Home Hand-Book of Domestic Hygiene and Rational Medicine* (London, 1906), pp. 356-57.

65. *Evening Telegram* cited by Clark, *Of Toronto the Good*, p. 124.

66. Cannon, "Septic Abortions," pp. 163-64.

67. See *Canada Lancet*, LX (1923), pp. 84-87; National Baby Week Council, *Some Maternity and Child Welfare Problems* (London, 1925), p. 39; Helen MacMurchy, *Maternal Mortality in Canada* (Toronto, 1928); Suzanne Buckley, "Efforts to Reduce Infant Mortality in Canada Between the Two World Wars," *Atlantis*, II (1977), pp. 76-84; Neil Sutherland, *Children in English-Canadian Society: Framing the Twentieth Century Consensus* (Toronto, 1976), pp. 56-70; Veronica Strong-Boag, *The Parliament of Women: The National Council of Women of Canada, 1893-1929* (Ottawa, 1976), pp. 206, 265.

68. J.T. Phair and A.H. Sellers, "A Study of Maternal Deaths in the Province of Ontario," *Canadian Public Health Journal*, XXV (1934), pp. 563-79; see also F.W. Jackson and R.D. Jeffries, "A Five Year Study of Maternal Mortality in Manitoba, 1928-1932," *Canadian Public Health Journal*, XXV (1934), p. 105; Helen MacMurchy, *Sterilization? Birth Control? A Book for Family Welfare and Safety* (Toronto, 1934), p. 97.

69. Scott, "Criminal Abortions," p. 78.

70. Cannon, "Septic Abortions," pp. 163-65.

71. A.B. Atherton, "The Causes of Degeneracy of the Human Race," *Canada Lancet*, XLI (1907-08), pp. 97-101; R.W. Bruce Smith, "Mental Sanitation, with Suggestions for the Care of the Degenerate, and Means for Preventing the Propagating of the Species," *ibid.*, XL (1906-07), pp. 969-76; James B. Watson, *Who Are the Producers of Human Damaged Goods?* (Toronto, 1913). See also Zlata Godler, "Doctors and the New Immigrants," *Canadian Ethnic Studies*, IX (1977), pp. 6-17; Terry L. Chapman, "Early Eugenics Movement in Western Canada," *Alberta History*, XXV (1977), pp. 9-17.

72. On the relationship of eugenics to contraception, see Angus McLaren, *Birth Control in Nineteenth Century England* (London, 1978).

73. A.T. Bond, "The Birth Rate," *Canadian Medical Monthly* (1920), p. 258. See also Bernarr McFadden, *Manhood and Marriage* (New York, 1916), pp. 87ff.

74. R.D. Defries, *The Development of Public Health in Canada* (Toronto, 1940), p. 78. The argument that a lower birth rate would reduce infant mortality was not accepted by all. Detecting this line of thought in the report of the City Improvement League of Montreal, a Catholic journalist replied: "Catholic mothers hold that to be born and baptised is a good compared with which the duration of mortal life is insignificant, for it means eternal life in heaven. Of course all wish to see infant mortality reduced as far as possible: but we do not want to see male and female professors of eugenics corrupting the morals of Catholic Canadian women,

and we are sure the clergy of Montreal will know how to silence them."
America: A Catholic Review of the Week, II (19 February 1910), p. 515.

Barber, Immigrant Domestics

1. *The Farmer's Advocate* (October, 1878), p. 237.
2. *Report of the Women's Institutes of the Province of Ontario, 1906*, Ontario, *Sessional Papers*, 1907, vol. XXXIX, part VI, no. 24, pp. 21-22.
3. *Census of Canada*, 1921, vol. IV, *Occupations*, pp. 2-3; *ibid.*, 1931, vol. VII, *Occupations*. According to the 1921 census, female servants were 41 per cent of the female work force in 1891, 34 per cent in 1901, 27 per cent in 1911, and 18 per cent in 1921. In 1931 the specific domestic servant category (excluding cooks and housekeepers) was 20 per cent of the female labour force. While the exact percentage can vary slightly depending on how the category of domestic servant is defined, the trend is clear.
4. David M. Katzman, *Seven Days a Week* (New York, 1976), pp. 87, 94.
5. *The Farmer's Advocate*, 20 November 1900, p. 639.
6. *Ibid.*
7. Maude Petitt Hill, "What's the Matter with Housework?" *Chatelaine* (March, 1928), p. 57.
8. PAC, RG76, Records of the Immigration Branch, file 356358-2, M. Agnes FitzGibbon to Scott, 31 August 1908. FitzGibbon cites the member to reinforce her appeal for payment of the government grant to the Toronto hostel.
9. *Ibid.*, file 22787-1, 3.
10. PAO, RG11, Department of Immigration, Correspondence, R.M. Persse, Ontario Immigration Agent, Quebec, to David Spence, 17 September 1881, 10 October 1881.
11. The exact amount of assistance fluctuated during the period. For example, in the mid-1870s British domestics going to Ontario were offered a special low passage fare of £2.5.0, including provisions, but not bedding or mess utensils, and an Ontario refund of $6, in addition to a free railway pass from Quebec provided by the Ontario government. See *Report of the Immigration Department for Ontario*, Ontario, *Sessional Papers*, for details.
12. *Report of the Department of Immigration for the Province of Ontario, 1882-83*, Ontario, *Sessional Papers*, 1883, no. 6, p. 5.
13. *Ibid.*, 1887, Ontario, *Sessional Papers*, 1888, no. 19, p. 8.
14. PAO, RG11, Immigration, Mrs. Duncan Matheson to Spence, 18 June 1878.
15. *Ibid.*, John Shier to Spence, 8 July 1885.
16. *Ibid.*, Rev. W.J. Smyth to Spence, 26 April 1878.
17. *Ibid.*, J. Stephenson, Grand Trunk Railway of Canada, to Spence, 10 July 1884.
18. *Ibid.*, R.M. Persse to Spence, 12 July 1883.
19. *The Imperial Colonist*, October, 1909, p. 147; Una Monk, *New Horizons* (London, 1963), p. 16.

20. *Annual Report of the Commissioner of Agriculture and Public Works for the province of Ontario on Immigration*, Ontario, *Sessional Papers*, no. 45, p. 9.

21. *The Imperial Colonist*, 1902-14; James Hammerton, *Emigrant Gentlewomen* (London, 1979), Ch. 6.

22. PAC, RG76, file 356358, *Annual Report of the Women's Welcome Hostel for 1912*, p. 16.

23. *Ibid.*, *Annual Report of the Women's Welcome Hostel for 1912*, M. Agnes FitzGibbon to Minister of the Interior, n.d. (received 19 January 1905).

24. H.J. Morgan, *The Canadian Men and Women of the Time*, 2nd edition (Toronto, 1912), p. 400.

25. PAC, RG76, file 356358, *Annual Report of the Women's Welcome Hostel, 1906-13*. The federal grant was given particularly because of the number of maids who went west after a year or two in Ontario. *Report*, 1908, p. 11.

26. *Ibid.*, 1906.

27. Public Records Office, CO721, Overseas Settlement, vol. 67, 1923, Reports on Visits to Canada.

28. PAC, RG76, file 22787, P.H. Bryce to Walker, 17 September 1906.

29. *Ibid.*, Report by Miss MacFarlane to Mr. Jolliff on the establishment and work of the women's division, 3 August 1944, pp. 1-2.

30. *Ibid.*, W.D. Scott to Cory, Memorandum, 23 November 1914.

31. *Ibid.*, Scott to Canadian agencies, 26 November 1914; Scott to J. Obed Smith, Assistant Superintendent of Emigration, London, 10 December 1914.

32. *Ibid.*, J. Obed Smith to Scott, 1 February 1917.

33. *Ibid.*, Report by Miss MacFarlane to Mr. Jolliff on women's division, 3 August 1944, p. 2.

34. *Ibid.*, Helen R.Y. Reid, Canadian Patriotic Fund, Montreal, to Calder, 16 July 1919.

35. *Ibid.*, J. Robson, Women's Branch, to Calder, 29 April 1920.

36. *Ibid.*, Conference on Immigration, 28 March 1919.

37. *Ibid.*, Memorandum, J.S. Robson to F.C. Blair, 27 January 1920.

38. *Ibid.*, Jessie Duff to Burnham, 16 April 1925.

39. In order to remove the burden of a large loan to be repaid from wages in Canada, the Empire Settlement ocean passage fare for houseworkers was set at £3 in 1926 and £2 in 1927. The regular fare in 1926 was £18.15.0.

40. Interview with a 1923 Empire Settlement Act immigrant, Victoria, B.C., 25 October 1979.

41. PAC, RG76, file 990380, Burnham to Duff, 15 March 1923; Duff to Burnham, 4 June 1923. In addition, Catholic women were sent to the Catholic Women's League Hostel in Toronto and Rosary Hall in Ottawa.

42. *Ibid.*, file 359252, Blair to Walker, 4 February 1929.

43. *Ibid.*, file 22787, Report by Miss MacFarlane to Mr. Jolliff on the establishment and work of the women's division, 3 August 1944, pp. 35-40.

44. *Ibid.*, file 35952, Charlesworth to Walker, 25 July 1929.

45. *Ibid.*, Report of Charlesworth attached to Burnham memo, 23 August 1929.

46. *Ibid.*, Blair to Little, 22 January 1930.

47. *Ibid.*, file 990380, Noxon to Burnham, 2 May 1923.

48. *Ibid.*, file 216882, Railways Agreement.

49. Glenbow Archives, CPR Records, box 149, Edith Robinson to Elsa Wares, Secretary, Central Women's Colonisation Board, 17 September 1928.

50. In 1921, 2.25 per cent of Ontario domestic servants were born in continental Europe whereas in 1931 the number had risen to 10.4 per cent. Immigrant domestic servants in Ontario were 89 per cent British and 6 per cent European in 1921, but 72.5 per cent British and 24.5 per cent European in 1931. (Statistics calculated from 1921 and 1931 census.)

51. *Census of Canada*, 1911, vol. VI, *Occupations*, Table VI.

52. PAC, RG76, file 22787, Little to Blair, 15 April 1924.

53. *Ibid.*, file 356358.

54. *Ibid.*, file 22787, Report by Miss MacFarlane to Mr. Jolliff on women's division, 3 August 1944, pp. 33-35.

55. *Ibid.*, file 359252, Kennedy to Burnham, 27 December 1929.

Danylewycz, Nuns and Feminists in Montreal

I would like to thank Marko Bojcun, Gail Brandt, Paul-André Linteau, and Alison Prentice for their comments on an earlier draft.

1. Michèle Jean, "Les Québécoises ont-elles une histoire?" in Jean, ed., *Québécoises du 20e siècle* (Montréal, 1974), pp. 13-36; Yolande Pinard, "Les débuts du mouvement des femmes," in Marie Lavigne et Yolande Pinard, eds., *Les femmes dans la société québécoise* (Montréal, 1977), pp. 61-87; Yolande Pinard, "Le féminisme à Montréal au commencement du XXe siècle, 1893-1920" (Thèse de maitrise, Université du Québec à Montréal, 1976); Marie Lavigne, Yolande Pinard, and Jennifer Stoddart, "The Fédération Nationale St-Jean-Baptiste," in Linda Kealey, ed., *A Not Unreasonable Claim: Women and Reform in Canada, 1880-1920s* (Toronto, 1979), pp. 71-87.

2. Micheline Dumont-Johnson, "Les communautés religieuses et la condition féminine," *Recherches sociographiques*, XIX (janvier-avril, 1978), pp. 79-102; Marta Danylewycz, "Taking the Veil in Montreal, 1850-1920: An Alternative to Migration, Motherhood and Spinsterhood," paper presented to the Canadian Historical Association, June, 1978, London, Ont.; Danielle Juteau Lee, "Les religieuses du Québec: leur influence sur la vie professionnelle des femmes, 1908-1954," *Atlantis*, 5 (Spring, 1980), pp. 29-33.

3. Bernard Denault, "Sociographie générale des communautés religieuses au Québec (1837-1970)," in Bernard Denault et Benoit Lévesque, *Éléments pour une sociologie des communautés religieuses au Québec* (Montréal, 1975), pp. 15-117.

4. For a general survey of the work of female religious communities, see *Le Diocése de Montréal à la fin du 19e siècle* (Montréal, 1900).

5. Elie J. Auclair, *Histoire des Soeurs de Miséricorde de Montréal* (Montréal, 1928); Léon Pouliot, *Monseigneur Bourget et son temps*, 5 tomes, Tome 3, *Évêque de Montréal* (Montréal, 1972), pp. 63-73, and Tome 2, *Évêque de*

Montréal, première partie (Montréal, 1979), pp. 86-109. For a corrective to Pouliot's interpretation of the role Mgr. Bourget played in the establishment of women's religious communities, see Marguerite Jean, s.c.i.m., *Évolution des communautés religieuses de femmes au Canada de 1639 à nos jours* (Montréal, 1977), pp. 79-92. As yet little is known about the impact of Mgr. Bourget's policy of encouraging the expansion of religious communities on lay activism. It remains to be seen whether he supported all types of Catholic charitable activities or whether, in building up the "clerical labour force," he consciously thwarted lay women's initiative in social service.

6.   Frédéric Langevin, s.j., *Mère Marie Anne, Fondatrice de l'Institut des Soeurs de Ste Anne, 1809-1890: Esquisse biographique* (Montréal, 1935); Albert Tessier, *Les Soeurs des Petites Écoles* (Rimouski, 1962).

7.   Marie-Claire Daveluy, *L'Orphelinat Catholique de Montréal* (Montréal, 1933), pp. 17-128.

8.   Thérèse Casgrain, *A Woman in a Man's World* (Toronto, 1972), p. 17; for a glimpse of the life of one married woman, see Mme. F.-L. Beique, *Quatre-vingts ans de souvenir: Histoire d'une famille* (Montréal, 1939), pp. 40-57.

9.   "Ce que nous ne serons pas," *Le Coin du Feu*, 1, 1 (janvier, 1893), p. 2.

10.   See Joséphine Dandurand's speeches to nuns and lay women in Joséphine Dandurand, "Le féminisme," in her *Nos travers* (Montréal, 1901), pp. 218-29; "Chronique," *Le Coin du Feu*, 2, 5 (mai, 1893), p. 130.

11.   Archives de l'Institut de Notre-Dame-du-Bon-Conseil (hereafter AIN-DBC). Brouillons de lettres, Marie Gérin-Lajoie à Léonie Morel, juillet, 1903.

12.   AINDBC, Marie Gérin-Lajoie, "Une pensée par jour (pages du journal de Maman, 1892-1898)," cahier manuscrit, 29 mars 1898.

13.   Françoise, "Vieilles Filles," *Le Journal de Françoise*, 4, 13 (7 octobre 1905), pp. 198-99; Robertine Barry, *Chroniques du lundi* (Montréal, n.d.), pp. 318-22; for a biographical sketch of Robertine Barry, see Renée des Ormes, *Robertine Barry en littérature: Françoise. Pionnière du journalisme au Canada 1863-1910* (Québec, 1949).

14.   In one of her first public statements Marie Gérin-Lajoie made the connection between feminism and changing material conditions. Mme. Gérin-Lajoie, "Le mouvement féministe," in *The Annual Report of the National Council of Women of Canada* (Ottawa, 1896), p. 287. Recent studies of the feminist movement have taken their cue from nineteenth-century feminists and have shown how a resolve to remedy the ills of industrial capitalism and a realization that participation in reform required the expansion of existing roles spurred the formation of the feminist movement. Pinard, "Les débuts du mouvement des femmes"; and Lavigne, Pinard, and Stoddart, "The Fédération Nationale."

15.   Marie Gérin-Lajoie, "Entre Nous," *La Bonne Parole*, 3, 12 (février, 1916), p. 2.

16.   Marie Gérin-Lajoie, "Fin d'année," *Le Journal de Françoise*, 2, 18-19 (19

décembre 1903), pp. 234-35: Françoise, "La charité canadienne," *Le Journal de Françoise*, 5, 1 (7 avril 1906), pp. 2-4.

17. Gérin-Lajoie, "Fin d'année," p. 233; she made the same point more poignantly in AINDBC, Marie Gérin-Lajoie à Léonie Morel, janvier, 1903.

18. Barry, *Chroniques du lundi*, p. 308; "Entre Nous: Le suffrage des femmes," *La Bonne Parole*, 11, 11 (novembre, 1921), pp. 3-4; Yvonne, "La condition privée de la femme," *Le Coin du Feu*, 11, 12 (décembre, 1894), p. 359.

19. "Notre Courrier," *La Bonne Parole*, 4, 3 (mai, 1918), p. 14.

20. Barry, *Chroniques du lundi*, p. 308.

21. Lavigne, Pinard, and Stoddart, "The Fédération Nationale," pp. 73-74.

22. The events leading up to the creation of the École ménagère were reported by Marie de Beaujeu in *Le Journal de Françoise*: "Les Écoles ménagères," 5, 9 (9 août 1906), pp. 131-33: "La popularité des écoles ménagères," 5, 10 (18 août 1906), pp. 151-53: "L'Utilité des écoles ménagères," 10, 11 (1 septembre 1906), pp. 166-68. For the cursory history of Montreal's École ménagère, see Béique, *Quatre-vingts ans*, pp. 244-57.

23. *The Annual Report of the National Council of Women of Canada* (Ottawa, 1896), p. 80.

24. AINDBC, Marie Gérin-Lajoie à Mlle. Morel, 22 décembre 1905.

25. Lavigne, Pinard, and Stoddart, "The Fédération Nationale," pp. 73-78. See the program of the first congress and the discussions leading up to it: Archives Nationales du Québec à Montréal. "Extrait du livre de minutes de l'Exécutif de la Fédération Nationale St-Jean-Baptiste," cahier no. 1, 19 octobre 1906-20 mai 1907.

26. For a breakdown of the types of organizations that federated in 1907, see Micheline Dumont-Johnson, "History of the Status of Women in the Province of Quebec," in *Cultural Tradition and Political History of Women in Canada. Study no. 8* (Ottawa, 1971), p. 24; the first page of each issue of *La Bonne Parole*, which began publication in 1912, listed member organizations; see also Marie Gérin-Lajoie's discussion of the Fédération's structure and purpose: "La Fédération Nationale St-Jean-Baptiste," *L'École Sociale Populaire*, 5 (Montréal, 1911).

27. "Chroniques des oeuvres," *La Bonne Parole*, 5, 2-3 (avril, 1917), p. 2.

28. Béique, *Quatre-vingts ans*, p. 257.

29. Archives Nationales du Québec à Montréal, "Extrait du livre de minutes de l'Exécutif de la Fédération Nationale St-Jean Baptiste," cahier no. 1, 1 mai 1909, et cahier no. 2, 2 mars 1912.

30. For examples of nuns and lay women co-operating, see *ibid.*, cahier no. 1, 11 avril 1907. cahier no. 2, 26 juin 1909, 2 mars 1912, cahier no. 3, 28 septembre 1912, 19 avril 1913, 13 décembre 1913. The Congregation of Notre Dame made the following remark about co-operation between the community and lay women: "Nous avons senti ensemble l'obligation de marcher la main dans la main avec toutes les oeuvres catholiques et militantes." Archives des Soeurs de la Congrégation de Notre-Dame (hereafter ACND), *Annales de la Maison Mère*, 24, 5 (mai, 1918), pp. 615-16.

31. For a history of the école ménagère movement, see Béique, *Quatre-vingts*

ans, pp. 244-64; Albert Tessier, *Souvenirs en vrac* (Montréal, 1975); Albert Tessier, "Les écoles ménagères au service du foyer," in Jean, ed., *Québécoises*, pp. 160-66.

32.   Barry, *Chroniques du lundi*, pp. 307-08; Joséphine Dandurand, "Les Professions féminines," *Le Coin du Feu*, 4, 8 (août, 1896), pp. 224-25.

33.   Joséphine Dandurand, "Les femmes savantes," *Le Coin du Feu*, 4, 1 (janvier, 1896), p. 4.

34.   Marie Gérin-Lajoie, "De l'Enseignement Supérieur pour les Femmes," *Le Journal de Françoise*, 4, 16 (18 novembre 1905), p. 246. Joséphine Dandurand made the same point in "Culture intellectuelle" in her *Nos Travers*, p. 18.

35.   Mention of Joséphine Dandurand's activities was made in "Le Concours Littérature," *Le Coin du Feu*, 4, 5 (mai, 1896), p. 141; Joséphine Dandurand, "Chronique – Un projet," *Le Coin du Feu*, 4, 1 (janvier, 1896), pp. 404-05; Joséphine Dandurand, "La Bibliothèque Publique," *Le Journal de Françoise*, 1, 9 (26 juillet 1902), pp. 98-99. At times it was simply noted that "Le prix que Mme Dandurand donne chaque année au Couvent de la Congrégation de Notre-Dame de cette ville pour la correction du langage a été gagné cette année par Mlle Jeannette d'Orsonnens": *Le Coin du Feu*, 4, 7 (juillet, 1896), p. 209.

36.   Françoise, "Les Jeunes Filles dans les bureaux," *Le Journal de Françoise*, 2, 23 (21 février 1903), pp. 269-70; Françoise, "Cours d'enseignement supérieur pour les jeunes filles," *Le Journal de Françoise*, 7, 14 (17 octobre 1908), p. 218.

37.   Marie Globensky Prévost, "Une Contemporaine d'Élite," *Le Journal de Françoise*, 2, 17 (5 décembre 1903), pp. 218-19.

38.   Marie Gérin-Lajoie, "De l'Enseignement Supérieur pour les Femmes," *Le Journal de Françoise*, 4, 15 (4 novembre 1905), pp. 227-30, and 4, 16 (18 novembre 1905), pp. 244-46.

39.   ACND, Journal de Mère St. Anaclet, 1894-1912, 5 cahiers manuscrits, cahier no. 2, 22 et 23 mai 1897.

40.   *Ibid.*, cahier no. 2, 14 et 28 janvier, 13 février 1902.

41.   *Ibid.*, cahier no. 4, 22 mars, 3 juin 1905, 17 avril 1906.

42.   *Ibid.*, cahier no. 4, 14 janvier 1907, et cahier no. 1, 8 mars 1896.

43.   *À la mémoire de Mère Ste. Anne Marie, Maîtresse Générale des Études de la Congrégation de Notre-Dame* (Montréal, 1938), pp. 1-30.

44.   *Ibid.*, pp. 30-36; Soeur Lucienne Plante, c.n.d., "La fondation de l'enseignement classique féminin au Québec" (Thèse de maîtrise, Université Laval, 1968), pp. 29-35.

45.   The official organ of the community congratulated Sister St. Anne Marie in *Annales de la Maison Mère*, 19 (juin, 1913), pp. 120-21. At the same time there were sisters who disagreed with the changes she had introduced. Plante, "La fondation," pp. 50-52.

46.   AINDBC, Marie Gérin-Lajoie à Léonie Morel, 25 avril 1904; Béique, *Quatre-vingts ans*, pp. 228-29.

47.   Plante, "La fondation," pp. 57-60; Françoise, "Un Lycée de Jeunes Filles," *Le Journal de Françoise*, 7, 6 (20 juin 1908), p. 92.

48. Soeur St. Stanislas de Jésus, c.n.d., "L'enseignement classique féminin en notre province," in Jean, ed., *Québécoises*, pp. 169-70.

49. ACND, *L'Annuaire de l'École d'enseignement supérieur pour les filles* (Montréal, 1910), pp. 95-96.

50. Plante, "La fondation," pp. 50-53; interview with Florence Fernet-Martel, one of the first graduates of the college and a close friend of many sisters of the Congregation of Notre Dame, 4 March 1980.

51. ACND, "Annales de l'École d'enseignement supérieur pour les filles," 1 (1908); St. Stanislas de Jésus, "L'enseignement classique," p. 173; former students of the École d'enseignement supérieur promoted higher education for women by conducting surveys and writing articles in its favour: Georgette Le Moyne, "Entre Nous," *La Bonne Parole*, 7, 1 (mars, 1919), pp. 1-2; Marie J. Gérin-Lajoie, "Entre Nous – La femme et l'université," *La Bonne Parole*, 8, 3 (mars, 1920), pp. 1-2; Mme. A. Lesage-Dérome, "Rapport du Congrès d'avril 1921; L'enseignement secondaire et la formation des classes dirigeantes," *La Bonne Parole*, 10, 9 (septembre, 1922), pp. 11-12.

52. Soeur Ste. Madeleine des Anges, c.n.d., *Soeur Ste Théophanie c.n.d., 1875-1948* (Montréal, 1949), p. 41; Plante, "La fondation," p. 106; Soeur Lucienne Plante, "L'Enseignement classique chez les Soeurs de la Congrégation de Notre-Dame, 1908-1971" (Thèse de doctorat, Université Laval, 1971), pp. 285-86.

53. Clippings of articles about college graduates can be found in "Annales de l'École d'enseignement supérieur," 5 (1912-13). See Henri Bourassa's articles in *Le Devoir*, 22, 28 janvier, 7 avril, 7 mai 1913, 11 septembre 1917, 28 mars 1918.

54. Interview with Florence Fernet-Martel, 4 March 1980.

55. ACND, "Annales de l'École d'enseignement supérieur," 16 (1923-24).

56. Feminists sensed that fear of competition drove men to deny women equal rights. AINDBC, Marie Gérin-Lajoie à Léonie Morel, 2 mai 1902. Robertine Barry made a similar observation in *Chroniques du lundi*, p. 307.

57. Marie Gérin-Lajoie, "Le Travail chez la Femme," *Le Coin du Feu*, 1, 3 (mars, 1893), pp. 67-68. Incidentally, Henri Bourassa used the same expression, "des fonctions lucratives jusqu'ici dévolues aux hommes," in one of his vitriolic attacks on feminism: quoted in Marie Lavigne and Jennifer Stoddart, "Women's Work in Montreal at the Beginning of the Century," in Marylee Stephenson, ed., *Women in Canada* (Toronto, 1977), p. 142.

58. Quoted in Plante, "La fondation," p. 53.

59. ACND, Correspondence, No. 19, A.P. Pelletier à Soeur Ste. Henriette, 18 novembre 1903.

60. Plante, "La fondation," p. 89, established that only 50 per cent of those who graduated between 1912 and 1926 married. Her study also provides information on the careers of the college's graduates. St. Stanislas de Jésus, "L'enseignement classique," p. 171, reported that as of February, 1954, only 676 out of the 1,494 women who graduated from women's colleges between 1912 and 1953 were married.

61. The program of the Fédération's first congress covered the following issues:

educational responsibility of mothers, domestic science education, condition of working women, protecting the morality of working women, preparing young girls for work. Archives Nationales du Québec à Montréal, "Extrait du livre de minutes de l'Exécutif de la Fédération Nationale St-Jean-Baptiste," cahier no. 1, 26-30 mai 1907; see also Béique, *Quatre-vingts ans*, pp. 232-35; Françoise, "Le Congrès Féminin," *Le Journal de Françoise*, 6, 6 (15 juin 1907), pp. 89-90.

62. For details of the circle's activities, see reports in "Annales de l'École d'enseignement supérieur," 1-16 (1909-25).

63. Marie J. Gérin-Lajoie, "Rapport de la journée d'études," *La Bonne Parole*, 10, 6 (juin, 1922), p. 11.

64. Georgette Le Moyne, "Journée d'études," *La Bonne Parole*, 3, 2 (juin, 1920), pp. 3-5; Georgette Le Moyne, "Les Cercles d'Études," *La Bonne Parole*, 8, 6 (juin, 1920), pp. 13-15; "Annales de l'École d'enseignement supérieur," 8 (1915-16).

65. Marie J. Gérin-Lajoie, "Nos Raisons d'Agir," *La Bonne Parole*, 10, 10 (octobre, 1922), p. 3; "Rapport du Cercle Notre-Dame," *La Bonne Parole*, 10, 4 (avril, 1922), p. 13; "Rapport du Comité Central," *La Bonne Parole*, 10, 6 (juin, 1922), pp. 12-13; "Pour les Cercles d'Études," *La Bonne Parole*, 11, 4 (avril, 1923), pp. 12-13. For an explanation of the study circles' purpose and an examination of their activities, see Marie J. Gérin-Lajoie, *Les Cercles d'Études Féminins*, L'École Sociale Populaire, 52 (Montréal, 1916).

66. The social background of 77 of the 125 women who graduated between 1911 and 1926 from l'École d'enseignement supérieur has been established by Plante, "La fondation," pp. 136-37. Their fathers' occupations were: accountant (3), businessman (25), civil servant (7), doctor (7), engineer (1), farmer (2), industrialist (4), insurance salesman (2), journalist (1), lawyer (6), hotel keeper (1), notary (15), plumber (1), school superintendent (1), travel agent (1).

67. Among the regular contributors to *La Bonne Parole* were M.J. Gérin-Lajoie, Yvonne Charette, Georgette Le Moyne, Irène Lesage, Evaline Zappa, all graduates of the École d'enseignement supérieur. Georgette Le Moyne, Jeanne Baril, Aline Sénécal, and M.J. Gérin-Lajoie were members of the Fédération's central committee; Florence Fernet worked for the passage of of women's suffrage in Quebec; Georgette Le Moyne was a member of the Ligue des droits de la femme and accompanied Marie Lacoste-Gérin-Lajoie on her pro-suffrage mission to Rome.

68. As M.J. Gérin-Lajoie stated it in *La Bonne Parole*: "Les Femmes à la Semaine Sociale," 8, 9 (septembre, 1920), p. 3; "Nos Raisons d'Agir," 10, 10 (octobre, 1922), p. 3; "Comment une Oeuvre de Charité devient Sociale;" 10, 12 (décembre, 1922), p. 3.

69. Marcienne Proulx, "L'Action sociale de Marie Gérin-Lajoie, 1910-1925" (Mémoire de maîtrise en théologie, Université de Sherbrooke, 1975), pp. 25-100.

70. AINDBC, M.J. Gérin-Lajoie, "Premières Gerbes," manuscrit, p. 3.

71. AINDBC, Lettres adressées à une religieuse auxiliatrice, mai, septembre,

1920; AINDBC, M.J. Gérin-Lajoie, "Mon itinéraire," manuscrit, 1915-16.

72. *Ibid.*, pp. 1-8.

73. Quoted in Evelyne Bissonnette Paquette et Johanne Cloutier Boucher, "Le suffrage féminin," in "La glace est rompue. Etat de recherche sur la vie de Marie Lacoste Gérin-Lajoie," Jennifer Stoddart *et al.* (1973), p. 103.

74. S.M. Gérin-Lajoie, "Notre rôle d'auxiliaire d'action catholique," *La Bonne Parole*, 20, 10 (novembre, 1932), pp. 1-2; Albertine Ferland-Anger, "L'Institut de Notre-Dame-du-Bon-Conseil," *La Bonne Parole*, 11, 5 (mai, 1923), p. 3.

75. Gérin-Lajoie, "Premières Gerbes," pp. 11-29.

76. Joséphine Dandurand, "Chronique," *Le Coin du Feu*, 11, 5 (mai, 1894), p. 130; *La Première Étape d'une fondation canadienne* (Montréal, 1929), pp. 9-11, 14.

77. AINDBC, Marie Gérin-Lajoie à Mlle. Morel, janvier, 1903.

Walsh, The Peacock and the Guinea Hen

1. Interview with Grace MacInnis, 18 November 1981.

2. *Vancouver Province*, 12 December 1936, p. 4.

3. *Vancouver Province*, 29 January 1944, p. 8.

4. MacInnis interview.

5. *Ibid.*

6. PAC, CCF/NDP Records, vol. 104, Mrs. D.G. Steeves, 1943-1950, Steeves to Betty Irwin, 29 November 1949.

7. *Ibid.*

8. PABC, Interview with Dorothy Steeves by Marlene Karnouk, 4 April 1975, track 1, p. 3.

9. PAC, Steeves to Irwin, 29 November 1949.

10. Karnouk interview, p. 6.

11. UBC, Special Collections, Steeves Papers, Box 2, Outgoing Correspondence, Steeves to Mrs. Biersteker, 26 March 1919.

12. PAC, CCF/NDP Records, vol. 144, Research: Biographies Misc., 1944-1953.

13. PAC, Steeves to Irwin, 29 November 1949.

14. Dorothy Steeves, *The Compassionate Rebel* (Vancouver, 1960), p. 79.

15. Interview with Mildred Farnhi, 31 March 1982.

16. *Vancouver Sun*, 18 February 1935, p. 1.

17. *Across Canada*, January, 1950. Interview with Harold and Jessie Mendels Winch, 18 May 1982.

18. *The Democrat*, April, 1975; see also Daisy Webster's biographical sketch of Steeves in *Growth of the NDP in BC, 1900-1970* (Vancouver, n.d.).

19. Winch interview.

20. PAC, MacInnis Papers, vol. 22, Personal and Political, MacInnis to David Lewis, 19 December 1939.

21. UBC Special Collections, Colin Cameron Papers, Box 1, Incoming Correspondence, Steeves to Cameron, 9 October 1955.

22. See *Victoria Times*, 17 March 1936; *Federationist*, 17 November 1938;

Victoria Times, 7 March 1943; *Vancouver Sun*, 12 May 1978; and Daisy Webster, "Women in Politics in British Columbia," UBC Special Collections (unpublished manuscript).

23.   *Vancouver Sun*, 9 October 1934, p. 8.
24.   *Ibid.*
25.   *Victoria Times*, 25 April 1935, p. 9.
26.   *Ibid.*
27.   *Ibid.*, 24 March 1936, p. 7.
28.   When asked about discrimination against women in the political arena, the then eighty-five-year-old Steeves replied: "Oh, not any more, I think. I think those women are looking for discrimination. I've always been of the opinion that I'm as good as any man." Karnouk interview.
29.   MacInnis interview.
30.   *Ibid.*
31.   *Ibid.*
32.   *Ibid.*
33.   *Vancouver News-Herald*, 16 February 1942, p. 7.
34.   MacInnis Papers, vol. 86, Correspondence Re: *CCF News*, MacInnis to the Editor of the *CCF News*, 1 October 1950.
35.   *Canadian Forum*, June, 1939.
36.   See Eleanor Godfrey's biographical sketch of MacInnis in the *New Commonwealth*, September, 1942.
37.   MacInnis Papers, vol. 86, MacInnis to Editor of *CCF News*, 1 October 1950.
38.   *Ibid.*
39.   MacInnis Papers, vol. 22, British Columbia, 1939-1951.
40.   Steeves Papers, folder on Cuba.
41.   MacInnis interview.
42.   See *Vancouver Province*, 13 March 1943, p. 9; *Vancouver Sun*, 26 September 1944, p. 7; *Victoria Colonist*, 13 February 1945, p. 7. Harold Winch remembers MacInnis as the one who was most pronounced on women's rights within the legislature. Winch interview.
43.   Grace MacInnis and Charles Woodsworth, *Canada: Through CCF Glasses* (Vancouver, 1935), p. 68.
44.   *Victoria Colonist*, 13 February 1945.
45.   MacInnis interview.
46.   *Ibid.*
47.   PAC, CCF/NDP Records, vol. 309. Grace MacInnis, "Frauen und Sozialisimus in Kanada," *Gleicher*, 1 January 1951. Translation for author by Elvira Eheman-Burklin, Simon Fraser University, 1981.
48.   MacInnis interview.
49.   *Ibid.*

Brandt, Female Cotton Workers in Quebec

1.   Gerda Lerner, "New Approaches to the Study of Women in American History," in Bernice A. Carroll, ed., *Liberating Women's History: Theoretical and Critical Essays* (Chicago, 1976), p. 353.

2. The project, "Women in the Quebec Cotton Industry, 1891-1951," is funded by the Social Sciences and Humanities Research Council of Canada. During the summer of 1980, fifty-six more interviews were conducted with women in Magog, and the information these contain corresponds with the Valleyfield data.
3. *Census of Canada*, 1911, vol. 3, Table V, pp. 216-17.
4. Edith Abbott, *Women in Industry* (New York, 1909), pp. 97-108.
5. *Report of the Royal Commission of Enquiry into the Textile Industry* (Ottawa, 1938), p. 151.
6. *Ibid.*, p. 149.
7. *Ibid.*, p. 148.
8. See, for example, *Relations* (mai, décembre, 1942, mai, 1943).
9. Worker employed at Montreal Cottons, 1943 to 1948.
10. It is indeed appropriate that the term "au coton" has also come to mean exhausted or worn out.
11. Worker employed from 1918 to 1929.
12. Worker employed from 1922 to 1941.
13. Worker employed from 1936 to 1941.
14. Among the larger industries established in the Valleyfield area during the war were Defence Industries Limited, Nichols Chemical Company, Colonial Dyeing and Finishing, and Quebec Distillers.
15. Tamara Hareven, "Family Time and Industrial Time: Family and Work in a Planned Corporation Town, 1900-1924," in Hareven, ed., *Family and Kin in Urban Communities, 1700-1930* (New York, 1977), p. 192.
16. Worker employed from 1908 to 1918.
17. Philippe Garigue, *La Vie familiale des canadiens français* (Montréal, 1970), p. 43.
18. Nicolas Zay, "Analyse statistique du travail de la femme mariée dans la province de Québec," in Michèle Jean, ed., *Québécoises du 20ᵉ siècle* (Montréal, 1974), pp. 124-40.
19. For a discussion of these views, see Veronica Strong-Boag, "The Girl of the New Day: Canadian Working Women in the 1920s," *Labour/Le Travailleur*, 4 (1979), pp. 152-58; Catherine McLeod, "Women in Production: the Toronto Dressmakers' Strike of 1931," in J. Acton *et al.*, eds., *Women at Work, Ontario, 1850-1930* (Toronto, 1974), pp. 324-25.
20. Royal Commission respecting industrial disputes in the Cotton Factories of the Province of Quebec (1908), vol. 1, "Minute Book," p. 9 (Public Archives of Canada).
21. *Le Fileur*, 1, 8 (juin, 1907).
22. According to information contained in the 1908 Royal Commission documents and in the files of the Ministry of Labour, women appear to have played an important role in at least nine work stoppages, and possibly an additional nine, out of a total of forty-two between 1900 and 1920.
23. *La Presse*, 2 février 1900.
24. The National Catholic Textile Federation was established in 1926 and was active in Valleyfield after 1934. The United Textile Workers of America were active there after 1942.
25. Of twenty-three work stoppages studied that occurred between 1920 and

1950, only four directly involved female workers.

26. CCCL, *Proceedings*, 1935, p. 39.

27. CCCL, *Proceedings*, 1939, p. 147. For a fuller discussion of the CCCL's attitudes toward women workers, see M.-J. Gagnon, "Les Femmes dans le mouvement syndical québécois," in Marie Lavigne et Yolande Pinard, eds., *Les Femmes dans la société québécoise: aspects historiques* (Montréal, 1977), pp. 145-68.

28. In 1946, only 17 per cent of the Quebec delegates to the national convention were women and only one woman served on a committee. By 1948, 30 per cent of the delegates and 30 per cent of the committee members were women. See PAC, Rowley-Parent Collection, vol. 5, file 3.

29. In case of sickness or accident, male workers received $12 compensation per week; female workers, $8.

30. PAC, Rowley-Parent Collection, vol. 5, file 27.

31. Worker employed from 1936 to 1941.

32. Worker employed from 1942 to 1955.

33. PAC, Rowley-Parent Collection, vol. 5, file 21, Jane Gray to Mr. Miller, n.d.

34. Worker employed from 1940 to 1947.

35. Worker employed from 1948 to 1961.

36. Worker employed from 1945 to 1947.

37. Worker employed from 1936 to 1941.

38. Royal Commission respecting industrial disputes in the Cotton Factories of the Province of Quebec, vol. 1, "Secretary's Minute Book," p. 8 (PAC).

39. *Ibid.*, vol. 2, "Dominion Textile Co. . . . Merchants Branch, Average Daily Wage of all Employees . . . May 4, 1908."

40. *Census of Canada*, 1931, vol. 7, Table 58, p. 786.

41. *Ibid.*, 1941, vol. 7, Table 21, p. 694.